ANCIENT CHRISTIAN
Devotional

A Year of Weekly Readings

General Editor Thomas C. Oden

Edited by Cindy Crosby

IVP Books

An imprint of InterVarsity Press
Downers Grove, Illinois

InterVarsity Press
P.O. Box 1400, Downers Grove, IL 60515-1426
Internet: www.ivpress.com
E-mail: email@ivpress.com

InterVarsity Press® is the book-publishing division of InterVarsity Christian Fellowship/USA®, a student
movement active on campus at hundreds of universities, colleges and schools of nursing in the United States
of America, and a member movement of the International Fellowship of Evangelical Students.
For information about local and regional activities, write Public Relations Dept., InterVarsity Christian
Fellowship/USA, 6400 Schroeder Rd., P.O. Box 7895, Madison, WI 53707-7895, or visit the IVCF website
at <www.intervarsity.org>.

Scripture quotations, unless otherwise noted, are from the Revised Standard Version of the Bible, copyright
1946, 1952, 1971 by the Division of Christian Education of the National Council of the Churches of Christ in
the U.S.A., and are used by permission.

Excerpts from The Handbook of Public Prayer by Roger Geffen are reprinted with the permission of
Scribner, an imprint of Simon & Schuster Adult Publishing Group. Copyright © 1963 by Roger Geffen. All
rights reserved.

The closing prayer on pp. 216-17 is taken from p. 63 of Prayers for the Heart by Richard Foster. Copyright
© 1994 by Richard Foster. Reprinted with permission of HarperCollins Publishers.

The opening prayer on p. 233 is quoted from A Free Church Book of Common Prayer. Reprinted with
permission of JM Dent, a division of The Orion Publishing Group.

Every effort has been made to contact copyright holders for materials quoted in this book. The editors will be
pleased to rectify any omissions in future editions if notified by the copyright holders.

Images: Scala/Art Resource, New York

Design: Cindy Kiple

ISBN 978-0-8308-3431-0

Printed in the United States of America ∞

Library of Congress Cataloging-in-Publication Data

Ancient Christian devotional: a year of weekly readings / edited by
Cindy Crosby; general editor, Thomas C. Oden.
    p. cm.
Includes bibliographical references and index.
ISBN 978-0-8308-3431-0 (pbk.: alk. paper)
1. Bible—Devotional literature. I. Crosby, Cindy, 1961- II. Oden,
Thomas C.
BS491.5.A52 2007
242'.3—dc22

    2006101569

P	18	17	16	15	14	13	12	11	10	9	8	7	6	5	4	3	2	1
Y	22	21	20	19	18	17	16	15	14	13	12	11	10	09	08	07		

CONTENTS

INTRODUCTION
page 7

DEVOTIONALS
page 11

ANCIENT CHRISTIAN COMMENTARY CITATIONS
page 269

PRAYER CITATIONS
page 271

BIOGRAPHICAL SKETCHES
page 283

INDEX OF NAMES AND SOURCES
page 293

Welcome to the
ANCIENT CHRISTIAN
DEVOTIONAL

For if the days of a person should be as many
as all the days of the world from Adam to the end of the ages
and he should sit and meditate on the holy Scriptures, he would not
comprehend all the force of the depth of the words.

APHRAHAT, DEMONSTRATIONS 22:26

Many Christians today lack grounding in the riches of church history. We may find ourselves "rootless and drifting in a barren secular and ecclesiastical landscape."* The church fathers offer us context and tradition that will help us establish the roots we need. They do so by taking us deeper into the rich resources of Scripture, helping us to read holy writings with ancient eyes.

This devotional combines excerpts from the writings of the church fathers as found in The Ancient Christian Commentary on Scripture with a simple structure of daily reading and prayer. It is designed to allow you to work through the material at your own pace. You can read a little each day, or, if you like to have a longer time of prayer once a week, it would work nicely in that format as well.

There are fifty-two weeks of readings, which follow the liturgical year. The year begins with the readings for the first Sunday in Advent, four Sundays before Christmas. Depending on where Easter falls in a given year, you may need to adjust your reading. The readings for the first Sunday of Lent begin in Week 13 and go through Week 18. Easter is in Week 19. Six weeks of Easter readings then follow. If Easter was early and you skipped some readings, you might at this point go back and pick them up. Pentecost is in Week 26. In Week 27 we then pick up the dating of the entries. You will also find a special week of readings in Week 48 for All Saints' Day—which is celebrated November first or the first Sunday in November.

Each week you will find the following elements.

THEME

An overview of the week's theme, drawing together the texts of the week. (The texts generally follow Lectionary Cycle A.)

OPENING PRAYER

A simple prayer taken from early church sources, which you can pray daily.

READINGS

Each week you will find an Old Testament, Epistle and Gospel reading, in keeping with the long tradition of the church lectionary cycles (depending on the liturgical cycle, some readings may differ slightly).

PSALM OF RESPONSE

The psalm can be used for prayer and meditation. It is there to help you offer words of petition and praise to God. You may want to pray through it daily.

REFLECTIONS FROM THE CHURCH FATHERS

These quotes offer insight on the Scripture passage. Read a few of these quotes each day, and stop when you feel stirred to pray or ponder. Give yourself time to reflect before God on what you are learning. You may want to journal your thoughts.

CLOSING PRAYER

This simple prayer drawn from ancient sources is designed to be used daily to close your time with God.

If you want to spend ten or fifteen minutes with this material each day, a suggested structure for your time would be to read the opening prayer, the psalm, one of the Scripture texts, two or three of the reflections from the church fathers, and the closing prayer. Feel free to write in the book to note the sections you have completed as you go.

Don't worry about getting through the material on any particular schedule. Allow God to speak to you. Listen. Rest. This book should not be a source of guilt but a resource of grace. May your reading draw you to dig deep into the riches of God's Word.

To search the sacred Scripture is very good and most profitable for the soul. For "like a tree which is planted near the running waters," so does the soul watered by sacred Scripture also grow hearty and bear fruit in due season. This is the orthodox faith. It is adorned with its evergreen leaves, with actions pleasing to God. (John of Damascus, *Orthodox Faith* 4.17)

*Robert Wilken, as quoted in Christopher Hall, *Reading Scripture with the Church Fathers* (Downers Grove, Ill.: InterVarsity Press, 1998).

Keep Watch

THEME

Scripture tells us that we are forgiven! It calls us to walk in the light of the Lord (Is 2:1-5), to pray for peace (Ps 122) and to keep watch for Christ's return (Mt 24:36-44), putting aside our deeds of darkness and living in the light (Rom 13:11-14). In this season of Advent, we celebrate the Child who is the Light. We thank God for forgiveness of sins and reaffirm our desire to walk with the Lord.

OPENING PRAYER: *First Sunday in Advent*

God is peace, the principle of all kinds of communion. Let us extol peace with songs of peaceful praise. It is God-who-is-Peace who brings all things into unity, who is the cause of every agreement, who is the author of all harmony. [Amen.] *Pseudo-Dionysius the Areopagite*

OLD TESTAMENT READING: *Isaiah 2:1-5*

REFLECTIONS FROM THE CHURCH FATHERS

Christ the Mountain. AUGUSTINE: The central place they are all coming to is Christ; he is at the center, because he is equally related to all; anything placed in the center is common to all. . . . Approach the mountain, climb up the mountain, and you that climb it, do not go down it. There you will be safe, there you will be protected; Christ is your mountain of refuge. And where is Christ? At the right hand of the

Father, since he has ascended into heaven. *Sermon 62A.3.*

Forgiveness Begins in Jerusalem. BEDE: It was opportune that the preaching of repentance and the forgiveness of sins through confession of Christ's name should have started from Jerusalem. Where the splendor of his teaching and virtues, where the triumph of his passion, where the joy of his resurrection and ascension were accomplished, there the first root of faith in him would be brought forth; [there] the first shoot of the burgeoning church, like that of some kind of great vine, would be planted. . . . It was opportune that the preaching of repentance and the forgiveness of sins, good news to be proclaimed to idolatrous nations and those defiled by various evil deeds, should take its start from Jerusalem, lest any of those defiled, thoroughly terrified by the magnitude of their offenses, should doubt the possibility of obtaining pardon if they performed fruits worthy of repentance, when it was a fact that pardon had been granted to those at Jerusalem who had blasphemed and crucified the Son of God. *Homilies on the Gospels 2.15.*

Peace Through Christ. ANTHANSIUS: Who is the one who has done this, or who is the one who has joined together in peace people who once hated one another, except for the beloved Son of the Father, the Savior of all, even Jesus Christ, who because of his own love suffered all things for our salvation? For from ages past the peace he would initiate was promised. *On The Incarnation 52.1.*

Walk in the Light. JEROME: For all who do evil hate the light and fail to come to the light lest their works be proven. But you, the house of Jacob, the house of my people, come with me and let us walk together in the light of the Lord. Let us accept the gospel of Christ and be illuminated by him who said, "I am the light of the world." *Commentary on Isaiah 1.2.5-6.*

⁑ PSALM OF RESPONSE: *Psalm 122*

NEW TESTAMENT READING: *Romans 13:11-14*

REFLECTIONS FROM THE CHURCH FATHERS

Full Time to Awake. CHRYSOSTOM: Paul is not trying to frighten his hearers but to encourage them, so as to detach them from their love of the things of this world. It was not unlikely that at the beginning of their endeavors they would be more dedicated and slacken off as time went on. But Paul wants them to do the opposite—not to slacken as time goes on but to become even more dedicated. For the nearer the King is, the more they ought to be ready to receive him. *Homilies on Romans 23.*

Cast Off Works of Darkness. ORIGEN: This may be understood in both a universal and in a particular sense. In the first instance, the light is dawning everywhere, and the reign of darkness over the world is rapidly coming to an end. . . . In the second instance, if we have Christ in our hearts he gives us light. Therefore if the reason of knowledge drives away our ignorance and if we turn away from unworthy deeds and do what is right, we are in the light and are walking honestly as if in the day. *Commentary on the Epistle to the Romans.*

Opportunities May Be Lost. DIODORE: The "day" is the time of this life which remains to us, in which we can do good works. The "night" is the future, in which it will no longer be possible to work. Then we shall lie in the darkness, having lost the chance to do good works. *Pauline Commentary from the Greek Church.*

Restraint of Excess. CHRYSOSTOM: Paul does not forbid alcohol; he is opposed only to its excessive use. Nor does he prohibit sexual intercourse; rather, he is against fornication. What he wants to do is to get rid of the deadly passions of lust and anger. Therefore he does not merely attack them but goes to their source as well. For nothing kindles lust or wrath so much as excessive drinking. *Homilies on Romans 24.*

Put on Christ. DIODORE: This means that we should imitate Christ in what we do and show him to others in the way we behave. *Pauline Commentary from the Greek Church.*

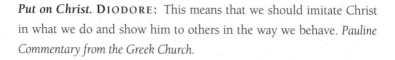 GOSPEL READING: *Matthew 24:36-44*

REFLECTIONS FROM THE CHURCH FATHERS

Whether the Son Knows the Day: HILARY OF POITIERS: When Christ taught us that no one knows the day on which the end of time will come, not the angels and not even himself, he removed from us any need to be concerned about its date. O immeasurable mercy of divine goodness! *On Matthew 26:4.*

They Did Not Know Until the Flood Came. ORIGEN: All who listen to the depths of the gospel and live it so completely that none of it remains veiled from them care very little about whether the end of the world will come suddenly and all at once or gradually and little by little. Instead, they bear in mind only that each individual's end or death will arrive on a day and hour unknown to him and that upon each one of us "the day of the Lord will come like a thief." *Commentary on Matthew 56.*

In the Field, at the Mill. CHRYSOSTOM: From both employees and employers some will be taken and some will be left. Among those who are at ease and those who labor, some will be taken, some left. Rank or station will not matter . . . he seems to indicate that the advent will come at night, like a thief, as Luke also indicates. It is amazing how fully he knows all things. *The Gospel of Matthew, Homily 77.2.*

Living in Expectation. ANONYMOUS: Why is the date of an individual's death hidden from him? Clearly it is so that he might always do good, since he can expect to die at any moment. The date of Christ's second advent is withheld from the world for the same reason, namely, so that every generation might live in the expectation of Christ's return. This is why, when his disciples asked him, "Lord, will you restore the kingdom to Israel at this time?" Jesus replied, "It is not for you to know the times and the seasons which the Father has established by his authority." *Incomplete Work on Matthew, Homily 51.*

⁜ CLOSING PRAYER

Therefore, we ask that we may know what we love, since we ask nothing other than that you give us yourself. For you are our all: our life, our light, our salvation, our food and our drink, our God. Inspire our hearts, I ask you, Jesus, with that breath of your Spirit. *Columbanus*

The Hope of the World

THEME

The prophet Isaiah foretells the coming of Christ (Is 11:1-10), who will defend the afflicted and crush the oppressor (Ps 72:1-7). In light of the Savior's arrival, John the Baptist calls us to repentance (Mt 3:1-12). We praise God for his marvelous deeds (Ps 18-19). Because of Christ, the root of Jesse, we have hope for the future through the power of the Holy Spirit (Rom 15:4-13).

OPENING PRAYER: *Second Sunday in Advent*

O God, who did look on humanity when they had fallen down into death and resolve to redeem them by the advent of your only-begotten Son, grant, we ask you, that they who confess his glorious incarnation may also be admitted to the fellowship of him their Redeemer; through the same Jesus Christ our Lord. Amen. *Ambrose*

OLD TESTAMENT READING: *Isaiah 11:1-10*

REFLECTIONS FROM THE CHURCH FATHERS

The Source of All Blessing. BEDE: The prophet Isaiah testified that it was necessary that our Redeemer be conceived in Nazareth when he said, "There will come forth a rod out of the root of Jesse, and a *nazareus* will go up from his root." *Nazareus* can be translated either as "flower" or as "pure." The Son of God who was made flesh for us can rightly be called by these names because he assumed a human nature which was pure of every vice and because he is the font and source of spiritual fruit for all who believe in him, to whom he also both showed an example and granted the gift of righteous and blessed living. *Homilies on the Gospels 1.6.*

The Spirit Rested. JUSTIN MARTYR: The Scriptures state that these gifts of the Holy Spirit were bestowed upon him, not as though he were in need of them but as though they were about to rest upon him, that is, to come to an end with him, so that there would be no more prophets among [his] people as of old. *Dialogue with Trypho 87.*

Distinguish Between Your Fears. AUGUSTINE: It is not the fear with which Peter denied Christ that we have received the spirit of, but that fear concerning which Christ himself says, "Fear him who has power to destroy both soul and body in hell; yes, I say to you, 'Fear him.' This, indeed, he said, lest we should deny him from the same fear which shook Peter; for such cowardice he plainly wished to be removed from us when he, in the preceding passage, said, "Be not afraid of them that kill the body, and after that have no more that they can do." It is not of this fear that we have received the spirit, but of power, and of love and of a sound mind. *On Grace and Free Will 39.*

His Hand. AMBROSE: Hear how the antidote was administered to the flesh: the Word of God became flesh, put his hand into the serpent's den, removed the venom and took away sin. In other words, "from sin, he condemned sin in the flesh." *Explanation of the Twelve Psalms 37.4.*

PSALM OF RESPONSE: *Psalm 72:1-7, 18-19*

NEW TESTAMENT READING: *Romans 15:4-13*

REFLECTIONS FROM THE CHURCH FATHERS

The Scriptures Enable Hope and Patience. CHRYSOSTOM: These things were written so that we might not fall away, for we have many battles to fight, both inward and outward. But being comforted by the Scriptures we can exhibit patience, so that by living in patience we might dwell in hope. For these things produce one another—hope brings forth patience, and patience, hope. *Homilies on Romans 27.*

The God of Steadfastness. [PSEUDO-]CONSTANTIUS: By "the God of steadfastness" Paul means the Holy Spirit. *The Holy Letter of St. Paul to the Romans.*

Bind Yourselves to One Another. CHRYSOSTOM: Let us obey this command and bind ourselves closely to one another. For it is no longer just the weak that he is encouraging, but everyone. If someone wants to break relations with you, do not do the same with him. . . . Rather, display even more love toward him, that you may draw him to you. For he is a member of the body, and when a member is cut off we must do everything we can to unite it again and then pay more attention to it. *Homilies on Romans 27.*

Jews and Gentiles Fellow Heirs. AMBROSIASTER: God long ago decreed in Psalm 116 that by the intervention of his mercy Jews and Gentiles would be united. The Gentiles would be granted grace to become fellow heirs with the Jews, who by the grace of God were long ago named as his people. While the Jews were noble, the Gentiles were ignoble, but now by God's mercy the Gentiles have been made noble as well, so that all may rejoice together by acknowledging the truth. *Commentary on Paul's Epistles.*

In Believing. CHRYSOSTOM: In other words, may you get rid of your heartlessness toward one another and not be cast down by temptations. You will achieve this by abounding in hope, which is the cause of all good things and comes from the Holy Spirit. It is not just from the Spirit, though, because you must do your part also. That is why Paul adds the words "in believing." *Homilies on Romans 28.*

GOSPEL READING: *Matthew 3:1-12*

REFLECTIONS FROM THE CHURCH FATHERS

Remove the Stones from the Road. CHROMATIUS OF AQUILEIA: Hence John prepared these ways of mercy and truth, faith and justice. Concerning them, Jeremiah also declared, "Stand by the roads, and look, and ask for the ancient paths, where the good way is, and walk in it." Because the heavenly kingdom is found along these ways, not without good reason John adds, "The kingdom of heaven is near." So do you want the kingdom of heaven to also be near for you? Prepare these ways in your heart, in your senses and in your soul. Pave within you the way of chastity, the way of faith and the way of holiness. Build roads of justice. Remove every scandal of offense from your heart. For it is written: "Remove the stones from the road." And then, indeed, through the thoughts of your heart and the very movements of your soul, Christ the King will enter along certain paths. *Tractate on Matthew 8.1.*

No Costly Attire. CHROMATIUS OF AQUILEIA: First, the heavenly life and glorious humility of John are demonstrated in his way of living. He who held the world in low regard did not seek costly attire. He who had no use for worldly delights did not have any desire for succulent foods. What need was there of fancy worldly clothing for one who was dressed with the cloak of justice? What dainty food of the earth could he desire who fed on divine discourses and whose true food was the law of Christ? Such a precursor ought to be the prophet of the Lord and the apostle of Christ who gave himself completely to his heavenly God and had contempt for the things of the world. *Tractate on Matthew 9.1.*

The Axe Laid to the Root. CHRYSOSTOM: He did not merely say that the axe was barely "touching the root" but "laid to the root"—it is poised right next to it and shows no sign of delay. Yet even while bringing the axe so near, he makes its cutting depend upon you. For if you turn around and become better persons, this axe will be laid aside with-

THE HOPE OF THE WORLD

19

out doing any harm. But if you continue in the same ways, it will tear up the tree by the roots. So note well that the axe is neither removed from the root nor too quickly applied to cut the root. He did not want you to become passive, yet he wanted to let you know that it is possible even in a short time to be changed and saved. He first heightened their fear in order to fully awaken them and press them on to repentance. *The Gospel of Matthew, Homily 11.3.*

Fire of the Spirit. CYRIL OF ALEXANDRIA: The blessed Baptist added to the word *spirit* the active and meaningful phrase "and with fire." This was not to imply that through Christ we shall all be baptized with fire but to indicate through the designation *fire* that the life-giving energy of the Spirit is given. *Fragment 27.*

The Threshing Floor. ANONYMOUS: The threshing floor is the church, the barn is the kingdom of heaven, and the field is the world. Therefore, like the head of the household who sends out reapers to mow down the stalks in the field and bring them to the threshing floor that he may thresh and winnow them there and separate the wheat from the chaff, the Lord sends out his apostles and other teachers as reapers. He will cut down all the people in the world and gather them onto the threshing floor of the church, where we are to be threshed at one point and then winnowed. As the grain of wheat enclosed in the chaff cannot escape unless it has been threshed, so too it is hard for one to escape worldly encumbrances and carnal affairs while one is enclosed in the chaff, unless one has been shaken by some hardship. Note that once the full grain has been slightly shaken it sheds its chaff. If it is flimsy, it takes longer to escape. If it is empty, it never emerges but is ground in its chaff and then thrown out with the chaff. In this way, all who take delight in carnal things will be like the grain and the chaff. But one who is faithful and has a good heart, once he experiences adversity, disregards those things that are carnal and hastens to God. If he has been somewhat unfaithful, however, only with great difficulty will he go back to God. As for him who is unfaithful and empty, though he may be sorry over his circumstances, like empty grain he will emerge from the chaff—he will never leave carnal things or worldly encumbrances behind, nor will he go over to God. Rather, he will be ground up with the things that are evil and thus be cast out with the unfaithful like the chaff. *Incomplete Work on Matthew, Homily 3.*

CLOSING PRAYER

O you who are everywhere present, filling yet transcending all things; ever acting, ever at rest; you who teach the hearts of the faithful without noise of words: teach us, we pray you, through Jesus Christ our Lord. Amen. *Augustine*

Wait for the Lord

THEME

The Lord is faithful forever and offers hope to those in difficult circumstances (Ps 146:5-10). Because God came in the flesh to save us, we can
experience great joy (Is 35:1-10). Jesus is the long-expected Savior of
the world (Mt 11:2-11), and following the example of the prophets,
who patiently awaited the Lord's coming, we must also patiently await
the time of his reappearance (Jas 5:7-10).

OPENING PRAYER: *Third Sunday in Advent*

Through him he has called us out of darkness into the light, out of ignorance into the knowledge of his glory, so that we might hope, Lord,
in your name, for it is the foundation of all creation. *Clement of Rome*

OLD TESTAMENT READING: *Isaiah 35:1-10*

REFLECTIONS FROM THE CHURCH FATHERS

The Soul That Is Parched. GREGORY OF NYSSA: For it is clear that
it is not without soul or sense that he proclaims the good tidings of joy,
but he speaks, by the figure of the desert, of the soul that is parched
and unadorned. *On the Baptism of Christ.*

The Lord. CYRIL OF ALEXANDRIA: Observe how he names him
Lord and calls him God, seeing that he speaks in the Spirit; note that

he knew the Emmanuel would not be simply a man bearing God nor, of a truth, as one assumed as an agent. But he knew that he was truly God and incarnate. *Letter 1.31.*

An Extreme Humility. AUGUSTINE: Christ, you see, was going to come in the flesh, not anyone at all, not an angel, not an ambassador; but "he himself will come and save you." *Sermon 293.8.*

The Strides of the Interior Life. CHROMATIUS OF AQUILEIA: Whoever has gone astray from the way of righteousness or from the way of truth is altogether lame, even if his feet and legs are healthy, since he limps with his mind and soul. For the journey of faith and truth is traveled not with bodily steps but with strides of the interior life. *Sermon 1.3-4.*

Toil and Groaning. AUGUSTINE: Certainly hope is very necessary for us in our exile. It is what consoles us on the journey. When the traveler, after all, finds it wearisome walking along, he puts up with the fatigue precisely because he hopes to arrive. Rob him of any hope of arriving, and immediately his strength for walking is broken. So the hope also which we have here is part and parcel of the justice of our exile and our journey. *Sermon 158.8.*

PSALM OF RESPONSE: *Psalm 146:5-10*

NEW TESTAMENT READING: *James 5:7-10*

REFLECTIONS FROM THE CHURCH FATHERS

God Waits for Repentance. CYRIL OF ALEXANDRIA: If God delays the punishment of sinners, waiting for them to repent, it is not because his character has changed, so that now he loves sin. Rather he is giving them time to repent. *Catena.*

He Will Come Quickly. BEDE: The just Judge will give you the rewards of your patience and will punish your adversaries with what they deserve. He sits at the door where he can watch everything you do, and he will come quickly to give each one whatever he or she deserves. *Concerning the Epistle of St. James.*

Stop Harming the Poor. ISHO'DAD OF MERV: James means that we should stop mocking the poor and doing them harm, complaining about them at the same time, because we shall be judged according to our cruelty and condemned by the righteous judge. *Commentaries.*

Without Complaint. BEDE: James tells us to look to the prophets, who never did anything wrong and who spoke the words of God's Spirit to the people but who nevertheless suffered a terrible end at the hands of unbelievers—Zechariah, Uriah and the Maccabees, for example, not to mention John the Baptist, Stephen, James the son of Zebedee and many others in the New Testament. They did not complain at such an end but were willing to endure it. *Concerning the Epistle of St. James.*

GOSPEL READING: *Matthew 11:2-11*

REFLECTIONS FROM THE CHURCH FATHERS

Are You He Who Is to Come? JEROME: John asks this not because he is ignorant but to guide others who are ignorant and to say to them, "Behold, the Lamb of God, who takes away the sin of the world!" And he had heard the voice of the Father saying, "This is my beloved Son, with whom I am well pleased." Rather, it is the same sort of question as when the Savior asked where Lazarus was buried. The people only meant to show him the tomb, but he wanted them to be brought to faith and see the dead man return to life. Similarly, when John was about to be killed by Herod, he sent his disciples to Christ, intending that when they met him, the disciples would observe his appearance and powers and believe in him, and they would tell this to their teacher when he questioned them. *Commentary on Matthew 2.11.3.*

Forerunner Even into Hell. GREGORY THE GREAT: It seems almost as if John did not know the one he had pointed out, as if he did not know whether he was the same person he had proclaimed by prophesying, by baptizing, by pointing him out! We can resolve this question more quickly if we reflect on the time and order of the events. For when John is standing beside the river Jordan, he declares that this is the Redeemer of the world. But when he has been thrown into jail, he asks whether they were to look for another or whether he had come. This is not because he doubts that he is the Redeemer of the world. John now wants to know whether he who had personally come into the world would also descend personally into the courts of hell. For John had preceded Christ into the world and announced him there. He was now dying and preceding him to the nether world. This is the context in which he asks, "Are you he who is to come, or shall we look for another?" But if he had spoken more fully he might have said, "Since you thought it worthy of yourself to be born for humanity, say whether you will also think it worthy of yourself to die for humanity. In this way I, who have been the herald of your birth, will also be the herald of your death. I will announce your arrival in the nether world as the One who is to come, just as I have already announced it on earth." *Forty Gospel Homilies 6.1.*

The Weakness of the Reed. GREGORY THE GREAT: He did not expect assent to this but denial. As soon as a slight breeze blows on a reed it bends away. What does the reed represent if not an unspiritual soul? As soon as it is touched by praise or slander, it turns in every direction. If a slight breeze of commendation comes from someone's mouth, it is cheerful and proud, and it bends completely, so to speak, toward being pleasant. But if a gust of slander comes from the source from which the breeze of praise was coming, it is quickly turned in the opposite direction, toward raving anger. John was no reed, shaken by the wind. No one's pleasant attitude made him agreeable, and no one's anger made him bitter. *Forty Gospel Homilies 6.2.*

The Least in the Kingdom. THEODORE OF MOPSUESTIA: If John is being judged against other people according to being born from a woman, he will be found to be the greatest of them all. He alone was filled with the Holy Spirit inside his mother's womb, so that he "leaped," and his mother prophesied because she partook in this as well. But if John is judged in relation to those who are to partake of the Spirit in the kingdom of heaven, Jesus says, he will be found to be least. Thus Jesus says that John by no means partakes of such great grace as those who will be reborn into immortality after Jesus' resurrection from the dead and that John will experience physical death. At that time, however, the Spirit's abundance toward people will be so great that no one who has partaken of even the least part of it can afterward fall into death. *Fragment 59.*

CLOSING PRAYER

We ask you, almighty God, let our souls enjoy this their desire, to be enkindled by your Spirit, that being filled as lamps by your divine gift, we may shine like burning lights before the presence of your Son Christ at his coming; through the same Jesus Christ our Lord. Amen. *The Gelasian Sacramentary*

Sources of Grace

THEME

The prophet Isaiah foretold the conception and birth of Jesus as a miraculous sign to us (Is 7:10-16), the way in which God would restore us to salvation (Ps 80:1-7, 17-19). God gives us grace through Jesus Christ, his Son (Rom 1:1-7), who was born of the Virgin Mary by the Holy Spirit (Mt 1:18-25).

OPENING PRAYER: *Fourth Sunday in Advent*

Open our hearts, O Lord, and enlighten us by the grace of your Holy Spirit, that we may seek what is well-pleasing to your will; and so order our doings after your commandments that we may be found meet to enter into your unending joys; through Jesus Christ our Lord. *Bede*

OLD TESTAMENT READING: *Isaiah 7:10-16*

REFLECTIONS FROM THE CHURCH FATHERS

Virgin and Sign. THEOPHYLACT: The Jews say that it is not written in the prophecy "virgin" but "young woman." To which it may be answered that "young woman" and "virgin" mean the same thing in Scripture, for in Scripture "young woman" refers to one who is still a virgin. Furthermore, if it was not a virgin that gave birth, how would it be a sign, something extraordinary? *Explanation of Matthew 23.*

The Message of the Miracles. AUGUSTINE: Christ was born a visible man of a human virgin mother, but he was a hidden God because God was his Father. So the prophet had foretold: "Behold, the virgin shall be with child and shall bring forth a son; and they shall call his name Emmanuel, which is interpreted, God with us." To prove that he was God, Christ worked many miracles, some of which—as many as seemed necessary to establish his claim—are recorded in the Gospels. Of these miracles the very first was the marvelous manner of his birth; the very last, his ascension into heaven in his body risen from the dead. *City of God 18.46.*

Many Longed to See His Day. AUGUSTINE: So do not let it surprise you, unbelieving soul, whoever you are, do not let it strike you as impossible that a virgin should give birth, and in giving birth remain a virgin. Realize that it was God who was born, and you will not be surprised at a virgin giving birth. *Sermon 370.3.*

Choosing Good Is Natural to God. JOHN OF DAMASCUS: Now, since the Lord was not a mere man but was also God and knew all things, he stood in no need of reflection, inquiry, counsel or judgment. He also had a natural affinity for good and antipathy for evil. Thus it is in this sense that the prophet Isaiah, too, says, "Before the child shall know to refuse the evil, he will choose the good." For before the child knows to refuse the evil and to choose the good, he will reject the evil by choosing the good. The "before" shows that he made no inquiry or investigation in a human manner but that since he was God and divinely subsisted in the flesh—that is to say, was personally united to the flesh—by the fact of his very being and his knowing all things he naturally possessed the good. *Orthodox Faith 3.14.*

✠ PSALM OF RESPONSE: *Psalm 80:1-7, 17-19*

⁜ NEW TESTAMENT READING: *Romans 1:1-7*

REFLECTIONS FROM THE CHURCH FATHERS

Never a Time When He Did Not Exist. ORIGEN: Without any doubt, he was made that which he had not previously been according to the flesh. But according to the Spirit he existed beforehand, and there was never a time when he did not exist. *Commentary on the Epistle to the Romans.*

Human and Divine. AUGUSTINE: Paul had to oppose the unbelief of those who accept our Lord Jesus Christ only according to the man whom he put on but do not understand his divinity, which sets him apart from every other creature. *Rudimentary Exposition of the Epistle to the Romans 4.*

Sonship in Power and Sonship by Grace. CYRIL OF ALEXANDRIA: As Christ was predestined to be the Son of God in power, so we too have been predestined to be sons of God, not however in power, but by grace, having been made worthy of such a calling and having received it only by the will of God the Father. . . . We stand in the same relation to him as images do to their original. *Commentary on Romans.*

Confirmation as the Son of God. JOHN OF DAMASCUS: By his miracles and resurrection and by the descent of the Holy Spirit, it was made plain and certain to the world that Christ was the Son of God. *Orthodox Faith 4.18.*

Called to Be Saints. CHRYSOSTOM: "Grace and Peace!" Christ told his apostles to make peace their first word when entering into houses. So it is from this that Paul always starts also, for it was no small war which Christ put an end to, but a many-sided and enduring conflict. And it was not because of anything we had done, but by his grace. *Homilies on Romans 1.*

GOSPEL READING: *Matthew 1:18-25*

REFLECTIONS FROM THE CHURCH FATHERS

The Simple Mystery of the Conception. CHRYSOSTOM: Do not speculate beyond the text. Do not require of it something more than what it simply says. Do not ask, "But precisely how was it that the Spirit accomplished this in a virgin?" For even when nature is at work, it is impossible fully to explain the manner of the formation of the person. How then when the spirit is accomplishing miracles, shall we be able to express their precise causes? *The Gospel of Matthew, Homily 4.3.*

The Mystery of His Divinity. ANONYMOUS: But in explaining that his birth happened in a way quite beyond human nature, he reveals the mystery of his divinity. It was not fitting that the only Son of God should be born in the human way. For he was born not for himself but for humanity. He was indeed born into flesh that would undergo corruption. But Christ was born in order to heal corruption itself. . . . Note that Mary was betrothed to a carpenter. Christ, betrothed to the church, was about to fashion for humanity salvation in its entirety and his entire work from the wood of the cross. *Incomplete Work on Matthew, Homily 1.*

His Corporeal Birth and His Divinity. CHROMATIUS OF AQUILEIA: John, however, addresses the issue of Jesus' divine birth in the preface to his Gospel: "In the beginning was the Word, and the Word was with God, and God was the Word. This was with God in the beginning. All things were made through him and without him nothing was made." The Evangelists help us to recognize both the divine and corporeal birth of the Lord, which they describe as a twofold mystery and a kind of double path. Indeed, both the divine and the bodily birth of the Lord are indescribable, but that from the Father vastly exceeds every means of description and wonder. The bodily birth of Christ was in time; his divine birth was before time. The one in this age, the other before the ages. The one from a virgin mother, the other from God the

Father. Angels and men stood as witnesses at the corporeal birth of the Lord, yet at his divine birth there was not witness except the Father and the Son, because nothing existed before the Father and the Son. But because the Word could not be seen as God in the glory of his own divinity, he assumed visible flesh to demonstrate his invisible divinity. He took from us what is ours in order to give generously what is his. *Tractate on Matthew 2.1.*

Not by Chance. ANONYMOUS: "Now all this came to pass." What is meant by "all"? That the virgin would marry her kinsman, that she would be preserved chaste, that the angel would speak to Joseph in a dream that he would be instructed to accept her as his wife, that the boy would be called Jesus and that the Virgin would bring forth the Savior of the world. "All this took place to fulfill what the Lord had spoken by the prophet, saying, 'Behold, the virgin shall be with child and shall bring forth a son.' Grace is witnessed through the prophets so that the Old and New Testaments may harmonize, grace may compensate for the weakness of the learned and what was predicted long ago might not seem to happen solely by chance. *Incomplete Work on Matthew, Homily 1.*

CLOSING PRAYER

Let us then rejoice in this grace, so that our glorying may bear witness to our good conscience by which we glory, not in ourselves but in the Lord. That is why Scripture says, "He is my glory, the one who lifts up my head." For what greater grace could God have made to dawn on us than to make his only Son become the Son of man, so that human beings might in their turn become children and heirs of God? Ask if this were merited; ask for its reason, for its justification, and whether you will find any other answer but sheer grace. *Augustine*

Unto Us a Child Is Born

THEME

We who have walked in deep darkness have seen a great light! For unto us a child is born, one who will bring eternal peace (Is 9:2-7). We celebrate Christ's birth (Lk 2:1-20) because he became what we are, giving his life freely that through his grace we might have the hope of salvation (Tit 2:11-14). Because of Jesus, we praise God and declare his glory (Ps 96).

OPENING PRAYER: *Christmas*

Bless, O Lord, the worship of your church this day, and bless our endeavors to glorify your name. Let not our hearts be unduly set on earthly things, but incline us to love things heavenly that even now, while we are placed among things that are passing away, we may cling to those that shall abide; through Jesus Christ our Lord, who lives and reigns with you and the Holy Spirit, one God, world without end. Amen. *The Leonine Sacramentary*

OLD TESTAMENT READING: *Isaiah 9:2-7*

REFLECTIONS FROM THE CHURCH FATHERS

Christ's Purity. CASSIODORUS: We often find the Lord Christ described as a child because of the purity of his innocence. The simplicity of youth bestows on a child the blessing of aversion from vices and from the malice of the world. *Exposition of the Psalms 68:18.*

The Mystery of Christ's Cross. CAESARIUS OF ARLES: When Isaac himself carried the wood for the sacrifice of himself, in this, too, he prefigured Christ our Lord, who carried his own cross to the place of his passion. Of this mystery much had already been foretold by the prophets: "And his government shall be upon his shoulders." Christ, then, had the government upon his shoulders when he carried his cross with wonderful humility. Not unfittingly does Christ's cross signify government: by it the devil is conquered and the whole world recalled to the knowledge and grace of Christ. *Sermon 84.3.*

The Wonder of His Birth. EPHREM THE SYRIAN: Today was born the child, and his name was called Wonderful! For a wonder it is that God should reveal himself as a baby. *Hymns on the Nativity.*

Christ's Peace Is Unending. CHRYSOSTOM: For Isaiah said, "There is no end of his peace." And what did happen makes it clear that this peace has spread over the whole earth and sea, over the world where people dwell and where no one lives, over mountains, woodlands and hills, starting from that day on which he was going to leave his disciples and said to them, "My peace I give to you; not as the world gives do I give to you." Why did Christ speak in this way? Because the peace which comes from a human being is easily destroyed and subject to many changes. But Christ's peace is strong, unshaken, firm, fixed, steadfast, immune to death and unending. *Demonstration Against the Pagans 2.8-10.*

PSALM OF RESPONSE: *Psalm 96*

NEW TESTAMENT READING: *Titus 2:11-14*

REFLECTIONS FROM THE CHURCH FATHERS

Sacrifices Disappeared Like Smoke. GREGORY OF NYSSA: Who does not know that the deceit of demons filled every corner of the world and held sway over human life by the madness of idolatry? Who does not realize that every people on earth was accustomed to worship demons under the form of idols, by sacrificing living victims and making foul offerings on their altars? But as the apostle says, from the moment that God's saving grace appeared among humanity and dwelled in human nature, all this vanished into nothing, like smoke. *Address on Religious Instruction 18.*

The Christmas Feast. LEO THE GREAT: It is, therefore, with an unmistakable tenderness that so great a wealth of divine goodness has been poured out on us, dearly beloved. Not only has the usefulness of foregoing examples served for calling us to eternity, but the Truth himself has even "appeared" in a visible body. We ought, then, to celebrate this day of the Lord's birth with no listless and worldly joy. *Sermons 23.5.*

True Renunciation. CHRYSOSTOM: Worldly passions are directed toward things that perish with the present life. Let us then have nothing to do with these. *Homilies on Titus 5.*

He Offered His Real Flesh. ATHANASIUS: How could he have given himself if he had not worn flesh? He offered his flesh and gave himself for us, in order that undergoing death in it, "He might bring to nothing the one who held the power of death, that is, the devil." For this reason we continually give thanks in the name of Jesus Christ. We do not bring to nothing the grace which came to us through him. For the coming of the Savior in the flesh has been the ransom and salvation of all creation. *Letter to Adelphus 60.6.*

GOSPEL READING: *Luke 2:1-20*

REFLECTIONS FROM THE CHURCH FATHERS

All Great Feasts Have Their Origin in Jesus' Nativity. CHRYSOS-TOM: A feast day is about to arrive, and it is the most holy and awesome of all feasts. It would be no mistake to call it the chief and mother of all holy days. What feast is that? It is the day of Christ's birth in the flesh. It is from this day that the feasts of the theophany, the sacred Pasch [Passover], the ascension and Pentecost had their source and foundation. Had Christ not been born in the flesh, he would not have been baptized, which is the theophany or manifestation. Nor would he have been crucified, which is the Pasch. Nor would he have sent down the Spirit, which is Pentecost. Therefore, just as different rivers arise from a single source, these other feasts have their beginnings in the birth of Christ. *On the Incomprehensible Nature of God 6.23-24.*

Bethlehem Has Opened Eden. ANONYMOUS: Bethlehem has opened Eden: Come, let us see! We have found joy hidden! Come, let us take possession of the paradise within the cave. There the unwatered stem has appeared, from which forgiveness blossoms forth! There the undug well is found from which David longed to drink of old! There the Virgin has borne a child, and at once the thirst of Adam and David is made to cease. Therefore let us hasten to this place where for our sake the eternal God was born as a little child! *Ikos of the Nativity of the Lord.*

Christ Became a Humble Child. AMBROSE: He was a baby and a child, so that you may be a perfect human. He was wrapped in swaddling clothes, so that you may be freed from the snares of death. He was in a manger, so that you may be in the altar. He was on earth that you may be in the stars. He had no other place in the inn, so that you may have many mansions in the heavens. He, being rich, became poor for your sakes, that through his poverty you might be rich. Therefore his poverty is our inheritance, and the Lord's weakness is our virtue. He chose to lack for himself, that he may abound for all. The sobs of that appalling infancy cleanse me, those tears wash away my sins. Therefore, Lord Jesus, I owe more to your sufferings because I was redeemed than I do to works for which I was created. . . . You see that he is in swaddling clothes. You do not see that he is in heaven. You hear the cries of an infant, but you do not hear the lowing of an ox recognizing its Master, for the ox knows his Owner and the donkey his Master's crib. *Exposition of the Gospel of Luke 2.41-42.*

Through Swaddling Clothes Jesus Looses the Bands of Sin. JOHN THE MONK: Rejoice, O Jerusalem, and celebrate, all who love Zion! Today the ancient bond of the condemnation of Adam is loosed. Paradise is opened to us. . . . Therefore let all creation sing and dance for joy, for Christ has come to restore it and to save our souls! *Stichera of the Nativity of the Lord.*

CLOSING PRAYER

Dearly beloved, today our Savior is born; let us rejoice. Sadness should have no place on the birthday of life. The fear of death has been swallowed up; life brings us joy with the promise of eternal happiness. No one is shut out from this joy; all share the same reason for rejoicing. Our Lord, victor over sin and death, finding no one free from sin, came to free us all. *Leo the Great*

The Shining Star

⁘ THEME

Isaiah foretells the coming of the wise men (Is 60:1-6); kings who will bring gifts and fall down and worship the Christ child (Ps 72:1-7, 10-14). The wise men come to Bethlehem from the East, following a star and seeking the newborn Jesus. On arriving, they rejoice and worship him (Mt 2:1-12). Through God's grace in sending Christ for us, we are given the mystery of the salvation of humanity (Eph 3:1-12).

⁘ OPENING PRAYER: *Epiphany*

Almighty and everlasting God, who has made known the incarnation of your Son by the bright shining of a star, which, when the wise men beheld, they presented costly gifts and adored your majesty; grant that the star of your righteousness may always shine into our hearts; and that, as our treasure, we may give ourselves and all we possess to your service; through Jesus Christ our Lord. Amen. *The Gelasian Sacramentary*

⁘ OLD TESTAMENT READING: *Isaiah 60:1-6*

REFLECTIONS FROM THE CHURCH FATHERS

Christian Illumination Makes a Difference to Lifestyle. ORIGEN: And the Logos, exhorting us to come to this light, says, in the prophecies of Isaiah, "Enlighten yourself, enlighten yourself. O Jerusalem; for your light is come and the glory of the Lord is risen upon you." Observe now the difference between the fine phrases of Plato respecting the "chief good" and the declarations of our prophets regarding the "light" of the blessed; and notice that the truth as it is contained in Plato concerning this subject did not at all help his readers to attain to a pure worship of God, nor even himself, who could philosophize so grandly about the "chief good," whereas the simple language of the Scriptures led to their honest readers being filled with a divine spirit; and this light is nourished within them by the oil, which in a certain parable is said to have preserved the light of the torches of the five wise virgins. *Against Celsus 6.5.*

Christ As God Is the Light Himself. METHODIUS: Hail and shine thou Jerusalem, for thy light is come, the Light eternal, the Light forever enduring, the Light supreme, the Light immaterial, the Light of same substance with God and the Father, the Light which is in the Spirit and which is the Father; the Light which illumines the ages; the Light which gives light to mundane and supramundane things, Christ our very God. *Oration Concerning Simeon and Anna 13.*

Divine Light Becomes the Outward Garment. METHODIUS: It is the church whose children shall come to her with all speed after the resurrection, running to her from all quarters. She rejoices, receiving the light that never goes down, and clothed with the brightness of the Word as with a robe. For with what other more precious or honorable ornament was it becoming that the queen should be adorned, to be led as a bride to the Lord, when she had received a garment of light and therefore was called by the Father? Come then, let us go forward in our discourse, and look upon this marvelous woman as upon virgins prepared for a marriage, pure and undefiled, perfect and radiating a permanent beauty, wanting nothing of the brightness of light; and instead of a dress, clothed with light itself; and instead of precious stones, her head adorned with shining stars. *Symposium or Banquet of the Ten Virgins 8.5.*

PSALM OF RESPONSE: *Psalm 72:1-7, 10-14*

NEW TESTAMENT READING: *Ephesians 3:1-12*

REFLECTIONS FROM THE CHURCH FATHERS

Fellow Heirs with Christ. JEROME: The Gentiles are fellow heirs with Israel. Put more precisely, they are fellow heirs with Christ. . . . It is not that some possession is divided among us but that God himself in his fullness is our inheritance and possession. *Epistle to the Ephesians 2.3.5.*

The Creator of All Works Through the Son. MARIUS VICTORINUS: Christ is the only-begotten Son of God, and through him all the rest are created. Through him the works of God are created, as God works in and through him. All ages of time are subsequent to Christ, being made by Christ. . . . Therefore, even though God is acknowledged as the Creator, God is nonetheless Creator through Christ. The term Creator therefore does not pertain simply to God as such but pertains to Christ and through Christ to God. Christ who was eternally begotten created all things in time. God worked and created all things through Christ. *Epistle to the Ephesians 1.3.9.*

Realized in Christ. AMBROSIASTER: The saving knowledge of the mystery of God is conferred upon the human race in this way: God bestows his grace on humanity as the firstfruits of Christ's coming kingdom. When Christ appeared God revealed his mystery for the salvation of humanity. *Epistle to the Ephesians 3.12.*

GOSPEL READING: *Matthew 2:1-12*

REFLECTIONS FROM THE CHURCH FATHERS

Distinguishing a Silent Sign from a Spoken Prophecy. GREGORY THE GREAT: We must ask what it means that when our Redeemer was born, an angel appeared to the shepherds in Judea, but a star and

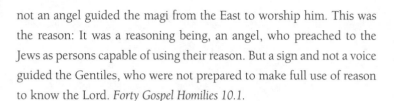

not an angel guided the magi from the East to worship him. This was the reason: It was a reasoning being, an angel, who preached to the Jews as persons capable of using their reason. But a sign and not a voice guided the Gentiles, who were not prepared to make full use of reason to know the Lord. *Forty Gospel Homilies 10.1.*

How the Church Became Israel. CYRIL OF ALEXANDRIA: Jacob was called the first Israel when he beheld the ladder and, on it, the "angels ascending and descending." He wrestled with the one who appeared to him. He heard him say, "Your name shall no more be called Jacob, but Israel." By this name the entire people of Israel was called, as if by a name divinely chosen, setting them apart from other nations. Now, Israel means "a mind that sees God." Thus the church from among the Gentiles is also called Israel, not according to the flesh but according to divine grace. *Fragment 11.*

They Found What They Sought. CHRYSOSTOM: In this way marvel was linked to marvel; the magi were worshiping, the star was going before them. All this is enough to captivate a heart made of stone. If it had been only the wise men or only the prophets or only the angels who had said these things, they might have been disbelieved. But now with all this confluence of varied evidence, even the most skeptical mouths are stopped. Moreover, the star, when it stood over the child, held still. This itself demonstrates a power greater than any star: first to hide itself, then to appear, then to stand still. From this all who beheld were encouraged to believe. This is why the magi rejoiced. They found what they were seeking. They had proved to be messengers of truth. Their long journey was not without fruit. Their longing for the Anointed One was fulfilled. He who was born was divine. They recognized this in their worship. *The Gospel of Matthew, Homily 7.4.*

With Great Joy. ANONYMOUS: By the sign of the star appearing to them at the time, they understood that the birth of the King was revealed to them by divine authority. Through the mystery of the star they understood that the dignity of the King who was born exceeded the measure of all earthly kings. For it was inevitable that they considered this King more glorious than the star, which devotedly paid homage to him. What else could these men do but submit to him when even the stars in the sky saw they were subject to him? How could the earth be rebellious against him upon whom the heavens waited? *Incomplete Work on Matthew, Homily 2.*

CLOSING PRAYER

Make us glad, O God, in recounting your mercies and adoring your holiness, and let it be our chief joy to glorify your holy name. Almighty and everlasting God, the brightness of faithful souls, who brought the Gentiles to your light and made known to them him who is the true Light, and the bright and morning Star: fill, we ask you, the world with your glory, and show yourself by the radiance of your light to all nations. *The Gregorian Sacramentary*

Trust

THEME

God tells us we need not be afraid: he is with us (Is 42:1-9)! He is powerful and full of majesty (Ps 29) and sent his only son, Jesus, who was baptized by John in order to fulfill the law, although he had no need of forgiveness of sins. The Spirit of God descended on Jesus like a dove, and God declared Jesus his "beloved Son, with whom I am well pleased" (Mt 3:13-17). We celebrate the good news that Christ, who was crucified, rose from the dead, and we may find forgiveness of our sins through him (Acts 10:34-43).

OPENING PRAYER

Almighty and merciful God, who wills the faults of sinners to perish, and not their souls; withhold from us the anger which we deserve, and pour out on us the mercy we implore, that through your mercy we may pass from sorrow into joy; through Jesus Christ our Lord. *The Gelasian Sacramentary, adapted*

OLD TESTAMENT READING: *Isaiah 42:1-9*

REFLECTIONS FROM THE CHURCH FATHERS

A Gentle and Peaceful Kingdom. IRENAEUS: By such means was the prophet—very indignant, because of the transgression of the people and the slaughter of the prophets—both taught to act in a more gentle manner, and the Lord's advent was pointed out, that it should be subsequent to that Law which was given by Moses, mild and tranquil, in which he would neither break the bruised reed nor quench the smoking flax. The mild and peaceful repose of his kingdom was indicated likewise. For after the wind which rends the mountains, and after the earthquake, and after the fire, come the tranquil and peaceful times of his kingdom, in which the Spirit of God does, in the most gentle manner, vivify and increase humankind. *Against Heresies 4.20.10.*

God's Judgment Established in Christ's Resurrection. EUSEBIUS OF CAESAREA: With truth and boldness to all he proclaims the judgment of God which has not ceased to operate. Rather it is like light that shines forth through the resurrection of the dead, which the prophetic word announced saying, "He will give light and not be crushed." For those who planned his death tried to crush him and extinguish him. For it is the nature of all mortal species to be crushed by death. But it did not crush him. Only he of all time was shown to be stronger than death. *Commentary on Isaiah 2.22.*

The Fullness of Christian Freedom. LACTANTIUS: Since, therefore, we were as though blind before, and when we sat as though enclosed by the prison house of foolishness in the darkness, not knowing God and his truth, we were enlightened by him who adopted us by his gracious treatment (his will in our favor), and when he had freed us as from evils and bonds and brought us into the light of wisdom, he recognized us as the heirs of his heavenly kingdom. *Divine Institutes 4.20.*

Behold the Father Through the Son. CLEMENT OF ALEXANDRIA: "The opened eyes of the blind" means he provided clear knowledge of the Father through the Son. *Stromateis 1.19.92.2.*

The Son Possesses Glory of the Father. THEODORET OF CYR: It is the Son who possesses the glory of the Father, and it is in the glory of the Father that he will manifest himself: for the divinity of the Son and

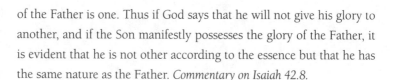

of the Father is one. Thus if God says that he will not give his glory to another, and if the Son manifestly possesses the glory of the Father, it is evident that he is not other according to the essence but that he has the same nature as the Father. *Commentary on Isaiah 42.8.*

PSALM OF RESPONSE: *Psalm 29*

NEW TESTAMENT READING: *Acts 10:34-43*

REFLECTIONS FROM THE CHURCH FATHERS

God Answers Our Prayers Freely. AMBROSE: Even if God is merciful, were he always granting the prayers of all he would seem no longer to act freely, but as it were, like someone under compulsion. Then, since all ask, if he were to hear all, no one would die. How many things do you not ask for daily? Must God's design be destroyed because of you? When you know that a petition cannot always be granted, why do you grieve that sometimes your petition is not obtained? *On His Brother Satyrus 1.65.*

God Rewards the Passionate Heart. CHRYSOSTOM: That is, God calls and attracts him to the truth. Can you see Paul? He was more vehement than anyone in warring and persecuting. Yet because he led an irreproachable life and did these things not through human passion, he was both received and reached a mark beyond all. *Homilies on 1 Corinthians 8.4.*

Baptized in the Name of the Trinity. BASIL THE GREAT: Do not be misled because the apostle frequently omits the names of the Father and the Holy Spirit when he speaks of baptism. Do not imagine because of this that the invocation of their names has been omitted. St. Paul says, "As many of you as were baptized into Christ have put on Christ" and . . . "all of us who have been baptized into Christ Jesus were baptized into his death." To address Christ in this way is a complete profession of faith, because it clearly reveals that God anoints the Son (the anointed One) with the unction of the Spirit. We can learn this from Peter's words in Acts, "God anointed Jesus of Nazareth with the Holy Spirit," or from Isaiah, "The Spirit of the Lord is upon me, because the Lord has anointed me," or from the Psalms, "Therefore God, your God has anointed you with the oil of gladness above your fellows." But the Scripture also speaks of baptism in the context of the Spirit alone, for example, "For by one Spirit we are all baptized into one body." There are other passages that agree with this: "You shall be baptized with the Holy Spirit," and "He will baptize you with the Holy Spirit." No one would claim that on the basis of these passages the invocation of the Spirit's name alone makes baptism complete and perfect. *On the Spirit 12.28.*

GOSPEL READING: *Matthew 3:13-17*

REFLECTIONS FROM THE CHURCH FATHERS

The Waters of Baptism Sanctified. HILARY OF POITIERS: In Jesus Christ we behold a complete man. Thus in obedience to the Holy Spirit the body he assumed fulfilled in him every sacrament of our salvation. He came therefore to John, born of a woman, bound to the law and made flesh through the Word. Therefore there was no need for him to be baptized, because it was said of him: "He committed no sin." And where there is no sin, the remission of it is superfluous. It was not because Christ had a need that he took a body and a name from our creation. He had no need for baptism. Rather, through him the cleansing act was sanctified to become the waters of our immersion. *On Matthew 2.5.*

All That Belongs to Human Nature. ANONYMOUS: How did Christ fulfill the righteousness of baptism? Without doubt according to the demands of human nature: people need to be baptized, for according to carnal nature they are all sinners. Even as he fulfilled the righteousness of baptism, he fulfilled also the righteousness of being born and growing, of eating and drinking, of sleeping and relaxing. He also fulfilled the righteousness of experiencing temptation, fear, flight and sadness, as well as suffering, death and resurrection: that is, according to the requirement of the human nature he took upon himself, he fulfilled all these acts of righteousness. *Incomplete Work on Matthew, Homily 4.*

The Father's Voice, the Son's Humanity, the Spirit's Descent. AUGUSTINE: Here then we have the Trinity presented in a clear way: the Father in the voice, the Son in the man, the Holy Spirit in the dove. This only needs to be barely mentioned, for it is so obvious for anyone to see. Here the recognition of the Trinity is conveyed to us so plainly that it hardly leaves any room for doubt or hesitation. The Lord Christ himself, who comes in the form of a servant to John, is undoubtedly the Son, for here no one can mistake him for either the Father or the Holy Spirit. It is the Son who comes. And who could have any doubt about the identity of the dove? . . . This ineffable Divinity, abiding ever in itself, making all things new, creating, creating anew, sending, recalling, judging, delivering, this Trinity, I say, we know to be at once indescribable and inseparable. *Sermon 2.1-2.*

❧ CLOSING PRAYER

O God, who through your only-begotten Son Jesus Christ our Lord has endowed the regenerating waters with the grace which hallows unto eternal salvation; and did yourself come on him by your Spirit, in the descent of the mysterious Dove on his head; grant, we ask you, that there may come on your whole church a blessing which may keep us all continually safe, may unceasingly bless all classes of your servants, may direct the course of those who follow you and open the door of the heavenly kingdom to all who are waiting to enter; through Jesus Christ our Lord. *Gothic Missal*

Light to the Nations

THEME

God promises us that his salvation will reach to the end of the earth (Is 49:1-7); he sent his only son Jesus, to take away the sin of the world (Jn 1:29-42). Because of God's grace and mercy toward us, we put our trust in him (Ps 40:1-11) and look to the second coming of Christ (1 Cor 1:1-9).

OPENING PRAYER: *Second Sunday After Epiphany*

O God, the light of the hearts that see you, the life of the souls that love you, the strength of the minds that seek you; from whom to turn is to fall, to whom to turn is to rise and in whom to abide is to stand fast forever: grant us your blessing as we offer up our confessions and supplications, and though we are unworthy to approach you or to ask anything of you at all, hear and forgive us, for the sake of our great High Priest and only Mediator, Jesus Christ your Son. Amen. *Augustine*

OLD TESTAMENT READING: *Isaiah 49:1-7*

REFLECTIONS FROM THE CHURCH FATHERS

The Preexistence of the Savior. CYRIL OF JERUSALEM: Consider how he who was not yet born could have a people, unless he were in being before he was born. The prophet says this in his person, "From my mother's womb he gave me my name," because the angel foretold that he would be called Jesus. Again, concerning the plots of Herod, he says, "He . . . concealed me in the shadow of his arm." *Catechetical Lectures 10.12.*

He Made My Mouth Like a Sharp Sword. ORIGEN: If anyone has been able to hold in the breadth of his mind and to consider the glory and splendor of all those things created in him, he will be struck by their very beauty and transfixed by the magnificence of their brilliance or, as the prophet says, "by the chosen arrow." And he will receive from him the saving wound and will burn with the blessed fire of his love. *Commentary on the Song of Songs, Prologue.*

The Salvation of the Nations. THEODORET OF CYR: Then Isaiah predicts the disobedience of the Jews and the salvation of the nations. "Behold, I have given you as a covenant of a race, as a light to the nations. . . ." The Lord's race according to the flesh was the entire race of human beings, yet his own and nearest was Israel. *Commentary on Isaiah 49.6.*

❦ **PSALM OF RESPONSE:** *Psalm 40:1-11*

❦ **NEW TESTAMENT READING:** *1 Corinthians 1:1-9*

REFLECTIONS FROM THE CHURCH FATHERS

The One Assembly All Over the World. CHRYSOSTOM: The church ought to be united because it belongs to God. It does not exist only in Corinth, but all over the world, and it is one, for the church's name (*ekklēsia*) means "assembly." It is not a name of separation, but a name of unity and concord. *Homilies on the Epistles of Paul to the Corinthians 1.1.*

Not by Works. CHRYSOSTOM: You were saved by grace, not by works. And who gave you this grace? It was not Paul, or another apostle, but Jesus Christ himself. *Homilies on the Epistles of Paul to the Corinthians 2.3.*

The Testimony Strengthened by Faith. AMBROSIASTER: The testimony of Christ has been confirmed in them because they have been strengthened by their faith. They had come to put no trust in human things. Rather, all their hope was in Christ, for they were ensnared neither by pleasure nor by the enticements of pleasure. *Commentary on Paul's Epistles.*

Sustained Forever. ORIGEN: Who sustains us? Christ Jesus, the Word and Wisdom of God. Moreover, he sustains us not merely for a day or two, but forever. *Commentary on 1 Corinthians 1.2.52-54.*

The Problem Is Not with God. CHRYSOSTOM: Paul says this so that the Corinthians will not fall into despair when he criticizes them. He reminds them that God is not the problem. We are, because of our sin and unbelief. *Homilies on the Epistles of Paul to the Corinthians 2.7.*

Called to Be One with Christ. ORIGEN: Believe in Christ always, because you were called for no other purpose than to be one with us in him. *Commentary on 1 Corinthians 1.3.*

GOSPEL READING: *John 1:29-42*

REFLECTIONS FROM THE CHURCH FATHERS

John's Task Is Finished with the Lamb's Arrival. CYRIL OF ALEXANDRIA: No longer does John need to "prepare the way," since the one for whom the preparation was being made is right there before his eyes. . . . But now he who of old was dimly pictured, the very Lamb, the spotless Sacrifice, is led to the slaughter for all, that he might drive away the sin of the world, that he might overturn the destroyer of the earth, that dying for all he might annihilate death, that he might undo the curse that is upon us. . . . For *one* Lamb died *for all,* saving the whole flock on earth to God the Father, one for all, that he might subject all to God. *Commentary on the Gospel of St. John 2.1.*

John's Baptism Did Not Endure. **AUGUSTINE:** John received the ministry of baptism so that by the water of repentance he might prepare the way for the Lord, not being himself the Lord. But where the Lord was known, it was superfluous to prepare for him the way, for to those who knew him he became himself the way. Therefore the baptism of John did not last long, but long enough to show our Lord's humility. . . . And did the Lord need to be baptized? I instantly reply to any one who asks this question: Was it needful for the Lord to be born? Was it needful for the Lord to be crucified? Was it needful for the Lord to die? Was it needful for the Lord to be buried? If he undertook for us so great a humiliation, might he not also receive baptism? *Tractates on the Gospel of John 4.12-14.*

Christ Did Not Lack the Holy Spirit. **CHRYSOSTOM:** In case any, however, think that Christ really lacked the Holy Spirit in the way that we do, [the Baptist] corrects this notion also by informing us that the descent of the Holy Spirit took place only for the purpose of making Christ known. *Homilies on the Gospel of John 17.2.*

John's Isolation in the Wilderness Testifies to His Veracity. **THEO-DORE OF MOPSUESTIA:** He revealed why he lived in the wilderness; this certainly happened through a special arrangement by God, in order that he might not have any relationship with the Messiah. And, John certainly would have had such a relationship if he had lived in town since they were of the same age, and they were related. The suspicion would have easily risen that he had testified those words because of that previous relationship, and because of their friendship and the fact that they were related. In order to remove this suspicion, John was segregated from adolescence onward and grew up in the wilderness. Therefore, with good reason he said: "I myself did not know him." I had no familiarity or friendship with him; but I was sent to baptize with water for him so that I might reveal him whom I did not know. He clearly showed that he baptized so that all the Jews who came because of the baptism might have an occasion to hear his doctrine, and to see him to whom he testified. *Commentary on the Gospel of John 1.1.33.*

✦ CLOSING PRAYER

Merciful Lord, the comforter and teacher of your faithful people, increase in your church the desires which you have given, and confirm the hearts of those who hope in you by enabling them to understand the depth of your promises, that all your adopted children may even now behold, with the eyes of faith, and patiently wait for, the light which as yet you do not openly manifest; through Jesus Christ our Lord. Amen. *Ambrose*

Unity in Christ the Light

⊰ THEME

Although we once walked in darkness, God has sent a great light, Jesus. The Lord himself is our light and our salvation (Is 9:1-4). God cares for us in times of trouble and calls for us to seek his face (Ps 27:1, 4-9). With this in mind, we need to put away our disagreements with others (1 Cor 1:10-18) and wholeheartedly follow Christ, repenting of our sins (Mt 4:12-23).

⊰ OPENING PRAYER: *Third Sunday After Epiphany*

O God, the enlightener of all nations, grant your people to enjoy perpetual peace; and pour into our hearts that radiant light which you did shed into the minds of the wise men; through Jesus Christ our Lord. *Trium Magorum, Gelasian*

⊰ OLD TESTAMENT READING: *Isaiah 9:1-4*

REFLECTIONS FROM THE CHURCH FATHERS

God's Grace. AMBROSE: Hence he was in the shadow of life, whereas sinners are in the shadow of death. According to Isaiah, the people who sinned sat in the shadow of death. For these a light arose, not by the merits of their virtues but by the grace of God. There is no distinction, therefore, between the breath of God and the food of the tree of life. No one can say that he can acquire more by his own efforts than what is granted him by the generosity of God. *On Paradise 5.29.*

Christ the Light. LEO THE GREAT: Although he filled all things with his invisible majesty, [Christ] came, nevertheless, to those who had not known him, as if from a very remote and deep seclusion. At that time, he took away the blindness of ignorance, as it has been written: "For those sitting in darkness and in the shadow of death, a light has risen." *Sermon 25.3.*

Spiritual Meaning of Darkness. ORIGEN: Now the expression *darkness* will likewise be used to refer to two corresponding concepts. The statement "And God called the light day, and the darkness he called night" is an example of the more common meaning. An example of the spiritual meaning occurs in the statement "The people who sat in darkness . . . and in the shadow of death, light has dawned on them." *Commentary on the Gospel of John 13.134.*

PSALM OF RESPONSE: *Psalm 27:1, 4-9*

NEW TESTAMENT READING: *1 Corinthians 1:10-18*

REFLECTIONS FROM THE CHURCH FATHERS

United in Judgment. CHRYSOSTOM: It is possible to agree on a form of words but still harbor dissent, which is why Paul speaks the way he does here. It is also possible to share the same opinion with someone but not the same feelings. For example, it is possible to be united in faith without being united in love. This is why Paul says that we must be united both in mind and in judgment. *Homilies on the Epistles of Paul to the Corinthians 3.2.*

How Christ Becomes Divided. AMBROSIASTER: By believing different things about Christ, the people have divided him. One person thought that Christ was a mere man, another than he was only God. One says that he was foretold by the prophets, while another denies it. Paul starts with himself, so that nobody will think that he is disparaging the status of others. If Christ died for us, how can we attribute his grace and blessing to men, thereby doing him a grave injustice? *Commentary on Paul's Epistles.*

The Question Rhetorical. CHRYSOSTOM: Whenever Paul uses rhetorical questions, as he does here, he implies that the whole argument is absurd. *Homilies on the Epistles of Paul to the Corinthians 3.5.*

Why Fishers Were Chosen to Preach. AMBROSIASTER: It was because Christian preaching does not need elaborate refinement of verbal expression that fishers, who were uneducated, were chosen to preach the gospel. In that way the truth of the message would be its own recommendation, and it would not depend on the cleverness or ingenuity of human wisdom. The false apostles were doing just that, and moreover they were omitting the things which the world does not believe, like the virgin birth of Christ and his resurrection from the dead. *Commentary on Paul's Epistles.*

⌘ GOSPEL READING: *Matthew 4:12-23*

REFLECTIONS FROM THE CHURCH FATHERS

Galilee of the Gentiles. ANONYMOUS: There indeed were many lights among the Jews: Moses and Aaron and Joshua and the judges and prophets were all lights. Every teacher is a light to them, whom he enlightens by teaching, as is written: "You are the light of the world." But Christ is the great light. *Incomplete Work on Matthew, Homily 6.*

The Gospel a Great Light. CYRIL OF ALEXANDRIA: And the "great light" is Christ our Lord and the brightness of the gospel preaching. . . . From the true light, indeed, the true light proceeded, and from the invisible, the visible. "He is the image of the invisible God," as the apostle notes. *Tractate on Matthew 15.1.*

How Much Did the Poor Fishermen Leave Behind? GREGORY THE GREAT: Someone may wonder: At the Lord's beckoning, what or how much did these two fishermen, who scarcely had anything, leave behind? On this, my beloved, we should attend to one's intention rather than one's wealth. That person has left behind a lot who keeps nothing for himself, who, though he has little, gives up everything. We tend to be attached to those things we own, and those things we scarcely own, we carefully hold on to. Therefore Peter and Andrew left much behind when they left behind covetousness and the very desire to own. *Forty Gospel Homilies 5.2.*

Jesus Chose the Lowly to Demonstrate Divine Grace. CHROMATIUS OF AQUILEIA: Oh, blessed are those fishermen whom the Lord chose from among so many doctors of the law and scribes, from among so many sages of the world, for the task of divine preaching and the grace of the apostolate! . . . Therefore he has not chosen the noble of the world or the rich, lest their preaching be suspect; not the wise of the world, lest people believe that they persuaded the human race with their wisdom; but he chose illiterate, unskilled and untutored fishermen, so that the Savior's grace might be open. *Tractate on Matthew 16.1.*

The Kingdom Worth Everything. GREGORY THE GREAT: The kingdom of heaven has no price tag on it: It is worth as much as you have. For Zacchaeus it was worth half of what he owned, because the other half that he had unjustly pocketed he promised to restore fourfold. For Peter and Andrew it was worth the nets and vessel they had left behind; for the widow it was worth two copper coins; for another it was worth a cup of cold water. So, as we said, the kingdom of heaven is worth as much as you have. *Forty Gospel Homilies 5.2.*

CLOSING PRAYER

Into your hands, O Lord, we commit ourselves this day. Grant to each one of us so to pass the waves of this troublous world, that finally we lose not the world eternal; through Jesus Christ our Lord. Amen. *Anonymous*

Blessed

⊰ THEME

God asks that we practice love, justice, kindness and humility (Mic 6:1-8). We are to be truthful, not slander others, protect the innocent and do what is right (Ps 15). God shows his strength through what the world considers weak or despised, so that he might be glorified (1 Cor 1:18-31). Thus, he calls "blessed" the poor in spirit, the meek, those who mourn, and the persecuted (Mt 5:1-12).

⊰ OPENING PRAYER: *Fourth Sunday After Epiphany*

Since this fountain, this source of life, this table surrounds us with untold blessings and fills us with the gifts of the Spirit, let us approach it with sincerity of heart and purity of conscience to receive grace and mercy in our time of need. Grace and mercy be yours from the only-begotten Son, our Lord and Savior Jesus Christ; through him and with him be glory, honor and power to the Father and the life-giving Spirit, now and always and forever. *Chrysostom*

⊰ OLD TESTAMENT READING: *Micah 6:1-8*

Sin Not Redeemed by Our Burnt Offerings. AMBROSE: For what is asked of you, O man? Only that you fear God: seek for him, walk after him, follow in his ways. "With what shall I win over the Lord? Shall I win him over with burnt offerings?" The Lord is not reconciled, nor are sins redeemed, with tens of thousands of young goats or thousands of rams or with the fruits of unholiness, but the grace of the Lord is won with a good life. *Flight from the World 6.33.*

Love of God and Neighbor. THEODORE OF MOPSUESTIA: Forget about burnt offerings, countless sacrifices and oblations of firstborn, he is saying. If you are concerned to appease the divinity, practice what God ordered you in the beginning through Moses. What in fact is that? To deliver fair judgment and decision in all cases where you have to choose better from worse, to continue giving evidence of all possible love and fellow-feeling to your neighbor, and be ready to put into practice what is pleasing to God in every way. He means, in short, "You will love God with all your heart, all your mind and all your soul, and you will love your neighbor as yourself," as was said of old through Moses. Do this, he is saying, as something preferable to sacrifices in God's eyes. *Commentary on Micah 6.6-8.*

The Lord Requires the Self. AUGUSTINE: You ask what you should offer: offer yourself. For what else does the Lord seek of you but you? Because of all earthly creatures he has made nothing better than you, he seeks yourself from yourself, because you have lost yourself. *Sermon 48.2.*

⊰ PSALM OF RESPONSE: *Psalm 15*

⊰ NEW TESTAMENT READING: *1 Corinthians 1:18-31*

REFLECTIONS FROM THE CHURCH FATHERS

A Divine Defense Against the Devil. ORIGEN: Who was capable of destroying the plague of ignorance, darkness and destruction? Not a prophet, nor an apostle, nor any other righteous man. Rather there had to be a divine power coming down from heaven, capable of dying on behalf of us all, so that by his death there might be a defense against the devil. *Commentary on 1 Corinthians 1.6.8-12.*

God's Wisdom Confounds Human Reasoning. AMBROSIASTER: When Paul speaks of the "foolishness of God," he is not implying that God is foolish. Rather he is saying that since God's way of reasoning is in accord with things of the spirit, it confounds the reasoning of this world. It is wiser than human reasoning, because spiritual things are wiser than carnal ones. Spiritual things do not exist through carnal ones, but the other way around. Therefore carnal things are understandable in relation to spiritual ones. Similarly, what belongs to heaven is stronger than what belongs to earth. So what seems like the weakness of God is not really weak at all. Christ appeared to be defeated when he was killed, but he emerged as the victor and turned the reproof back on his persecutors. *Commentary on Paul's Epistles.*

Worldly Standards. CHRYSOSTOM: The man who is wise according to the standards of this world is really very foolish, because he will not cast away his corrupt teaching. A little learning is a dangerous thing, because it makes those who have it unwilling to learn more. The unlearned are more open to conviction, because they are not so foolish as to think that they are wise. *Homilies on the Epistles of Paul to the Corinthians 5.2.*

The Harm of Boasting. THEODORE OF MOPSUESTIA: Boasting, even if it is of good works, harms the soul of the boaster. Anyone who boasts of worldly achievements is highly worldly himself. *Pauline Commentary from the Greek Church.*

Our Redemption. AMBROSIASTER: Christ did what he did in order to strengthen believers, for no one can redeem something which did not originally belong to him. *Commentary on Paul's Epistles.*

GOSPEL READING: *Matthew 5:1-12*

REFLECTIONS FROM THE CHURCH FATHERS

The Blessed Poor, Rich in God. CHROMATIUS OF AQUILEIA: We know many poor people, indeed who are not merely poor but blessed. For the necessity of poverty does not produce blessedness in each of us, but a devout trust sustained through poverty does. Some, having no worldly resources, continue to sin and remain without faith in God. Clearly we cannot call these people blessed. We must inquire just who are these blessed of whom the Lord says, "Blessed are the poor in spirit, for theirs is the kingdom of heaven." Jesus means that those persons are truly blessed who, having spurned the riches and resources of the world to become rich in God, desire to be poor in the world. Indeed, such people seem to be poor in the sight of the world, but they are rich in God, needy in the world but wealthy in Christ. *Tractate on Matthew 17.2.1-2.*

A Greater Blessedness. ANONYMOUS: Those who mourn their own sins are indeed blessed, but blessed in a less wonderful way than those who mourn the sins of others. Those who mourn the sins of others are less likely to have sins of their own to mourn. These are the ones who should be called teachers. They are with the Lord on the mountain. *Incomplete Work on Matthew, Homily 9.*

Imitating the Lord's Meekness. CHROMATIUS OF AQUILEIA: The meek are those who are gentle, humble and unassuming, simple in faith and patient in the face of every affront. *Tractate on Matthew 17.4.1-2.*

Mercy Toward Enemies. ANONYMOUS: The kind of compassion referred to here is not simply giving alms to the poor or orphan or widow. This kind of compassion is often found even among those who hardly know God. But that person is truly compassionate who shows compassion even to his own enemy and treats the enemy well. *Incomplete Work on Matthew, Homily 9.*

Where Peace Is. AUGUSTINE: There is in the inner person a kind of daily quarrel; a praiseworthy battle acts to keep what is better from being overcome by what is worse. The struggle is to keep desire from conquering the mind and to keep lust from conquering wisdom. This is the steadfast peace that you ought to develop in yourself, that what is better in you may be in charge of what is worse. The better part in you, moreover, is that part in which God's image is found. This is called the mind, the intellect. There faith burns, there hope is strengthened, there charity is kindled. *Sermon 53A.12.*

Weigh Earthly Disturbance Against Heavenly Glory. ANONYMOUS: One who desires what is in heaven does not fear reproaches on earth. He does not care about what people say about him but rather how God judges him. But one who rejoices in the praise of others and how much they praise him is saddened when he receives no praise. He feels sad at other's reproaches. But a person who is not lifted up by others' praise is not lowered by their reproach. Wherever any one seeks his own glory, just there he also fears reproach. A person who constantly seeks glory on earth constantly fears troubles on earth. But a person who seeks glory only with God fears no disturbance except for God's judgment. *Incomplete Work on Matthew, Homily 9.*

CLOSING PRAYER

O Lord, from whom all good things do come; grant to us, your humble servants, that by your holy inspiration we may think those things that be good, and by your merciful guiding may perform the same, through Jesus Christ our Lord. Amen. *The Gelasian Sacramentary*

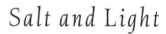

Salt and Light

❧ THEME

How do we please God? By caring for the poor and working toward justice (Is 58:1-9, 12), exhibiting courage, fearing the Lord and following his commandments (Ps 112:1-9, 10) and living in the Spirit, depending on the power of God rather than the power of rhetoric (1 Cor 2:1-12, 13-16). In this way, we become the salt of the earth and the light of the world (Mt 5:13-20).

❧ OPENING PRAYER: *Fifth Sunday After Epiphany*

We ask you, O Lord, give strength to the weary, aid to the sufferers, comfort to the sad, help to those in tribulation. *The Ambrosian Sacramentary*

❧ OLD TESTAMENT READING: *Isaiah 58:1-9, 12*

REFLECTIONS FROM THE CHURCH FATHERS

Fasting No Ground for Pride. JEROME: If you have fasted two or three days, do not think yourself better than others who do not fast. You fast and are angry; the other eats and wears a smiling face. You work off your irritation and hunger in quarrels. He uses food in moderation and gives God thanks. *Letter 22.37.*

God Glorifies Our Efforts. THEODORET OF CYR: The light is desirable, but more desirable still is the dawn which appears after the night.

This he has called "the morning light." . . . Aquila has, "Then your light will break through like the dawn." For just as the dawn tears away the curtain of the night, so, he says, the night of your misfortunes, your life lived under the law will disperse and the light of my providence will be supplied to you. *Commentary on Isaiah 58.8.*

The Need for Compassionate Mediators of God. JEROME: One who is not bound by such chains of sin is found only with difficulty. And a soul is rarely discovered who does not have this extremely heavy collar around its neck . . . unable to look toward heaven. . . . In this way, if we refrain from doing the things just mentioned and if we accomplish the deeds which are to be outlined, so that we would give food to the hungry not as in the case mentioned above, but with our very soul, helping them in whichever way we are able to help, and this "not begrudgingly or under compulsion," but giving from the soul, thus receiving more benefits than we give. . . . And if we suffer with the suffering and mourn with those who mourn, then our light will arise in the darkness, that light which said: "I am the light which came into the world so that all who believe in me would not remain in the darkness" but "have the light of life." *Commentary on Isaiah 16:20-22.*

PSALM OF RESPONSE: *Psalm 112:1-9, 10*

NEW TESTAMENT READING: *1 Corinthians 2:1-16*

REFLECTIONS FROM THE CHURCH FATHERS

In Much Fear. CHRYSOSTOM: Was Paul really afraid of danger? Yes, he was, for even though he was Paul, he was still a man. This is not to say anything against him but rather about the infirmity of human nature. Indeed it is to the credit of his sense of determination that even when he was afraid of death and beatings, he did nothing wrong because of this fear. *Homilies on the Epistles of Paul to the Corinthians 6.2.*

The Mature. **AMBROSIASTER:** The mature are those who preach the cross as wisdom because of the witness of Christ's power at work. They know that actions speak louder than words. Their wisdom is not of this age but of the age to come, when the truth of God will be manifested to those who now deny it. *Commentary on Paul's Epistles.*

The Limits of Human Searching. **ORIGEN:** Only the Spirit can search everything. The human soul cannot do this, which is why it needs to be strengthened by the Spirit if it is ever going to penetrate the depths of God. *Commentary on 1.10.6-10.*

The Unspiritual Try to See Without Light. **CHRYSOSTOM:** God gave us a mind in order that we might learn and receive help from him, not in order that the mind should be self-sufficient. Eyes are beautiful and useful, but if they choose to see without light, their beauty is useless and may even be harmful. Likewise, if my soul chooses to see without the Spirit, it becomes a danger to itself. *Homilies on the Epistles of Paul to the Corinthians 7.9.*

⸙ GOSPEL READING: *Matthew 5:13-20*

REFLECTIONS FROM THE CHURCH FATHERS

Resistance to Corruption. **HILARY OF POITIERS:** The salt of the earth, I suppose, seems at first like nothing special. So what did Jesus mean when he called the apostles the "salt of the earth"? We must look for the words' appropriate meaning. Both the apostles' task and the nature of salt itself will reveal this. The element of water and the element of fire are combined and united in salt. So ordinary salt, made for the use of the human race, imparts resistance to corruption to the meats on which it is sprinkled. And, of course, it is very apt to add the sensation of hidden flavor. Likewise the apostles are the preachers of surprising heavenly things and eternity. Like sowers, they sow immortality on all bodies on which their discourse has been sprinkled. They are perfected by the baptism of water and fire. *On Matthew 4.10.*

Do Not Fence in Goodness. CHRYSOSTOM: The person characterized by humility, gentleness, mercy and righteousness does not build a fence around good deeds. Rather, that one ensures that these good fountains overflow for the benefit of others. One who is pure in heart and a peacemaker, even when persecuted for the sake of truth, orders his way of life for the common good. *The Gospel of Matthew, Homily 15.7.*

Good Works to Glorify God. AUGUSTINE: One must look deeply into the human heart to see in what direction it is turned and on what point its gaze is fixed. Suppose someone desires that his good work be seen by others. Suppose he regards his glory and profit according to the estimation of others and seeks to be elevated in the sight of others. By doing so he fulfills neither of the commands that the Lord has given in this text. . . . He did not wish to have glory rendered to God but to himself. . . . It is only for the sake of God's glory that we should allow our good works to become known. *Sermon 54.3.*

Law Summed Up in the Gospel. JEROME: We are promised a new heaven and a new earth, which the Lord God will make. If new ones are to be created, the old ones will therefore pass away. As for what follows, "Not one iota, not a dot, shall be lost from the law until all is accomplished," this literally shows that even what is considered least important in the law is full of spiritual sacraments, and it is all summed up in the gospel. *Commentary on Matthew 1.5.18.*

CLOSING PRAYER

We most earnestly ask you, O Lover of humankind, to bless all your people, the flocks of your fold. Send down into our hearts the peace of heaven, and grant us also the peace of this life. Give life to the souls of all of us, and let no deadly sin prevail against us or any of your people. Deliver all who are in trouble, for you are our God, who sets the captives free; who gives hope to the hopeless, and help to the helpless; who lifts up the fallen; and who is the haven of the shipwrecked. Give your pity, pardon and refreshment to every Christian soul, whether in affliction or error. Preserve us in our pilgrimage through this life from hurt and danger, and grant that we may end our lives as Christians, well-pleasing to you and free from sin, and that we may have our portion and lot with all your saints. *Liturgy of St. Mark*

A Righteous Life

THEME

God gave us instructions about how to live a righteous life (Ex 24:12-18). God is holy and loves justice, and we offer him our worship and praise (Ps 99). We pay close attention to Scripture and the words of Jesus (2 Pet 1:16-21), who is the beloved Son of God and takes away our fear (Mt 17:1-9).

OPENING PRAYER: *Last Sunday After Epiphany, Transfiguration Sunday*

O Lord our God, teach us, we ask you, to ask you aright for the right blessings. Steer the vessel of our life toward yourself, you tranquil haven of all storm-tossed souls. Show us the course wherein we should go. Renew a willing spirit within us. Let your Spirit curb our wayward senses, and guide and enable us unto that which is our true good, to keep your laws, and in all our works evermore to rejoice in your glorious and gladdening presence. For yours is the glory and praise from all your saints, for ever and ever. Amen. *Basil the Great*

OLD TESTAMENT READING: *Exodus 24:12-18*

REFLECTIONS FROM THE CHURCH FATHERS

The Stone of the Law. BEDE: Mystically the rolling away of the stone implies the disclosure of the sacraments, which were formerly hidden and closed up by the letter of the law. The law was written on stone. Indeed in the case of each of us, when we acknowledge our faith in the Lord's passion and resurrection, his tomb, which had been closed, is opened up. *Homilies on the Gospels 2.10.*

To Have God as a Friend. AMBROSE: If anyone therefore desires to behold this image of God, he must love God so as to be loved by him, no longer as a servant but as a friend who observes his commandments, that he may enter the cloud where God is. *On His Brother Satyrus 2.110.*

Moses Was Transfigured. PETER CHRYSOLOGUS: Moses himself was so purified and freed from his body by a fast of forty days that his whole self took on a glorious appearance of divinity. Still in the darkness of our body, he gleamed with the full radiance of divinity. The eyes of mortals could not gaze upon him who, long nourished by the substance of God, had forgotten all about the aids provided by mortals' food. From this he learned that the sustenance of life does not fail those who live in God's sight and with him. *Sermon 166.*

PSALM OF RESPONSE: *Psalm 99*

NEW TESTAMENT READING: *2 Peter 1:16-21*

REFLECTIONS FROM THE CHURCH FATHERS

No Cleverly Devised Myths. OECUMENIUS: Peter says that he has not invented stories like those of the Valentinians but merely handed on the teaching of Christ in simple and humble words, as Paul also told the Corinthians he was doing. *Commentary on 2 Peter.*

Three Times Confirmed. THEOPHYLACT: Peter knew that Jesus received the Father's confirmation from heaven on three different occasions, in his baptism, at his passion and on the mountain. However, this was the one which he himself witnessed. *Commentary on 2 Peter.*

Until the Morning Star Rises in Your Hearts. **BEDE:** In the night of this world, so full of dark temptations, where there is hardly anyone who does not sin, what would become of us if we did not have the lamp of the prophetic word? Will this word always be necessary? No. It is only necessary until the daylight comes. Right now we have a night lamp because we are children of God, and in comparison with the ungodly, we are the very daylight itself. But if we compare what we are now with what we shall be in the future, then we are still in darkness and need this lamp. *On 2 Peter.*

No Attempt to Tilt Its Meaning. **OECUMENIUS:** This means that the prophets received their prophecies from God and transmitted what he wanted to say, not what they wanted. They were fully aware that the message had been given to them, and they made no attempt to put their own interpretation on it. *Commentary on 2 Peter.*

The Spirit Speaks in Us. **SYMEON THE NEW THEOLOGIAN:** You see that it is not I who speak great and extraordinary things to your charity, but the Spirit of God who speaks in us. To this Peter, the chief apostle, bears witness when he says that no prophecy ever came by man, but holy men of God spoke, moved by the Holy Spirit. For though we are insignificant and unworthy, far from all holiness and from the holy men of God, yet we cannot deny the power that has been given to us by God. *Discourses 34.5.*

GOSPEL READING: *Matthew 17:1-9*

REFLECTIONS FROM THE CHURCH FATHERS

The Sun of Righteousness. **ORIGEN:** Do you wish to see the transfiguration of Jesus? Behold with me the Jesus of the Gospels. Let him be simply apprehended. There he is beheld both "according to the flesh" and at the same time in his true divinity. He is beheld in the form of God according to our capacity for knowledge. This is how he was be-

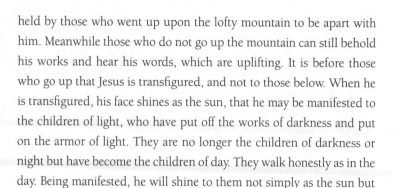

held by those who went up upon the lofty mountain to be apart with him. Meanwhile those who do not go up the mountain can still behold his works and hear his words, which are uplifting. It is before those who go up that Jesus is transfigured, and not to those below. When he is transfigured, his face shines as the sun, that he may be manifested to the children of light, who have put off the works of darkness and put on the armor of light. They are no longer the children of darkness or night but have become the children of day. They walk honestly as in the day. Being manifested, he will shine to them not simply as the sun but as he is demonstrated to be, the sun of righteousness. *Commentary on Matthew 12-37.*

I Will Make Three Booths. **JEROME:** You go astray, Peter, just as the other Evangelist attests: you do not know what you are saying. Do not seek three tabernacles. Seek only the tabernacle of the gospel in which the law and the prophets are to be recapitulated. By seeking three tabernacles you appear to be comparing incommensurably the two servants with the one Lord. Seek only the Father and the Son and the Holy Spirit, for in these there is one God, who is to be worshiped in the tabernacle of your heart. *Commentary on Matthew 3.17.4.*

Listen to Him. **LEO THE GREAT:** A voice from the cloud said, This is my beloved Son, with whom I am well pleased; listen to him. I am manifested through his preaching. I am glorified through his humility. So listen to him without hesitation. He is the truth and the life. He is my strength and wisdom. "Listen to him" whom the mysteries of the law foreshadowed, of whom the mouths of the prophets sang. "Listen to him" who by his blood redeemed the world, who binds the devil and seizes his vessels, who breaks the debt of sin and the bondage of iniquity. "Listen to him" who opens the way to heaven and by the pain of the cross prepares for you the steps of ascent into his kingdom. *Sermon 38.7.*

Jesus Came and Touched Them. **JEROME:** For three possible reasons they were petrified with fear: either because they knew they had sinned or because the bright cloud covered them or because they had heard the voice of God the Father speaking. Human weakness is not strong enough to bear the sight of such great glory but trembles with its whole heart and body and falls to earth. . . . "And Jesus came up and touched them." Because they were lying down and could not rise, he mercifully came up and touched them so that through his touch he might put to flight their fear and strengthen their weakened limbs. "And he said to them, 'Rise, and don't be afraid.'" Those whom he had healed with his hand, he heals with his command, "Have no fear." First fear is expelled so that afterwards doctrine may be imparted. *Commentary on Matthew 3.17.6-7.*

⸎ CLOSING PRAYER

Grant us, even us, O Lord, to know you, and love you and rejoice in you. And if we cannot do these perfectly in this life, let us, at least, advance to higher degrees every day, till we can come to do them in perfection. Let the knowledge of you increase in us here, that it may be full hereafter. Let the love of you grow every day more and more here, that it may be perfect hereafter; that our joy may be great in itself and full in you. We know, O God, that you are a God of truth. O make good your gracious promises to us, that our joy may be full. To your honor and glory, who with the Father and the Holy Spirit lives and reigns one God, world without end. Amen. *Augustine*

The Remedy Against Sin

THEME

Adam succumbed to temptation and brought sin on all generations of people (Gen 2:15-17; 3:1-7). We confess our sin and rejoice in God's forgiveness (Ps 32). Just as Adam's sin brought sin on all humankind, so is Christ's redemption of sin available for all (Rom 5:12-19), because Jesus alone was able to resist temptation (Mt 4:1-11).

OPENING PRAYER: *First Sunday in Lent*

Grant to us, O almighty God, that by the annual exercise of Lenten observances we may advance in knowledge of the mystery of Christ and follow his mind by conduct worthy of our calling, through the same Jesus Christ our Lord. *The Gelasian Sacramentary*

OLD TESTAMENT READING: *Genesis 2:15-17; 3:1-7*

REFLECTIONS FROM THE CHURCH FATHERS

The Tree of Life. JOHN OF DAMASCUS: Some have imagined paradise to have been material, while others have imagined it to have been spiritual. However, it seems to me that just as man was created both sensitive and intellectual, so did this most sacred domain of him have the twofold aspect of being perceptible both to the senses and to the mind. For while in his body he dwelled in this most sacred and superbly beautiful place, as we have related, spiritually he resided in a loftier and far more beautiful place. There he had the indwelling God as a dwelling place. *Orthodox Faith 2.11.*

Pride Is the Beginning of All Sin. AUGUSTINE: But it is most truly said . . . "Pride is the beginning of all sin," for it was this sin that overthrew the devil, from whom arose the origin of sin and who, through subsequent envy, overturned the man who was standing in the righteousness from which he had fallen. For the serpent, seeking a way to enter, clearly sought the door of pride, when he declared, "You shall be as gods." That is why it is written, "Pride is the beginning of all sin," and "The beginning of the pride of man is to fall away from God." *On Nature and Grace 29.33.*

Christ Is the Remedy Against Sin. GREGORY OF NYSSA: Those who have been tricked into taking poison offset its harmful effect by another drug. The remedy, moreover, just like the poison, has to enter the system, so that its remedial effect may thereby spread through the whole body. Similarly, having tasted the poison, that is, the fruit, that dissolved our nature, we were necessarily in need of something to reunite it. Such a remedy had to enter into us, so that it might by its counteraction undo the harm the body had already encountered from the poison. And what is this remedy? Nothing else than the body that proved itself superior to death and became the source of our life. *Address on Religious Instruction 37.*

Why Tempted? AUGUSTINE: If someone asks, therefore, why God allowed man to be tempted when he foreknew that man would yield to the tempter, I cannot sound the depths of divine wisdom, and I confess that the solution is far beyond my powers. . . . I do not think that a man would deserve great praise if he had been able to live a good life for the simple reason that nobody tempted him to live a bad one. *On the Literal Interpretation of Genesis 11.4.6.*

⁜ PSALM OF RESPONSE: *Psalm 32*

⁜ NEW TESTAMENT READING: *Romans 5:12-19*

REFLECTIONS FROM THE CHURCH FATHERS

Original Sin. AUGUSTINE: These words clearly teach that original sin is common to all, regardless of the personal sins of each one. *Against Julian 6.20.64.*

Before the Law of Moses, Not of Nature. DIODORE: Sin was in the world before the law of Moses came, and it was counted, though not according to that law. Rather it was counted according to the law of nature, by which we have learned to distinguish good and evil. This was the law of which Paul spoke above. *Pauline Commentary from the Greek Church.*

In What Sense Was Adam the Type of Christ? DIODORE: Adam was a type of Christ not with respect to his sin or his righteousness—in this respect the two men were opposites—but with respect to the effects of what he did. For just as Adam's sin spread to all, so Christ's life also spread to all. *Pauline Commentary from the Greek Church.*

One Man. THEODORET OF CYR: Paul calls Jesus a man in this passage in order to underline the parallel with Adam, for just as death came through one man, so the cure for death came through one man as well. *Interpretation of the Letter to the Romans.*

No Trace of Death. CHRYSOSTOM: Paul speaks of an abundance of grace to show that what we have received is not just a medicine sufficient to heal the wound of sin, but also health and beauty and honor, and glory and dignity far transcending our natural state. Each of these in itself would have been enough to do away with death, but when they are all put together in one there is not a trace of death left, nor can any shadow of it be seen, so entirely has it been done away with. *Homilies on Romans 10.*

By One Man's Obedience. [PSEUDO-]CONSTANTIUS: In this Adam was a type of Christ, because just as by his disobedience death entered the world, so life and resurrection came by the obedience of Christ. *The Holy Letter of St. Paul to the Romans.*

GOSPEL READING: *Matthew 4:1-11*

REFLECTIONS FROM THE CHURCH FATHERS

Not by Bread Alone. THEODORE OF HERACLEA: The first Adam sinned by eating. Christ prevailed by self-control. *Fragment 22.*

Temptation Overcome by Forbearance. CHRYSOSTOM: What does Christ then do? He is neither indignant nor provoked but with extreme gentleness reasons with him again from the Scriptures, saying, "You shall not tempt the Lord your God," teaching us that we must overcome the devil not by miracles but by forbearance and long-suffering and that we should do nothing at all for display and vainglory. *The Gospel of Matthew, Homily 13.4.*

The Three Temptations. GREGORY THE GREAT: When the Lord was tempted by the devil, he answered him with the commands of sacred Scripture. By the Word that he was, he could have easily plunged his tempter into the abyss. But he did not reveal the power of his might, but he only brought forth the precepts of Scripture. This was to give us an example of his patience, so that as often as we suffer something from vicious persons we should be aroused to teach rather to exact revenge. *Forty Gospel Homilies 16.2-3.*

CLOSING PRAYER

Shed your light on us, O Lord, that, being rid of the darkness of our hearts, we may come into the true light which is Christ, the light of the world, who lives and reigns with you in the unity of the Holy Spirit, one God, world without end. *Anonymous*

A Spiritual Journey

⊰ THEME

Just as Abraham was called by God, so we are called to a spiritual journey (Gen 12:1-4a). Our help comes from the Lord, who made all things and who keeps us in his watchful care (Ps 121). God's promises to Abraham are also for believers who have faith (Rom 4:1-5, 13-17) and through baptism are made new (Jn 3:1-17).

⊰ OPENING PRAYER: *Second Sunday in Lent*

O Lord, we ask you mercifully to receive the prayers of your people who call upon you; and grant that they may both perceive and know what things they ought to do, and also may have grace and power faithfully to fulfil the same; through Jesus Christ our Lord. *The Gregorian Sacramentary*

⊰ OLD TESTAMENT READING: *Genesis 12:1-4a*

REFLECTIONS FROM THE CHURCH FATHERS

Abraham Believed God's Promise. AUGUSTINE: The right thing to do, brothers and sisters, is to believe God before he pays up anything, because just as he cannot possibly lie, so he cannot deceive. For he is God. That's how our ancestors believed him. That's how Abraham believed him. There's a faith for you that really deserves to be admired and made widely known. He had received nothing from him, and he believed his promise. We do not yet believe him, though we have already received so much. Was Abraham ever in a position to say to him, "I will believe you, because you promised me that and paid up"? No, he believed from the very first command given, without having received anything else at all. *Sermon 113A.10.*

In Baptism Our Land Is Our Body. CAESARIUS OF ARLES: Now everything that was written in the Old Testament, dearly beloved, provided a type and image of the New Testament. As the apostle says, "Now all these things happened to them as a type, and they were written for our correction, upon whom the final age of the world has come." Therefore, if what happened corporally in Abraham was written for us, we will see it fulfilled spiritually in us if we live piously and justly. "Leave your country," the Lord said, "your kinsfolk and your father's house." We believe and perceive all these things fulfilled in us, brothers, through the sacrament of baptism. Our land is our body; we go forth properly from our land if we abandon our carnal habits to follow the footsteps of Christ. Does not one seem to you happily to leave his land, that is, himself, if from being proud he becomes humble; from irascible, patient; from dissolute, chaste; from avaricious, generous; from envious, kind; from cruel, gentle? Truly, brothers, one who is changed thus out of love for God happily leaves his own land. *Sermon 81.1.*

PSALM OF RESPONSE: *Psalm 121*

NEW TESTAMENT READING: *Romans 4:1-5, 13-17*

REFLECTIONS FROM THE CHURCH FATHERS

Justification by Works and by Faith. ORIGEN: In this whole passage it seems that the apostle wants to show that there are two justifications, one by works and the other by faith. He says that justification by works has its glory but only in and of itself, not before God. Justification by faith, on the other hand, has glory before God, who sees our hearts and knows those who believe in secret and those who do not believe. Thus it is right to say that it has glory only before God, who sees the hidden power of faith. But the one who looks for justification by works may expect honor mainly from other persons who see and approve of them. *Commentary on the Epistle to the Romans.*

Rain Waters the Root and Bears Fruit: ORIGEN: Faith, which believes in the justifier, is the beginning of justification before God. And this faith, when it is justified, is like a root in the soil of the soul, which the rain has watered, so that as it begins to grow by the law of God, branches appear, which bring forth fruit. The root of righteousness does not spring from works; rather, the fruit of works grows from the root of righteousness, namely, by that root of righteousness by which God brings righteousness to the one whom he has accepted apart from works. *Commentary on the Epistle to the Romans.*

Righteousness Greater Than Reward. CHRYSOSTOM: Think how great a thing it is to be persuaded and have complete confidence that God is able not only to set an ungodly man free from punishment but also to make him righteous and count him worthy to receive these immortal honors. *Homilies on Romans 8.*

How Faith Brings Joy. AMBROSIASTER: But faith is the gift of God's mercy, so that those who have been made guilty by the law may obtain forgiveness. Therefore faith brings joy. Paul does not speak against the law but gives priority to faith. It is not possible to be saved by the law, but we are saved by God's grace through faith. *Commentary on Paul's Epistles.*

Seed of Abraham Not Merely a Racial Definition. THEODORET OF CYR: Paul humbled the pride of the Jews by calling all those who imitated Abraham's faith "the seed of Abraham," even if they were of a different race. For if the law punished those who break it, grace gives forgiveness of sins and confirms the promise of God, giving a blessing to the Gentiles. *Interpretation of the Letter to the Romans.*

GOSPEL READING: *John 3:1-17*

REFLECTIONS FROM THE CHURCH FATHERS

Children of God by Virtue of Being Born Again. BASIL THE GREAT: And by the blood of Christ, through faith, we have been cleansed from all sin, and by water we were baptized in the death of the Lord. We have made an avowal . . . that we are dead to sin and to the world, but alive unto righteousness. Thus, baptized in the name of the Holy Spirit, we were born anew. Having been born, we were also baptized in the name of the Son, and we put on Christ. Then, having put on the new man according to God, we were baptized in the name of the Father and called sons of God. *Concerning Baptism.*

The Story of Moses and the Brass Serpent. CYRIL OF ALEXANDRIA: [This story is a type of] the whole mystery of the incarnation. For the serpent signifies bitter and [deadly] sin, which was devouring the whole race upon the earth . . . biting the soul of man, and infusing [it with the venom] of wickedness. [And there is no way that we could have escaped being conquered by it], save by the [relief] which [only comes] from heaven. The Word of God then was made in the likeness of sinful flesh, "that he might condemn sin in the flesh," as it is written. *Commentary on the Gospel of St. John 2.1.*

He Gave What Was Most Precious to Show His Abundant Love. ISAAC OF NINEVEH: The sum of all is God, the Lord of all, who from love of his creatures has delivered his Son to death on the cross. For God so loved the world, that he gave his only-begotten Son for it. Not that he was unable to save us in another way, but in this way it was possible to show us his abundant love abundantly, namely, by bringing us near to him by the death of his Son. If he had anything more dear to him, he would have given it to us, in order that by it our race might be his. And out of his great love he did not even choose to urge our freedom by compulsion, though he was able to do so. But his aim was that we should come near to him by the love of our mind. And, our Lord obeyed his Father out of love for us. *Mystical Treatise 74 [509].*

The Sick Who Resist the Physician's Help Destroy Themselves.
AUGUSTINE: As far as it lies in the power of the physician, he has come to heal the sick. Whoever does not observe his orders destroys himself. Why would he be called the Savior of the world except because he saves the world? *Tractate on the Gospel of St. John 12.12.*

⌐CLOSING PRAYER

O you who behold all things, we have sinned against you in thought, word and deed; blot out our trangressions, be merciful to us sinners and grant that our names may be found written in the book of life, for the sake of Christ Jesus our Savior. Amen. *Nerses of Clajes*

Living Water

THEME

Water is used throughout Scripture as a symbol of faith. In the Old Testament, it sometimes foreshadows Christ's sacrifice for our sins (Ex 17:1-7). In the New Testament, Jesus offers forgiveness to all, regardless of race or past misdeeds, and "living water," which is the Holy Spirit and eternal life (Jn 4:5-42). Through his death, we are reconciled to God (Rom 5:1-11), our Creator and King, to whom we offer praise and thanks for our salvation (Ps 95).

OPENING PRAYER: *Third Sunday in Lent*

Almighty and everlasting God, by whom that begins to be which was not and that which lay hidden is made visible, cleanse away the folly of our heart and purify us from our secret vices, that we may be able to serve you, O Lord, with a pure mind; through Jesus Christ our Lord. [Amen.] *The Gelasian Sacramentary*

OLD TESTAMENT READING: *Exodus 17:1-7*

REFLECTIONS FROM THE CHURCH FATHERS

For What Did the People Thirst? CAESARIUS OF ARLES: What then does Scripture mention in what follows? "In their thirst for water, the people grumbled against Moses." Perhaps this word that he said may seem superfluous, that the people thirsted for water. For since he said, "In their thirst," what need was there to add "for water"? Thus indeed the ancient translation has it. Why did he add this, except because they thirsted for water when they should have thirsted for justice? "Blessed are they who hunger and thirst for justice"; and again, "thirsty is my soul for the living God." Many people are thirsty, both the just and sinners; the former thirst after justice, the latter after dissipation. The just are thirsty for God; sinners for gold. For this reason the people thirsted after water when they should have thirsted after justice. *Sermon 103.2.*

Christ the Rock Had to Suffer. CAESARIUS OF ARLES: Then the Lord said to Moses, "Take the staff and strike the rock, that it may produce water for the people." Behold, there is a rock, and it contains water. However, unless this rock is struck, it does not have any water at all. But when it has been struck, it produces fountains and rivers, as we read in the Gospel: "He who believes in me, from within him there shall flow rivers of living water." When Christ was struck on the cross, he brought forth the fountains of the New Testament. Therefore it was necessary for him to be pierced. If he had not been struck, so that water and blood flowed from his side the whole world would have perished through suffering thirst for the word of God. *Sermon 103.3.*

The Rock and the Virgin Mary. AMBROSE: It does not surpass faith that a virgin gave birth, when we read that even a rock poured out water and that the waves of the sea were made solid in the form of a wall. *Letter 15.*

⁂ PSALM OF RESPONSE: *Psalm 95*

⁂ NEW TESTAMENT READING: *Romans 5:1-11*

REFLECTIONS FROM THE CHURCH FATHERS

God Reconciled Us to Himself. CHRYSOSTOM: What does it mean to have peace? Some say that it means that we should not fall out with one another because of disagreements over the law. But it seems to me that he is speaking much more about our current behavior. . . . Paul means here that we should stop sinning and not go back to the way we used to live, for that is to make war with God. How is this possible? Paul says that not only is it possible, it is also reasonable. For if God reconciled us to himself when we were in open warfare with him, it is surely reasonable that we should be able to remain in a state of reconciliation. *Homilies on Romans 9.*

Like Exercise for Athletes. **BASIL THE GREAT:** For those who are well prepared, tribulations are like certain foods and exercises for athletes which lead the contestant on to the inheritance of glory. When we are reviled, we bless; maligned, we entreat; ill-treated, we give thanks; afflicted, we glory in our afflictions. *Homily 16.*

The Greatest Gift Possible. **CHRYSOSTOM:** God has given us the greatest gift possible and in profusion. . . . What is this gift? It is the Holy Spirit. *Homilies on Romans 9.*

Moral Progress. **AUGUSTINE:** Who can hurt such a man? Who can subdue him? In prosperity he makes moral progress, and in adversity he learns to know the progress he has made. When he has an abundance of mutable goods he does not put his trust in them, and when they are taken away he gets to know whether or not they have taken him captive. *Of True Religion 92.*

If He Died for Enemies, Think of What He Will Do for Friends. **AMBROSIASTER:** If Christ gave himself up to death at the right time for those who were unbelievers and enemies of God . . . how much more will he protect us with his help if we believe in him! . . . So if he died for his enemies, just think what he will do for his friends! *Commentary on Paul's Epistles.*

GOSPEL READING: *John 4:5-42*

REFLECTIONS FROM THE CHURCH FATHERS

Divine Majesty Beheld in the Feelings of Our Human Nature.
AMBROSE: Many things we read and believe, in the light of the sacrament of the incarnation. But even in the very feelings of our human
nature we may behold the divine majesty. Jesus is wearied with his
journey, that he may refresh the weary; he desires to drink when about
to give spiritual drink to the thirsty; he was hungry, when about to supply the food of salvation to the hungry. *Of the Christian Faith 5.4.54.*

Human Nature Buds into a Virtuous Life Watered by Living Water.
CYRIL OF ALEXANDRIA: Jesus calls the quickening gift of the Spirit
"living water" because mere human nature is parched to its very roots,
now rendered dry and barren of all virtue by the crimes of the devil.
But now human nature runs back to its pristine beauty, and drinking
in that which is life-giving, it is made beautiful with a variety of good
things and, budding into a virtuous life, it sends out healthy shoots of
love toward God. *Commentary on the Gospel of St. John 2.4.*

Benefits of the Godhead Come Through the Spirit. AUGUSTINE: So
let us believe also in the Holy Spirit. He is God, you see, because it is
written, "God is spirit." Through him we have received the forgiveness
of sins, through him we believe in the resurrection of the flesh, through
him we hope for life everlasting. But take care you don't fall into error
by counting, and imagine that I have said there are three gods, because
I have given the one God a third name. There is one substance of godhead in the Trinity, one power, one might, one majesty, one name of divinity; just as he himself said to his disciples when he had risen from
the dead: "Go, baptize the nations," not in several names, but "in the
one name of the Father and the Son and the Holy Spirit." *Sermon 215.8.*

ᛜCLOSING PRAYER

O Lord, we ask you favorably to hear the prayers of your people; that we, who are justly punished for our offenses, may be mercifully delivered by your goodness, for the glory of your name; through Jesus Christ our Savior, who lives and reigns with you and the Holy Spirit ever, one God, world without end. [Amen.] *The Gregorian Sacramentary*

Light Dispels Darkness

⛨ THEME

God looks at our hearts, not our outward appearances, as he showed when choosing David as king, prefiguring Christ (1 Sam 16:1-13). Like David, we trust God; we have confidence in his protection even when we are in the midst of great difficulty (Ps 23). The light of Christ's grace and forgiveness dispels the darkness of sin (Eph 5:8-14)—he is the light of the world (Jn 9:1-41).

⛨ OPENING PRAYER: *Fourth Sunday in Lent*

Permit us not, O Lord, to hear your word in vain. Convince us of its truth, cause us to feel its power and bind us to yourself with cords of faith and hope and love that never shall be broken. We bind to ourselves today, you our God: your power to hold us, your hand to guide us, your eye to watch us, your ear to hear us, your wisdom to teach us, your word to give us speech, your presence to defend us, this day and every day; in the name of the blessed Trinity, Father, Son and Holy Spirit, to whom be the kingdom, and the power and the glory, forever and forever. Amen. *Patrick*

⛨ OLD TESTAMENT READING: *1 Samuel 16:1-13*

REFLECTIONS FROM THE CHURCH FATHERS

David's Kingly Anointing Prefigures Christ's. LACTANTIUS: The Jews had before been directed to compose a sacred oil, with which those who were called to the priesthood or to the kingdom might be anointed. And as now the robe of purple is a sign of the assumption of royal dignity among the Romans, so with them the anointing with the holy oil conferred the title and the power of king. . . . On this account we call him Christ, that is, the Anointed, who in Hebrew is called the Messiah. *Epitome of the Divine Institutes 4.7.*

The Eyes of the Lord. TERTULLIAN: You are human, and so you know other people only from the outside. You think as you see, and you see only what your eyes let you see. But "the eyes of the Lord are lofty." "Man looks on the outward appearance, God looks on the heart." So "the Lord knows them that are his" and roots up the plant which he has not planted. He shows the last to be first, he carries a fan in his hand to purge his floor. Let the chaff of light faith fly away as it pleases before every wind of temptation. So much the purer is the heap of wheat which the Lord will gather into his garner. *Prescriptions Against Heretics 3.*

⊰ **PSALM OF RESPONSE:** *Psalm 23*

⊰ **NEW TESTAMENT READING:** *Ephesians 5:8-14*

REFLECTIONS FROM THE CHURCH FATHERS

Light Exposes Darkness. CHRYSOSTOM: He has said, *you are light.* Light exposes what takes place in darkness. Insofar as you are light your goodness shines forth. The wicked are not able to hide. Their actions are illuminated as though a lamp were at hand. *Homily on Ephesians 18.5.11-13.*

The Metaphors of Sleeping and Death. AMBROSIASTER: By *sleep* he signifies a stupor of the mind. The sleepers are lost from the true path. This estrangement is a kind of death, from which he calls them to rise that they may repent and acknowledge the truth, which is Christ. Thus the faithless and vicious, steeped as they are in mud without hope of life, are called to rise and come out and have a share in life with Christ, so as to pass from the shadows out to the light and from death to life. *Epistle to the Ephesians 5.14.*

Addressed Also to Believers Who Sleep in Sin. CHRYSOSTOM: He is not speaking only to unbelievers. For there are many believers, no less than unbelievers, who remain still trapped in various sins. There are indeed some who do so all the more. Therefore it was necessary to call these to *awake,* etc. *Homily on Ephesians 18.4.14.*

GOSPEL READING: *John 9:1-41*

REFLECTIONS FROM THE CHURCH FATHERS

Nothing Happens Without a Purpose. THEODORE OF MOPSUESTIA: Since the disciples had this opinion about the blind man, the Lord appropriately adjusts his speech in order to answer their question: "Who sinned, this man or his parents?" They were asking, in other words, whether this happened to him because of the sins of his parents, or because of the man's sin—as if there was no other cause for such an event. After they asked this, the Lord taught them that there are many reasons for all these events, and that they are certainly secret and unexplainable. And so, we always complain about events whose causes we ignore, but then we also learn that nothing happens in vain. This knowledge will be given to us in the future world, because what is hidden now will be revealed to us. *Commentary on the Gospel of John IV (9:3).*

What Is the Cause of Suffering? CYRIL OF ALEXANDRIA: Truly, by our minds we cannot comprehend those things which are far above us. And, I should advise the prudent and myself above all to abstain from wishing to thoroughly scrutinize them. For we should recall to mind what we have been commanded and not curiously examine things which are too deep or pry into those which are too hard, or rashly attempt to discover those things which are hidden in the Divine and ineffable counsel alone. Rather concerning such matters we should piously acknowledge that there are certain wondrous things which God alone understands. At the same time we should maintain and believe that since God is the fountain of all righteousness, God will neither do nor determine anything whatsoever in human affairs, or in those of the rest of creation which is unbecoming to God or differs at all from the true righteousness of justice. *Commentary on the Gospel of St. John 6.1.*

You Too Come to Siloam. AMBROSE: Again, I ask you: What is he trying to convey to us by spitting on the ground, mixing his saliva with clay and putting it on the eyes of a blind man, saying: "Go and wash yourself in the pool of Siloam (a name that means 'sent')?" What is the meaning of the Lord's action in this? Surely one of great significance, since the person whom Jesus touches receives more than just his sight. In one instant we see both the power of his divinity and the strength of his holiness. As the divine light, he touched this man and enlightened him; as priest, by an action symbolizing baptism he wrought in him his work of redemption. They only reason for his mixing clay with the saliva and smearing it on the eyes of the blind man was to remind you that he who restored the man to health by anointing his eyes with clay is the very one who fashioned the first man out of clay, and that this clay that is our flesh can receive the light of eternal life through the sacrament of baptism. You, too, should come to Siloam, that is, to him who was sent by the Father, as he says in the Gospel, "My teaching is not my own, it comes from his who sent me." Let Christ wash you and you will then see. Come and be baptized, it is time; come quickly, and you too will be able to say, "I went and washed"; you will be able to say, "I was blind, and now I can see." And, as the blind man said when his eyes began to receive the light, you too can say, "The night is almost over and the day is at hand." *Letter 67.4-6.*

Two Recoveries of Sight, Two Types of Blindness. CHRYSOSTOM: In this passage he speaks of two recoveries of sight and of two types of blindness: one sensory and the other spiritual. . . . But they were intent only on the sensory things and were ashamed only of sensory blindness. *Homilies on the Gospel of John 59.1-2.*

CLOSING PRAYER

Christ with me, Christ before me, Christ behind me,
Christ within me, Christ beneath me, Christ above me,
Christ on my right, Christ on my left. . . .
Christ in the heart of everyone who thinks of me,
Christ in the mouth of everyone who speaks to me,
Christ in every eye that sees me,
Christ in every ear that hears me.
[Amen.]
The Canticle of St. Patrick

The Giver of Life

THEME

God is all-powerful, bringing life from death (Ezek 37:1-14), just as his
Son, Jesus, has the power over life and death (Jn 11:1-45). We wait patiently for him to help us in the midst of our troubles, knowing that his
love for us is unwavering (Ps 130); we submit to God, setting our
minds on spiritual things, rather than the things of the flesh, and letting
Christ dwell in us (Rom 8:6-11). Jesus is the giver of life and has the
power over life and death (Jn 11:1-45).

OPENING PRAYER: *Fifth Sunday in Lent*

O God, who has given us the great and saving truths of your gospel:
grant us, we ask you, to live amid these things, to meditate on them and
to seek them; for one who goes on seeking, finds. Help us, therefore,
to learn those things on earth, the knowledge of which shall abide with
us in heaven. Grant this for Jesus Christ's sake. Amen. *Jerome*

OLD TESTAMENT READING: *Ezekiel 37:1-14*

REFLECTIONS FROM THE CHURCH FATHERS

**The Church Is a Community Where the Weak Are Supported by the
Strong.** BASIL THE GREAT: According to the same reasoning there
should also be certain bones of the inner man in which the bond of
union and harmony of spiritual powers is collected. Just as the bones

by their own firmness protect the tenderness of the flesh, so also in the church there are some who through their own constancy are able to carry the infirmities of the weak. And as the bones are joined to each other through articulations by sinews and fastenings which have grown upon them, so also would be the bond of charity and peace, which achieves a certain natural junction and union of the spiritual bones in the church of God. *Homily 16.*

The Vision Portrays Future Judgment. JUSTIN MARTYR: The prophets have foretold two comings of Christ: the one, which already took place, was that of a dishonored and suffering man; the other coming will take place, as it is predicted, when he gloriously comes from heaven with his angelic army, when he also raises to life the bodies of all the men that ever were, cloaks the worthy with immortality, and relegates the wicked, who will be subjected to pain for all eternity, into the eternal fire, together with the evil demons. We will now show how these things also have been predicted as yet to happen. Thus spoke the prophet Ezekiel, "And the bones came together, bone to its bone." *Apology 1.52.*

PSALM OF RESPONSE: *Psalm 130*

NEW TESTAMENT READING: *Romans 8:6-11*

REFLECTIONS FROM THE CHURCH FATHERS

Life and Peace. GENNADIUS OF CONSTANTINOPLE: "Death" is estrangement and punishment from God; "life" is immortality and "peace" is fellowship with him. *Pauline Commentary from the Greek Church.*

Whether the Flesh Can Please God. CHRYSOSTOM: What Paul means by the flesh in this passage is not the essence of the body but a life which is carnal and worldly, serving self-indulgence and extravagance to the full. *Homilies on Romans 13.*

Your Bodies Are Dead Because of Sin. CHRYSOSTOM: Paul is not saying here that the Spirit is Christ but is showing rather that anyone who has the Spirit has Christ as well. For where the Spirit is, there Christ is also. Wherever one person of the Trinity is present, the whole Trinity is present too. For the Trinity is undivided and has a perfect unity in itself. *Homilies on Romans 13.*

He Who Raised Christ Will Raise You. POLYCARP: But he who raised Christ up from the dead will raise us up also if we do his will and walk in his commandments and love what he loved, keeping ourselves from all unrighteousness, covetousness, love of money, evil speaking, false witness, "not rendering evil for evil, or railing for railing," or blow for blow or cursing for cursing, but being mindful of what the Lord said in his teaching. *The Epistle to the Philippians 2.*

GOSPEL READING: *John 11:1-45*

REFLECTIONS FROM THE CHURCH FATHERS

Jesus Grants Free Reign to the Grave. PETER CHRYSOLOGUS: You see how he gives full scope to death. He grants free reign to the grave; he allows corruption to set normal course; he allows the realm of darkness to seize his friend, drag him down to the underworld and take possession of him. He acts like this so that human hope may perish entirely and human despair reach its lowest depths. The deed he is about to accomplish may then clearly be seen to be the work of God, not of man. He waited for Lazarus to die, staying in the same place until he could tell his disciples that he was dead; then he announced his intention of going to him. "Lazarus is dead," he said, "and I am glad." Was this a sign of his love for his friend? Not so. Christ was glad because their sorrow over the death of Lazarus was soon to be changed into joy at his restoration to life. "I am glad for your sake," he said. Why for their sake? Because the death and raising of Lazarus were a perfect prefiguration of the death and resurrection of the Lord himself. *Sermon 63.2.*

Resurrecting Adam and His Descendants. ROMANUS THE MELODIST: In order that he might bring an end to the mourning of Martha,
The Savior of all spoke to her and addressed
These divine words to her:
"I exist as the Light of the world
And the resurrection of all from the dead;
It was for this end that I appeared in order to resurrect Adam
And the descendants of Adam
And on the fourth day to resurrect Lazarus
Taking pity, as a Merciful One, on
The tears of Mary and Martha." *Kantakion 15.8.*

We Are Alive If We Believe. AUGUSTINE: "Whoever believes in me," he said, "even though he dies, is alive." He both proclaims life and does not deny death. What does it mean, "even though he dies, is alive?" Even though he dies in the body, he is alive in the spirit. Then he adds, "and whoever is alive and believes in me, will not die forever." Well now, "even though he dies;" but how is it the case if "he will not die?" Yes, but even though he dies for a time, "he will not die forever." That is how we solve that problem. And see how the words of Truth do not contradict each other, and how they can support our loving devotion. So then, although we are going to die in the body, we are alive if we believe. *Sermon 173.1.*

Jesus Weeps for All Humanity. CYRIL OF ALEXANDRIA: The Jews thought that Jesus wept on account of the death of Lazarus, but in fact he wept out of compassion for all humanity, not mourning Lazarus alone, but all of humanity which is subject to death, having justly fallen under so great a penalty. *Commentary on the Gospel of St. John 7.1.*

CLOSING PRAYER

Almighty God, who sees that we have no power of ourselves to help ourselves: Keep us, both outwardly in our bodies and inwardly in our souls, that we may be defended from all adversities which may happen to the body and from all evil thoughts which may assault and hurt the soul; through Jesus Christ our Lord. [Amen.] *The Gregorian Sacramentary*

Humbled for Our Sake

THEME

God is with us in our suffering (Is 50:4-9a), and we petition him to protect us from those who wish us harm (Ps 31:9-16). Yet, the innocent Jesus, God's only Son, was crucified so that we might have eternal life and forgiveness of sins (Mt 27:11-54). Because he defeated death, his name is above all names, and we give God glory (Phil 2:5-11).

OPENING PRAYER: *Palm or Passion Sunday*

We ask you, O Lord, in your forgiving love, turn away what we deserve for our sins, nor let our offenses prevail before you; but let your mercy always rise up to overcome them; through Jesus Christ our Lord. Amen. *The Leonine Sacramentary*

OLD TESTAMENT READING: *Isaiah 50:4-9a*

REFLECTIONS FROM THE CHURCH FATHERS

Be Silent So We Can Speak. AMBROSE: Now what ought we to learn before everything else, but to be silent, that we may be able to speak? Lest my voice should condemn me, before that of another acquits me; for it is written: "By your words you shall be condemned." What need is there, then, that you should hasten to undergo the danger of condemnation by speaking, when you can be more safe by keeping silent? How many have I seen to fall into sin by speaking, but scarcely one by keeping silent; and so it is more difficult to know how to keep silent than how to speak. . . . He is wise, then, who knows how to keep silent. Lastly, the Wisdom of God said: "The Lord has given to me the tongue of learning, that I should know when it is good to speak." Justly, then, is he wise who has received of the Lord to know when he ought to speak. Wherefore the Scripture says well: "A wise man will keep silence until there is opportunity." *Duties of the Clergy 1.2.*

Prophecy Fulfilled in the Gospels. THEODORET OF CYR: This whole recital is taught by the holy Gospels. For the servant of the high priest gave him a blow on the cheek; some struck his face, saying; "Prophesy to us, Christ! Who is the one who struck you?" Others spat in his face; as for Pilate, he had him scourged and delivered him to be crucified. So, all this he predicts in the prophecy to teach of his own patience. *Commentary on Isaiah 50.6.*

PSALM OF RESPONSE: *Psalm 31:9-16*

NEW TESTAMENT READING: *Philippians 2:5-11*

REFLECTIONS FROM THE CHURCH FATHERS

What the Hymn as a Whole Tells Us. EPIPHANIUS THE LATIN: You see that he reveals Christ to be a man but not merely so, since he is the mediator of God and humanity. . . . He is trueborn God by nature with respect to his Father, but with respect to humanity he is Mary's trueborn son by nature, begotten without the seed of a man. *Ancoratus 44.*

The Sovereignty Temporarily Under Submission. NOVATIAN: The sovereignty of the divine Word temporarily submitted to assume a man and for a season humbled himself and abased himself, not exercising his nature through his powers, while he bore the man that he had assumed. He emptied himself when he bowed to injuries and slanders, when he heard unspeakable insults and suffered indignities. *On the Trinity 22.8-9.*

His Humbling Becomes Our Example. CYRIL OF ALEXANDRIA: He humbled himself, according to the Scriptures, taking on himself the form of a slave. He became like us that we might become like him. The work of the Spirit seeks to transform us by grace into a perfect copy of his humbling. *Festal Letter 10.4.*

He Put Death to Death. EPIPHANIUS THE LATIN: The Word tasted death once on our behalf, the death of the cross. He went to his death so that by death he might put death to death. The Word, becoming human flesh, did not suffer in his divinity but suffered with humanity. *Ancoratus 92.*

This Is the Name of God. NOVATIAN: He received *the name that is above every name,* which we must certainly understand as nothing other than the name of God. For it belongs to God to be above all. So it follows that the name that is above all belongs to him who is above all, namely, God. *On the Trinity 22.10.*

GOSPEL READING: *Matthew 27:11-54*

REFLECTIONS FROM THE CHURCH FATHERS

Barabbas or Jesus? CHRYSOSTOM: Note how far Pilate goes to give the crowd a chance to relieve themselves from blame. Observe how they did not leave themselves so much as a shadow of an excuse. *The Gospel of Matthew, Homily 86.2.*

He Washed His Hands. CHRYSOSTOM: Why then did Pilate allow him to be sacrificed? Why didn't he rescue him, like the centurion had rescued Paul? For that man too was aware that he could have pleased the Jews and that a sedition may have taken place and a riot; nevertheless he stood firm against all these. But not so Pilate. He was extremely cowardly and weak. He joined in their corruption. *The Gospel of Matthew, Homily 86.2.*

And on Our Children. CHRYSOSTOM: What then did they do? When they saw the judge washing his hands and saying, "I am innocent," they cried out, "His blood be on us and on our children.". . . Note how great is their madness. For passion and evil desire work on us like this. They did not permit anyone to see anything of what was right. They not only curse themselves, they draw down the curse upon their own children as well. *The Gospel of Matthew, Homily 86.2.*

Wine Mingled with Gall. CHROMATIUS OF AQUILEIA: When they had come to Golgotha, the Gospel says, "They gave him vinegar mixed with gall, but when he tasted it, he refused to drink." This event was foretold by David when he wrote, "They gave me gall for food, and they gave me vinegar to slake my thirst." Take note of the mystery revealed here. Long ago, Adam tasted the sweetness of the apple and obtained the bitterness of death for the whole human race. In contrast to this, the Lord tasted the bitterness of gall and obtained our restoration from death's sting to the sweetness of life. He took on himself the bitterness of gall in order to extinguish in us the bitterness of death. *Tractate on Matthew 19.7.*

He Laid Down His Life. CHRYSOSTOM: "When Jesus had cried out with a loud voice, he yielded up the spirit." This refers to what he had earlier said: "I have power to lay down my life and I have power to take it again," and "I lay it down of myself." So for this cause he cried with the voice, that it might be shown that the act is done by his own power. *The Gospel of Matthew, Homily 88.1.*

Graves Were Opened. HILARY OF POITIERS: The earth shook. For the earth could not hold this dead man. Rocks were split, for the Word of God and the power of his eternal goodness rushed in, penetrating every stronghold and principality. Graves were opened, for the gates of death had been unlocked. And a number of the bodies of the saints who had fallen asleep arose. Dispelling the shadows of death and illuminating the darkness of hell, Christ destroyed the spoils of death itself at the resurrection of the saints, who saw him immediately. The centurion and the guards who witnessed this disturbance of the entire natural order confessed him to be the Son of God. *On Matthew 23.7.*

CLOSING PRAYER

Speak to our hearts, O Christ our overseer; say to us, "Hail, be strong and of good courage." You who did this of old, can you not do the same now? You can, you can indeed! For you are almighty. You can, O most Loving, you can do what we cannot conceive; for nothing is impossible to you, almighty God! Truly, O Savior, for us your body is red with blood; you have "washed your garment in wine and your clothes in the blood of grapes"; for you are God alone, crucified for us, whom the old transgression gave over to death; by your wound have been healed the countless wounds of our sins. And now, O loving and crucified Christ, redeem us with your own; save us, O loving Goodness, O God, who reigns with the Father and the Holy Spirit, one God forever, throughout all ages. [Amen.] *Old Gallican Missal*

Christ Is Risen!

⊣ THEME

Jesus has risen (Acts 10:34-43)! God's love for us is unshakeable. In the most desperate situations, he will be victorious (Ps 118:1-2, 14-24). Let us then also walk in new life, putting away the old things (Col 3:1-4). Let us celebrate with the two women at the tomb Jesus' triumph over death. He is risen, as he said (Mt 28:1-10).

⊣ OPENING PRAYER: *Resurrection Sunday: Easter*

O God, who by your only-begotten Son has overcome death and opened to us the gate of everlasting life, grant us, we ask you, that we who celebrate the solemnities of our Lord's resurrection may by the renewing of your Spirit arise from the death of the soul; through the same Jesus Christ our Lord. [Amen.] *The Gelasian Sacramentary*

⊣ READING FROM ACTS: *Acts 10:34-43*

REFLECTIONS FROM THE CHURCH FATHERS

All May Receive Forgiveness of Sins. BEDE: He says, "It is clear that God is no respecter of persons, for he sent his only-begotten Son, who is the Lord and creator of all, to make peace with the human race. In his name, as the prophets bore witness, not only the Jews, but all who believe, may receive forgiveness of sins." *Commentary on the Acts of the Apostles 10.36.*

By Death He Conquered the Death of Humanity. GREGORY OF NYSSA: Therefore, since it was necessary that the good shepherd lay down his life on behalf of the sheep, so that through his own death he might destroy death, the captain of our salvation, by bringing death to pass, becomes a composite in his human nature, both as a priest and a lamb in the ability to receive a share of suffering. *Against Apollinaris.*

The Lord Provided Proof of His Resurrection. THEODORET OF CYR: For since eating is proper to them that live this present life, of necessity the Lord by means of eating and drinking proved the resurrection of the flesh to those who did not acknowledge it to be real. This same course he pursued in the case of Lazarus and of Jairus' daughter. For when he had raised up the latter he ordered that something should be given her to eat and he made Lazarus sit with him at the table and so showed the reality of the rising again. *Dialogue 2.*

PSALM OF RESPONSE: *Psalm 118:1-2, 14-24*

NEW TESTAMENT READING: *Colossians 3:1-4*

REFLECTIONS FROM THE CHURCH FATHERS

Look at Heavenly Things. ISAAC OF NINEVEH: What is the resurrection of the soul, of which the apostle speaks, saying, "If then you have been raised with Christ"? When the apostle said, "God who commanded the light to shine out of darkness, has shined into our heart," he showed this resurrection to be the exodus from the old state which in the likeness of Sheol incarcerates a man so that the light of the gospel will not shine mystically upon him. This is a breath of life through hope in the resurrection, and by it the dawning of divine wisdom shine in his heart, so that a man should become new, having nothing of the old man. Then the image of Christ is formed in us through the Spirit of wisdom and revelation of the knowledge of him. *Ascetical Homilies 37.*

A Sobering Reminder. SEVERIAN OF GABALA: Our life is hidden until the blessing of eternal life shall be revealed to all, when the glory of Christ shall appear in his second coming. *Pauline Commentary from the Greek Church.*

Solid Encouragement. AUGUSTINE: But what did he go on to say? "When Christ appears, your life, then you also will appear with him in glory." So now is the time for groaning, then it will be for rejoicing; now for desiring, then for embracing. What we desire now is not present; but let us not falter in desire; let long, continuous desire be our daily exercise, because the one who made the promise doesn't cheat us. *Sermons 350A.4.*

GOSPEL READING: *Matthew 28:1-10*

REFLECTIONS FROM THE CHURCH FATHERS

Why Was the Stone Rolled Back? PETER CHRYSOLOGUS: An angel descended and rolled back the stone. He did not roll back the stone to provide a way of escape for the Lord but to show the world that the Lord had already risen. He rolled back the stone to help his fellow servants believe, not to help the Lord rise from the dead. He rolled back the stone for the sake of faith, because it had been rolled over the tomb for the sake of unbelief. He rolled back the stone so that he who took death captive might hold the title of Life. Pray, brothers, that the angel would descend now and roll away all the hardness of our hearts and open up our closed senses and declare to our minds that Christ has risen, for just as the heart in which Christ lives and reigns is heaven, so also the heart in which Christ remains dead and buried is a grave. May it be believed that just as he died, so was he transformed. Christ the man suffered, died and was buried; as God, he lives, reigns, is and will be forever. *Sermons 75.4.*

Jesus Met Them. PETER CHRYSOLOGUS: While they were going, the Lord "met them" and said, "Hail!" When he meets them, he does not frighten them with his power but comes before them with the ardor of his love. He does not startle them with his authority but greets them warmly. He binds them by the covenant of the bridegroom, not by the right of the ruler. He honors them with the love of a brother. He greets them with a gracious salutation. At one time he had said to his disciples, "Salute no one on the road." So why is it that here along the way this visitor is so quick to salute them? He does not wait to be recognized. He does not demand to be understood. He does not allow himself to be questioned. Rather, he extends this greeting immediately, enthusiastically. He does this because the force of his love overcomes and surpasses all. *Sermons 75.2.*

They Worship Him. CHRYSOSTOM: Some among you may desire to be like these faithful women. You too may wish to take hold of the feet of Jesus. You can, even now. You can embrace not only his feet but also his hands and even his sacred head. You too can today receive these awesome mysteries with a pure conscience. You can embrace him not only in this life but also even more fully on that day when you shall see him coming with unspeakable glory, with a multitude of the angels. If you are so disposed, along with him, to be compassionate, you shall hear not only these words, "All hail" but also those others: "Come, you blessed of my Father, inherit the kingdom prepared for you before the foundation of the world." *The Gospel of Matthew, Homily 89.3.*

CLOSING PRAYER

O God, who for our redemption gave your only-begotten Son to the death of the cross, and by his glorious resurrection has delivered us from the power of the enemy, grant us to die daily to sin, that we may evermore live with him, in the joy of his resurrection; through the same Jesus Christ our Lord. Amen. *Gregory the Great*

Confidence Through Christ

⟨ THEME

Jesus has risen from the dead (Acts 2:14a, 22-32). With this in mind, God deserves our confidence. He will bring us through any difficulties, and we will once again be joyful (Ps 16) because of our hope through the resurrection of salvation of eternal life (1 Pet 1:3-9). Until Jesus comes again, he has left us with the Holy Spirit to guide us and help us on our spiritual journey (Jn 20:19-31).

⟨ OPENING PRAYER: *Second Sunday of Easter*

Lamb of God, who takes away the sin of the world, look on us and have mercy on us, you who are both victim and priest, reward and redeemer; keep safe from all evils those whom you have redeemed, O Savior of the world. *Old Gallican Missal*

⟨ READING FROM ACTS: *Acts 2:14a, 22-32*

REFLECTIONS FROM THE CHURCH FATHERS

Once Fearful, Peter Is Now Bold. CHRYSOSTOM: What is meant by "with the eleven"? They expressed themselves through a common voice, and he spoke for everyone. The eleven stood by as witnesses to what he said. "He raised his voice," that is, he spoke with great confidence, that they might perceive the grace of the Spirit. He, who could not endure the questioning of a poor girl, now discourses with such great confidence in the middle of people all breathing murder upon him. This in itself became an indisputable proof of the resurrection. He spoke [among] people who could deride and make a joke of such things! . . . For wherever the Holy Spirit is present, people of clay are changed into people of gold. Look at Peter now, if you would, and scrutinize the timid one, the man without understanding (as Christ said, "Are you also still without understanding?"). This is the man who was called Satan after that marvelous confession. Consider also the unanimity of the apostles. Of their own accord they yielded to him the office of speaking, for there was no need for them all to speak. So "he raised his voice and addressed them" with every confidence. *Homilies on the Acts of the Apostles 4.*

He Died and Rose As Man. THEODORET OF CYR: Peter said, "God has made this Jesus both Lord and Christ" and said too, "This Jesus whom you crucified God has raised up." Now it was the manhood, not the Godhead, that became a corpse, and he who raised it was the Word, the power of God, who said in the Gospel, "Destroy this temple, and in three days I will raise it up." So when it is said that God has made him who became a corpse and rose from the dead both Lord and Christ, what is meant is the flesh, and not the Godhead of the Son. *Dialogue 3.*

Not Abandoned to Hell. BEDE: Christ did indeed descend, with respect to his soul, to those in hell so that he might come to the aid of those for whom it was necessary; but he was not abandoned in hell, because returning immediately he sought his body, which was to rise again. *Commentary on the Acts of the Apostles 2.31.*

PSALM OF RESPONSE: *Psalm 16*

NEW TESTAMENT READING: *1 Peter 1:3-9*

REFLECTIONS FROM THE CHURCH FATHERS

His Mercy Great Enough. **HILARY OF ARLES:** Peter means that God has acted to redeem us without any help from us. His mercy is great enough to forgive every sin which has been committed in thought, word and deed, from the beginning to the end of the world. *Introductory Commentary on 1 Peter.*

Make Yourself Ready. **BEDE:** Your place in the kingdom of heaven is ready, your room in the Father's house is prepared, your salvation in heaven awaits you. All you have to do, if you want to receive them, is to make yourself ready. But since no one can do this by his own efforts, Peter reminds us that we are kept in the power of God by faith. Nobody can keep doing good works in the strength of his own free will. So we must all ask God to help us, so that we may be brought to perfection by the one who made it possible for us to do good works in the first place. *On 1 Peter.*

Trials for a Time. **BEDE:** Peter says that we must still suffer for a little while, because it is only through the sadness of the present age and its afflictions that it is possible to reach the joys of eternity. He stresses the fact that this is only "for a little while," because once we have entered our eternal reward, the years spent suffering here below will seem like no time at all. *On 1 Peter.*

GOSPEL READING: *John 20:19-31*

REFLECTIONS FROM THE CHURCH FATHERS

Death's Power Banished from the Body. **CYRIL OF ALEXANDRIA:** By his unexpected entry through closed doors Christ proved once more that by nature he was God and also that he was none other than the one who had lived among them. By showing his wounded side and the marks of the nails, he convinced us beyond a doubt that he had raised the temple of his body, the very body that had hung upon the cross. He restored that body which he had worn, destroying death's power over all flesh, for as God, he was life itself. Why would he need to show them his hands and side if, as some perversely think, he did not rise again bodily? And if the goal was not to have the disciples think about him in this way, why not appear in another form and, disdaining any likeness of the flesh, conjure up other thoughts in their minds? But he obviously thought it was that important to convince them of the resurrection of his body that, even when events would have seemed to call for him to change the mode of his body into some more ineffable and surpassing majesty, he nonetheless resolved in his providence to appear once more as he had been in the past [i.e., in the flesh] so that they might not think he was wearing any other form than the one in which he had suffered crucifixion. *Commentary on the Gospel of St. John 12.1.*

The Peace of Christ. CYRIL OF ALEXANDRIA: When Christ greeted his holy disciples with the words, "Peace be with you," by peace he meant himself, for Christ's presence always brings tranquility of soul. This is the grace Saint Paul desired for believers when he wrote, "The peace of Christ which passes all understanding, will guard your hearts and minds." The peace of Christ which passes all understanding is in fact the Spirit of Christ, who fills those who share in him with every blessing. *Commentary on the Gospel of St. John 12.1.*

Reopening Old Wounds. PETER CHRYSOLOGUS: Why does the hand of a faithful disciple in this fashion retrace those wounds which an unholy hand inflicted? . . . Why, Thomas, do you alone, a little too clever a sleuth for your own good, insist that only the wounds be brought forward in testimony to faith? . . . But Thomas was curing not only the uncertainty of his own heart, but also that of all human beings; and since he was going to preach this message to the Gentiles, this conscientious investigator was examining carefully how he might provide a foundation for the faith needed for such a mystery. . . . For the only reason the Lord had kept his wounds was to provide evidence of his resurrection. *Homily 84.8.*

Courageous Endurance. JOHN OF CARPATHOS: Blessed are those who, when grace is withdrawn, find no consolation in themselves, but only continuing tribulation and thick darkness, and yet do not despair; but, strengthened by faith, they endure courageously, convinced that they do indeed see him who is invisible. *Texts for the Monks in India 71.*

CLOSING PRAYER

We bless you, almighty Lord God, for that you have counted [us] worthy to be born again and that you have poured out thy Holy Spirit over them in order to unite them to the body of the church, never to be separated from it by alien works. Grant also to them to whom you have already given remission of sins the earnest of your kingdom: through our Lord Jesus Christ, through whom, with the Holy Spirit, be glory to you to ages of ages. [Amen.] *Canons of Hippolytus*

Breaking Bread

⊰ THEME

Jesus offers forgiveness of sins, which we embrace through baptism (Acts 2:14a, 36-41), and his presence with us today through the breaking of bread in the sacrament of communion (Lk 24:13-25). Because of Christ's perfect life, laid down for our imperfect ones, we are to purify our souls through love and obedience (1 Pet 1:17-23). In the midst of personal affliction and difficulty, we call on the Lord for help, knowing he loves us (Ps 116:1-4, 12-19).

⊰ OPENING PRAYER: *Third Sunday of Easter*

Holy Father, we come before you with humble hearts, confessing our sins. We have chased after the vanities of the world and have wandered from our heart's true home; and, forgetful of you, the living God, we have burned the incense of the soul before false gods that cannot deliver. Deal not with us as we deserve, but pardon our foolish and perverse ways. Of your clemency wash us clean from all sin, for no adversity shall harm us if no wickedness has dominion over us; through Jesus Christ our Lord. Amen. *The Leonine Sacramentary*

⊰ READING FROM ACTS: *Acts 2:14a, 36-41*

REFLECTIONS FROM THE CHURCH FATHERS

The Crucified One Is Exalted. IRENAEUS: Thus the apostles did not preach another God or another Fullness or that the Christ who suffered and rose again was one, while he who flew off on high was another and remained impassible; but that there was one and the same God the Father, and Christ Jesus who rose from the dead. They preached faith in him to those who did not believe on the Son of God and exhorted them out of the prophets, that the Christ whom God promised to send, he sent in Jesus, whom they crucified and God raised up. *Against Heresies 3.12.2.*

The Gentleness of Peter. CHRYSOSTOM: Do you see what a great thing gentleness is, how it stings our hearts more than vehemence? It inflicts indeed a keener wound. For in the case of bodies that have become callous, a blow does not affect the sense so powerfully, but if someone first softens them and makes them tender, then a stab is effective. Likewise here one must first soften, and that which softens is not wrath, not vehement accusation, not reproach, but gentleness. . . . For notice how he gently reminded them of the outrages they have committed, adding no comment. He spoke of the gift of God, he brought in the grace that bears witness to the event, and he drew out his discourse to still greater length. They stood in awe of the gentleness of Peter, because he was speaking like a father and caring teacher to them who crucified his master and breathed murder against himself and his companions. They were not merely persuaded; they even condemned themselves. They came to a sense of their past behavior. *Homilies on the Acts of the Apostles 7.*

Fulfillment of Prophecy. BEDE: Behold the fulfillment of the prophecy of Joel. Notice that after the fire of the Holy Spirit there followed the vapor of compunction, for smoke tends to cause tears. Those who have laughed in ridicule begin to weep. They beat their breasts. They present their prayer to God as a sacrifice, so that as people who are to be saved they may be able to taste of that blood that before, when they were damned, they had called down upon themselves and their children. *Commentary on the Acts of the Apostles 2.37.*

Proved by Their Deeds. CHRYSOSTOM: "What shall we do?" They did what must be done, but we the opposite. They condemned themselves and despaired of their salvation. This is what made them such as they were. They knew what a gift they had received. But how will you become like them, when you do everything in an opposite spirit? As soon as they heard, they were baptized. They did not speak these cold words that we do now, nor did they contrive delays, even though they heard all the requirements. For they did not hesitate when they were commanded to "save yourselves from this generation" but welcomed it. They showed their welcome through action and proved through deeds what sort of people they were. *Homilies on the Acts of the Apostles 7.*

PSALM OF RESPONSE: *Psalm 116:1-4, 12-19*

NEW TESTAMENT READING: *1 Peter 1:17-23*

REFLECTIONS FROM THE CHURCH FATHERS

The Price of Your Redemption. BEDE: The greater the price of your redemption, the more respectful to God you out to be, and not risk offending your Redeemer by falling back into your previous life of wickedness. *On 1 Peter.*

Fully and Perfectly Revealed. OECUMENIUS: Christ existed in earlier times and even before the foundation of the world, when he was hidden by divine providence until the right time should come. *Commentary on 1 Peter.*

Birth from the Spirit. DIDYMUS THE BLIND: Peter uses the words *regeneration* and *restitution* to signify the introduction of birth after the destruction of the first generation of mankind. For how could that not have been destroyed, seeing that it is corrupt, in order to make room for the incorruptible which is coming and which will remain forever? For there is a first birth, in the descent of Adam, which is mortal and therefore corruptible, but there is also a later birth which comes from the Spirit and the ever-living Word of God. *Commentary on 1 Peter.*

GOSPEL READING: *Luke 24:13-35*

REFLECTIONS FROM THE CHURCH FATHERS

Jesus Is to Be Recognized in the Breaking of the Bread. AUGUSTINE: Ah yes, brothers and sisters, but where did the Lord wish to be recognized? In the breaking of bread. We're all right, nothing to worry about—we break bread, and we recognize the Lord. It was for our sake that he didn't want to be recognized anywhere but there, because we weren't going to see him in the flesh, and yet we were going to eat his flesh. So if you're a believer, any of you, if you're not called a Christian for nothing, if you don't come to church pointlessly, if you listen to the Word of God in fear and hope, you may take comfort in the breaking of bread. The Lord's absence is not an absence. Have faith, and the one you cannot see is with you. *Sermon 235.2-3.*

Everything in Scripture Speaks of Christ. AUGUSTINE: All that we read in holy Scripture for our instruction and salvation demands an attentive ear. You have just heard how the eyes of those two disciples whom the Lord joined on their way were kept from recognizing him. . . . He opened their minds to understand the Scriptures. And so let us pray that he will open our own. *Homily 2.1 on 1 John.*

Broken Bread the Key to Open Eyes. EPHREM THE SYRIAN: When the disciples' eyes were held closed, bread too was the key whereby their eyes were opened to recognize the omniscient: saddened eyes beheld a vision of joy and were instantly filled with happiness. *Hymns on Paradise 15.4.*

The Breaking of the Bread Is the Sacrament. AUGUSTINE: And no one should doubt that his being recognized in the breaking of bread is the sacrament, which brings us together in recognizing him. *Letter 149.*

⚜ CLOSING PRAYER

O God, who opens the entrance of the kingdom of heaven to those only who are born again of water and the Holy Spirit, increase evermore on your servants the gifts of your grace, that they who have been cleansed from all sins may not be defrauded of any promises; through our Lord Jesus Christ. [Amen.] *The Gelasian Sacramentary*

Fellowship and Communion

THEME

As the early church did, we are to gather together in fellowship, communion and prayer (Acts 2:42-47). Just as Christ unjustly suffered, we may also experience injustice and suffering (1 Pet 2:19-25). God watches over us; he protects us and leads us in the right direction if we trust him to do so (Ps 23). Christ has come that we might live life to the fullest (Jn 10:1-10).

OPENING PRAYER: *Fourth Sunday of Easter*

We ask you, Lord and Master, to be our help and succor. Save those who are in tribulation; have mercy on the lonely; lift up the fallen; show yourself to the needy; heal the ungodly; convert the wanderers of your people; feed the hungry; raise up the weak; comfort the faint-hearted. Let all the peoples know that you are God alone, and Jesus Christ is your Son, and we are your people and the sheep of your pasture; for the sake of Christ Jesus. Amen. *Clement of Rome*

READING FROM ACTS: *Acts 2:42-47*

REFLECTIONS FROM THE CHURCH FATHERS

Double Ardor of Love. BEDE: If the love of God pervades our hearts, without a doubt it will soon engender affection for our neighbor as well. Hence, because of the double ardor of one and the same love, we read that the Holy Spirit was given twice to the apostles, and the possession of everything without [anyone] having anything of his own is a great token of brotherly love. *Commentary on the Acts of the Apostles 2.44.*

Gladness and Simplicity of Heart. CHRYSOSTOM: Do you see that the words of Peter contain this also, namely, the regulation of life? ["And singleness of heart."] For no gladness can exist where there is no simplicity. *Homilies on the Acts of the Apostles 7.*

Rejoice. AUGUSTINE: One who wishes to make a place for the Lord should rejoice not in private joy but in the joy of all (*gaudio communi*). *Explanation of Psalm 131.5.*

Unity of the Trinity. AUGUSTINE: If, as they drew near to God, those many souls became, in the power of love, but one soul and these many hearts but one heart, what must the very source of love effect between the Father and the Son? Is not the Trinity for even greater reasons, but one God? . . . If the love of God poured forth in our hearts by the Holy Spirit, who is given to us, is able to make of many souls but one soul and of many hearts but one heart, how much more are the Father and the Son and Holy Spirit but one God, one Light, one Principle? *Tractates on the Gospel of John 39.5.*

All in Common. AUGUSTINE: First of all, because you are gathered together in one that you might live harmoniously (*unanimes*) and that there be one soul and one heart toward God. And you should not call anything your own, but let all things be common to you and distributed to each one of you according to need. *Letter 211.5.*

⊰ PSALM OF RESPONSE: *Psalm 23*

⊰ NEW TESTAMENT READING: *1 Peter 2:19-25*

REFLECTIONS FROM THE CHURCH FATHERS

God Too Suffered Unjustly. HILARY OF ARLES: You will be approved by God if you suffer unjustly, because you know that that is exactly what he did. *Introductory Commentary on 1 Peter.*

The Guardian of Your Souls. HILARY OF ARLES: Error has three causes—darkness, loneliness and ignorance. The Gentile sheep were wandering among idols because of their foolish ignorance, and they found themselves lost in the darkness of sin and in the loneliness of a strange nation. Peter goes on to add that now they have turned to the guardian [bishop] of their souls, because although there are many guardians around who care about the things of the flesh, there are few who can look deep into the soul and take care of it. *Introductory Commentary on 1 Peter.*

Shepherd and Guardian. BEDE: Here Peter alludes to the parable in the Gospels where the Good Shepherd leaves the ninety-nine sheep in the desert and goes after the one who has gone astray. For as it is said there, when he finds it he puts it on his shoulder and rejoices. Jesus wanted to redeem us so much that he put our sins on his shoulder and bore them for us on the tree, in order to give us eternal life as well as blessings in this world. He comes to us daily to visit the light which he has given us, in order to tend it and to help it grow. This is why he is called not only the shepherd but also the guardian of our souls. *On 1 Peter.*

⊰ GOSPEL READING: *John 10:1-10*

REFLECTIONS FROM THE CHURCH FATHERS

Scripture Is the Door. CHRYSOSTOM: Observe the marks of a robber. First, that he does not enter openly. Second, he does not enter according to the Scriptures, for this is, "not by the door." Here also, Jesus refers to those who had been before, and to those who would come after him: antichrist and the false christs, Judas and Theudas, and whoever else there have been of the same kind. And he rightly calls the Scriptures "a door," for they bring us to God and open to us the knowledge of God. . . . In that he introduces us to the Father, he is the door, in that he takes care of us, he is the shepherd. *Homilies on the Gospel of John 59.2-3.*

The Shepherd Still Defends His Sheep. GREGORY OF NAZIANZUS: The good shepherd who laid down his life for the sheep has not left us even now. He is present and tends and guides and knows his own, and is known by his own. And, though bodily invisible, [he] is spiritually recognized, and defends his flock against the wolves, and allows no one to climb over into the fold as a robber and traitor. *On the Death of His Father, Oration 18.4.*

An Early Shepherd Hymn. CLEMENT OF ALEXANDRIA:
Bridle of colts untamed,
Over our wills presiding;
Wing of unwandering birds,
Our flight securely guiding.
Rudder of youth unbending,
Firm against adverse shock;
Shepherd, with wisdom tending
Lambs of the royal flock:
Your simple children bring
In one, that they may sing
In solemn lays
Their hymns of praise
With guileless lips to Christ their King. *A Hymn to Christ the Savior 1.*

Sheep Need a Shepherd. CLEMENT OF ALEXANDRIA: In our sickness we need a savior, in our wanderings a guide, in our blindness someone to show us the light, in our thirst the fountain of living water which quenches forever the thirst of those who drink from it. We dead people need life, we sheep need a shepherd, we children need a teacher, the whole world needs Jesus! *Christ the Educator 1.9.83.*

Christ Is the Way to the Kingdom. MAXIMUS THE CONFESSOR: He is the way, the door, the key and the kingdom, all alike; a way as guide; a key as the one who opens and who is opened for those who are worthy of divine treasures; a door as the one who gives entry; a kingdom as the one who is inherited and who comes to be present in all through participation. *Chapters on Knowledge 2.69.*

CLOSING PRAYER

Almighty God, who knows our necessities before we ask and our ignorance in asking: set free your servants from all anxious thoughts for the morrow. Give us contentment with your good gifts. Confirm our faith that, according as we seek your kingdom, you will not suffer us to lack any good thing. Provide, therefore, whatever you see to be necessary for our health and salvation. Of your fatherly love and compassion, give us whatever else would truly bless us. All our desire is known, O Lord, to you. Therefore perfect in us what your Spirit has awakened us to ask in prayer. [Amen.] *Augustine*

Boldness in Faith

THEME

We are not offered an easy life; we may suffer, like Stephen did, for our faith (Acts 7:55-60). However, we put ourselves in God's hands, trusting him to care for us and to give us refuge (Ps 31:1-5, 15-16). Jesus is the cornerstone of our salvation, and he calls us to declare the good news, no matter what the cost (1 Pet 2:2-10). And, Jesus has promised he prepares a place for us in heaven (Jn 14:1-14).

OPENING PRAYER: *Fifth Sunday of Easter*

Grant, O Lord, to your servants and followers who are persecuted for righteousness' sake that their conversation may be as becomes the gospel of Christ; that they may stand fast in one spirit, with one mind striving together for the faith of the gospel; that terrified in nothing by their adversaries they may be bold in the behalf of Christ, not only to believe on him but also to suffer for his sake, who lives and reigns, ever one God, world without end. Amen. *Paul*

READING FROM ACTS: *Acts 7:55-60*

REFLECTIONS FROM THE CHURCH FATHERS

Jesus Stood As His Helper. AMBROSE: Jesus stood as a helpmate; he stood as if anxious to help Stephen, his athlete, in the struggle. He stood as though ready to crown his martyr. Let him then stand for you that you may not fear him sitting, for he sits when he judges. . . . He sits to judge, he stands to give judgment, and he judges the imperfect, but gives judgment among the gods. *Letter 59 (63).*

Bold Speech Without Anger. CHRYSOSTOM: This is the boldness of speech that belongs to a man who is carrying the cross. Let us then also imitate this. For although it is not a time for war, it is always the time for boldness. "For I spoke," he says, "in your testimonies before kings and I was not ashamed." If we happen to be among Gentiles, let us silence them likewise, without anger and without harshness. For if we do this with anger, it is no longer boldness, but appears rather as raw passion. If, however, it is done with gentleness, that is true boldness. For in one and the same thing success and failure cannot possibly go together. Boldness of speech is success; anger is failure. Therefore, if we should aspire to boldness, we must be free from anger, in case anyone should attribute our words to anger. For no matter how just your words may be, when you speak with anger, you ruin everything. This is true no matter how boldly you speak or how fairly you admonish—in short, no matter what you do. . . . The Holy Spirit does not dwell where anger is and cursed is the wrathful. Nothing wholesome can proceed from where anger issued forth. *Homilies on the Acts of the Apostles 17.*

PSALM OF RESPONSE: *Psalm 31:1-5, 15-16*

NEW TESTAMENT READING: *1 Peter 2:2-10*

REFLECTIONS FROM THE CHURCH FATHERS

Long for Spiritual Milk. HILARY OF ARLES: Milk has three forms which can be compared to doctrine, that is, the liquid, cheese and butter. Liquid milk is the literal sense of Scripture, cheese is the moral sense, and butter is the spiritual sense. Find a good teacher and you will soon learn these things. *Introductory Commentary on 1 Peter.*

In One Edifice. **BEDE:** The temple which Christ built is the universal church, which he gathers into the one structure of his faith and love from all the believers throughout the world, as it were from living stones. *Homilies on the Gospels 2.24.*

A Royal People. **CLEMENT OF ALEXANDRIA:** That we are a chosen people is clear enough, but Peter said that we are a royal people because we have been called to share Christ's kingdom and we belong to him. We are a priesthood because of the offering which is made in prayers and in the teachings by which souls which are offered to God are won. *Adumbrations.*

The Altar Fire Maintained. **ORIGEN:** If you want to exercise the priesthood of your soul, do not let the fire depart from your altar. *Sermons on Leviticus 4.2.*

One Holy People. **ANDREAS:** When people from different races and nations are called to abandon all their differences and to take on one mind, drawing near to him by one faith and one teaching, by which the soul and the heart become one, they are one holy people. *Catena.*

GOSPEL READING: *John 14:1-14*

REFLECTIONS FROM THE CHURCH FATHERS

Faith More Powerful Than Anything. **CHRYSOSTOM:** He shows the power of the Godhead within him, discerning their inward feelings when he says, "Let not your heart be troubled. Believe in God, believe also in me." Faith, too, in me, and in the Father that begat me, is more powerful than anything that shall come upon you; and it will permit no evil thing to prevail against you. *Homilies on the Gospel of John 73.1.*

The Perfect Way. **BASIL THE GREAT:** We understand by "Way" that advance to perfection which is made stage by stage, and in regular order, through the works of righteousness and "the illumination of knowledge"; ever longing after what is before, and reaching forward to those things which remain until we have reached the blessed end, the knowledge of God. . . . For our Lord is an essentially good Way, where erring and straying are unknown, to that which is essentially good—to the Father. For "no one," he says, "comes to the Father but through me." Such is our way up to God "through the Son." *On the Spirit 8.18.*

Jesus Does Not Mislead Us. HILARY OF POITIERS: He who is the way leads us not into by-paths or trackless wastes: he who is the truth mocks us not with lies; he who is the life betrays us not into delusions which are death. He himself has chosen these winning names to indicate the methods which he has appointed for our salvation. As the way, he will guide us to the truth; the truth will establish us in the life. And therefore it is all-important for us to know what is the mysterious mode which he reveals, of attaining this life. "No one comes to the Father except through me." The way to the Father is through the Son. *On the Trinity 7.33.*

The Divine Three Are Inseparable. AUGUSTINE: So then, with all these ways of speaking we still have to understand that the activities of the divine three are inseparable, so that when an activity is attributed to the Father he is not taken to engage in it without the Son and the Holy Spirit; and when it is an activity of the Son, it is not without the Father and the Holy Spirit; and when it is an activity of the Spirit, it is not without the Father and the Son. That being the case, those who have the right faith, or better still the right understanding as far as they can, know well enough that the reason it is said about the Father, "He does the works," is that the works have their origin in the one from whom the co-working persons have their very existence; the Son, you see, is born of him, and the Holy Spirit proceeds primarily from him of whom the Son is born, being the Spirit common to them both. *Sermon 71.26.*

CLOSING PRAYER

Lord Jesus, we follow you, but we can only come at your bidding. No one can make the ascent without you, for you are our way, our truth, our life, our strength, our confidence, our reward. Be the way that receives us, the truth that strengthens us, the life that invigorates us. [Amen.] *Ambrose*

God Is Near

THEME

We seek God, remembering that he is always near (Acts 17:22-31), even when we suffer for his sake (1 Pet 3:13-22). We seek him through prayer, knowing that he listens to our prayers. In turn, we tell others what he has done for us and stories of our experiences (Ps 66:8-20). When we love Jesus, we joyfully submit to his will and diligently try to keep his commandments, with the help of the Holy Spirit (Jn 14:15-21).

OPENING PRAYER: *Sixth Sunday of Easter*

O God, who by the life and death and rising again of your dear Son has consecrated for us a new and living way into the holiest of all: cleanse our minds, we ask you, by the inspiration of your Holy Spirit, that drawing near to you with a pure heart and conscience undefiled, we may receive these gifts without sin and worthily magnify your holy name. *Liturgy of St. James*

READING FROM ACTS: *Acts 17:22-31*

REFLECTIONS FROM THE CHURCH FATHERS

Our Great Need of Revelation. CLEMENT OF ALEXANDRIA: To talk about God is most difficult. . . . For how can that be expressed which is neither genus, nor difference, nor species, nor individual, nor number; nay more, is neither an event, nor that to which an event happens? No one can rightly express him wholly. For on account of his greatness he is ranked as the All, and is the Father of the universe. Nor are any parts to be predicated of him. For the One is indivisible, and therefore also is infinite, not considered with reference to inscrutability, but with reference to its being without dimensions, and not having a limit. And therefore it is without form and name. And if we name it, we do not do so properly, terming it either the One, or the Good, or Mind, or Absolute Being, or Father, or God, or Creator or Lord. We speak not as supplying his name; but for want, we use good names, in order that the mind may have these as points of support, so as not to err in other respects. For each one by itself does not express God; but all together are indicative of the power of the Omnipotent. *Stromateis 5.12.*

All Creation Is in God. BEDE: Since this verse is difficult to understand, it should be explained in the words of the blessed Augustine, who says, the apostle shows that "God is ceaselessly at work in the things which he has created. It is not with respect to his substance that we are in him. For instance, it has been said that he has life in himself, but since we are certainly different from him, we are not in him in any other way except that he brings it [our existence] about; and this is his work, whereby he contains all things. And it has been said that his wisdom reaches mightily from one end of the earth to the other and orders all things well. It is through this ordering that in him we live and move and are. Hence we infer that if he withdrew this work of his from things, we would neither live nor move nor be." *Commentary on the Acts of the Apostles 17.28a.*

The Resurrection: Universal Call to Repentance. CHRYSOSTOM: What? Are none of these to be punished? No, not if they are willing to repent. He says this not of the departed but of those whom he is addressing. He does not [yet] call you to account, Paul says. He does not say, "He neglected" or "He permitted," but "You were ignorant. He overlooked."

That is, he does not exact punishment from you as from men deserving punishment. You were ignorant. *Homilies on the Acts of the Apostles 38.*

꙰ PSALM OF RESPONSE: *Psalm 66:8-20*

꙰ NEW TESTAMENT READING: *1 Peter 3:13-22*

REFLECTIONS FROM THE CHURCH FATHERS

You Will Never Lose God. AUGUSTINE: If you love the good, you will suffer no loss, because whatever you may be deprived of in this world, you will never lose God, who is the true good. *Sermons 335C.5.*

Conscience Defined. HILARY OF ARLES: Do not get angry or threaten anyone. Your conscience is the part of you which embraces what is good and which rejects evil. It is like the doorkeeper of a house which is open to friends and closed to enemies. *Introductory Commentary on 1 Peter.*

Whether Injustice Is Ever Useful. AUGUSTINE: Everyone who lies acts unjustly, and if lying ever seems to be useful to someone, it may be that injustice sometimes seems useful to him. But in fact injustice is never useful, and lying always does harm. *On Christian Doctrine 1.40.*

Unjust Suffering Is Still Meaningful. ANDREAS: Once again, Peter exhorts us not to grieve over unjust suffering, if that is God's will for us. He teaches us that we suffer for the specific purpose of being trained for what we are meant to be according to the mercy of God. *Catena.*

Reversing the Mandate. PRUDENTIUS: Into hell with love he entered. To him the broken gates yield. The bolts and massive hinges fall asunder at his word. Now the door of ready entrance but forbidding all return outward swings. Bars are loosened and send forth the prisoned souls by reversal of the mandate, treading its threshold once more. *Hymns 9.70-75.*

GOSPEL READING: *John 14:15-21*

REFLECTIONS FROM THE CHURCH FATHERS

To Love Is to Submit to Christ. CHRYSOSTOM: At all times it is works and actions that we need, not a mere show of words. It is easy for anyone to say or promise something, but it is not so easy to act on that word or promise. . . . "If you love me," Christ said, "keep my commandments." . . . I have commanded you to love one another and to do to one another as I have done to you. To love me is to obey these commands and to submit to me, your beloved. *Homilies on the Gospel of John 75.1.*

Spirit of the Trinity. AUGUSTINE: We have here, at all events, the Holy Spirit in the Trinity whom the catholic faith acknowledges to be consubstantial and coeternal with the Father and the Son. *Tractates on the Gospel of John 74.1.*

The Holy Spirit Comforts in a Different Way Than the Son. DIDYMUS THE BLIND: But the Holy Spirit was another Comforter differing not in nature, but in operation. For whereas our Savior in his office of Mediator, and of Messenger, and as High Priest, made supplication for our sins, the Holy Spirit is a Comforter in another sense, that is, as consoling our griefs. But do not infer from the different operations of the Son and the Spirit a difference of nature. For in other places we find the Holy Spirit performing the office of intercessor with the Father, as when "The Spirit himself intercedes for us." And the Savior, on the other hand, pours consolation into those hearts that need it: as in Maccabees, he strengthened those of the people who were brought low. *On the Holy Spirit 27.*

The Favoring Breeze of the Spirit of Truth. CLEMENT OF ALEXANDRIA: As the general directs the phalanx, consulting the safety of his soldiers, and the pilot steers the vessel, desiring to save the passengers; so also the Instructor [i.e., Jesus] guides the children to a saving course of conduct through his concern for us. And, in general, whatever we ask within reason from God to be done for us, will happen to those who believe in the Instructor. And just as the helmsman does not always yield to the winds, but sometimes, turning the prow toward them, opposes the whole force of the hurricanes, so the Instructor never yields to the blasts that blow in this world, nor commits the child to them like a vessel to make shipwreck on a wild and licentious course of life. Rather, wafted on by the favoring breeze of the Spirit of truth, he stoutly holds on to the child's helm—his ears, I mean—until he brings him safely to anchor in the haven of heaven. *The Instructor 1.7.*

Holy Spirit Seen in the Conscience. AUGUSTINE: "He shall be in you." He is seen, therefore, in an invisible way. And we can have no knowledge of him unless he is in us. For it is in a similar way that we come to see our conscience within us: for we see the face of another but we cannot see our own; but it is our own conscience we see, not another's. And yet conscience is never anywhere but within us. But the Holy Spirit can also exist apart from us since he is given that he may also be in us. But we cannot see and know him in the only way in which he may be seen and known, unless he is in us. *Tractates on the Gospel of John 74.5.*

CLOSING PRAYER

Save us while waking, and defend us while sleeping, that when we awake we may watch with Christ, and when we sleep we may rest in peace. Amen. *Anonymous*

Jesus Ascends to Heaven

𝕵 THEME

Jesus ascended to heaven (Acts 1:1-11), fulfilling everything written about him in the Scriptures (Lk 24:44-53). The "eyes of our hearts" are opened by faith to him whose "name is above all names" (Eph 1:15-23), and acknowledging his authority as ruler of creation, we offer God our praise (Ps 93).

𝕵 OPENING PRAYER: *Seventh Sunday of Easter*

O Lord Jesus Christ, who after your resurrection from the dead gloriously ascended into heaven, grant us the aid of your loving-kindness, that, according to your promise, you may ever dwell with us on earth, and we with you in heaven, where, with the Father and the Holy Spirit, you live and reign one God for ever and ever. Amen. *The Gelasian Sacramentary*

𝕵 READING FROM ACTS: *Acts 1:1-11*

REFLECTIONS FROM THE CHURCH FATHERS

Lover of God. BEDE: Theophilus means lover of God, or beloved of God. Therefore, anyone who is a lover of God may believe that this work was written for him, because the physician Luke wrote it in order that the reader might find health for his soul. Note also that he says, "all that Jesus began to do and teach," first "do" and then "teach," because

Jesus, establishing the pattern of a good teacher, taught nothing except those things which he did. *Commentary on the Acts of the Apostles 1.1.*

Teaching First by Conduct, Then Words. CHRYSOSTOM: Consider how Christ validated his words through actions. "Learn from me," he said, "for I am gentle and humble in heart." He taught us to be poor and demonstrated this through action, for "the Son of man," he says, "has no place to lay his head." Again, he commanded us to love our enemies and taught this lesson on the cross, when he prayed for those who were crucifying him. . . . He bid also the others to teach in this way. Therefore Paul also said, "as you have an example in us." For nothing is more insipid than a teacher who shows his wisdom only in words, since he is then not a teacher, but a hypocrite. *Homilies on the Acts of the Apostles 1.*

Why the Spirit Was Not Poured Out Until the Son Departed. CHRYSOSTOM: But why did the Holy Spirit not come to them while Christ was present, rather than immediately after his departure? Instead, although Christ ascended on the fortieth day, the Spirit came to them when the day of Pentecost had come. . . . It was necessary for them to have a longing for the event, and so receive the grace. For this reason Christ himself departed, and then the Spirit came. For if he had been present, they would not have expected the Spirit so earnestly as they did. *Homilies on the Acts of the Apostles 1.*

Keeping Watch. EPHREM THE SYRIAN: "It is not for you to know times or seasons." He has hidden that from us so that we might keep watch, and that each of us might think that this coming would take place during our life. For, if the time of his coming were to be revealed, his coming would be in vain, and it would not have been desired by the nations and the ages in which it was to take place. He has indeed said that he will come, but he did not define when, and thus all generations and ages thirst for him. *Commentary on Tatian's Diatessaron.*

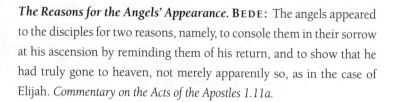

The Reasons for the Angels' Appearance. BEDE: The angels appeared to the disciples for two reasons, namely, to console them in their sorrow at his ascension by reminding them of his return, and to show that he had truly gone to heaven, not merely apparently so, as in the case of Elijah. *Commentary on the Acts of the Apostles 1.11a.*

☙ PSALM OF RESPONSE: *Psalm 93*

☙ NEW TESTAMENT READING: *Ephesians 1:15-23*

REFLECTIONS FROM THE CHURCH FATHERS

For What Does Paul Pray? AMBROSIASTER: The hope of their faith lies in a heavenly reward. When they truly know what the fruit of believing is, they will become more eager in acts of worship. *Epistle to the Ephesians 1.18.1.*

The Eyes of the Heart. JEROME: His phrase *eyes of the heart* clearly refers to those things we cannot understand without sense and intelligence. . . . Faith sees beyond what the physical eyes see. Physical eyes are in the heads of not only the wise but the unwise. *Epistle to the Ephesians 1.1.15.*

That You May Know by Insight and Revelation. MARIUS VICTORINUS: Let us understand that we arrive at the full mystery of God by two routes: We ourselves by rational insight may come to understand and discern something of the knowledge of divine things. But when there is a certain divine self-disclosure God himself reveals his divinity to us. Some may directly perceive by this revelation something remarkable, majestic and close to truth. . . . But when we receive wisdom we apprehend what is divine both through our own rational insight and through God's own Spirit. When we come to *know* what is true in the way this text intends, both these ways of knowing correspond. *Epistle to the Ephesians 1.1.17-18.*

The Immeasurable Greatness of His Power. THEODORET OF CYR: The name "Father of glory" embraces the hope of our calling and the riches of the glory of our inheritance, the exceeding greatness of his power and the good pleasure of his will, and all that goes with it. But *the immeasurable greatness of his power* ironically now comes to mind as he thinks of the dishonor of the cross and considers how much was achieved through it. *Epistle to the Ephesians 1.19.*

Far Above Every Sovereignty. CHRYSOSTOM: He says not merely "above" but *far above.* For God is higher than the powers on high. So he led him up there, the very one who shared our lowly humanity. He led him from the lowest depth to the highest sovereignty, beyond which there is no higher honor. *Above every sovereignty,* he says: not merely compared with this or that. . . . What gnats are compared with humans, so is the whole creation compared with God. *Homily on Ephesians 3.1.20-23.*

Nothing Further Is to Be Added or Received. MARIUS VICTORINUS: All these statements about the magnificence and power of Christ have this purpose: To prove that nothing further is to be received, no other thought required to complete the revelation. *Epistle to the Ephesians 1.1.20-23.*

GOSPEL READING: *Luke 24:44-53*

REFLECTIONS FROM THE CHURCH FATHERS

Proclamation Begins at Pentecost. AUGUSTINE: The Lord did not only shed his blood, but he also applied his death to the preparation of the cure. He rose again to present us with a sample of resurrection. He suffered with patience all his own to teach us the patience we should have. In his resurrection, he showed us the reward of patience. As you know and we all confess, he ascended into heaven, and then he sent the Holy Spirit as he had previously promised. *Sermon 175.3.*

At Bethany, Jesus Gives His Blessing. BEDE: The Lord himself was made obedient to his Father even unto death, so that he might restore the lost grace of blessing to the world. He gives the blessing of heavenly life only to those who strive in the holy church to comply with the divine commands. *Homilies on the Gospels 11.15.*

Creating a New Pathway for Us. CYRIL OF ALEXANDRIA: Having blessed them and gone ahead a little, he was carried up into heaven so that he might share the Father's throne even with the flesh that was united to him. The Word made this new pathway for us when he appeared in human form. After this, and in due time, he will come again in the glory of his Father with the angels and will take us up to be with him. Let us glorify him. *Commentary on Luke 24.*

The Joy of Entering Heaven Through the Flesh of Jesus. LEO THE GREAT: Dearly beloved, through all this time between the resurrection of the Lord and his ascension, the providence of God thought of this, taught this and penetrated their eyes and heart. He wanted them to recognize the Lord Jesus Christ as truly risen, who was truly born, truly suffered and truly died. The manifest truth strengthened the blessed apostles and all the disciples who were frightened by his death on the cross and were doubtful of his resurrection. The result was they were not only afflicted with sadness but also were filled with "great joy" when the Lord went into the heights of heaven. *Sermon 73.3-4.*

CLOSING PRAYER

Hear us, O merciful God, and grant our minds to be lifted up to where our Redeemer has ascended; that at the second coming of the Mediator we may receive from your manifested bounty what we now venture to hope for as a promised gift; through the same Jesus Christ our Lord. [Amen.] *The Leonine Sacramentary*

The Gift of the Holy Spirit

THEME

On Pentecost, we celebrate the gift of the Holy Spirit (Acts 2:1-21). Through Christ, we are given the living water of the Holy Spirit, poured out on believers on Pentecost, so that we might "thirst" no more (Jn 7:37-39) and that we might use the spiritual gifts we are given to his glory (1 Cor 12:3b-13). We look at the wonders of creation and cannot help but praise God for his wisdom, originality and the beauty of the world around us (Ps 104:24-34, 35b).

OPENING PRAYER: *Pentecost*

O Holy Spirit of God, very God, who descended on Christ at the river Jordan and on the apostles in the upper chamber, we have sinned against heaven and before you; purify us again, we ask you, with your divine fire, and have mercy on us; for Christ's sake. Amen. *Nerses of Clajes*

READING FROM ACTS: *Acts 2:1-21*

REFLECTIONS FROM THE CHURCH FATHERS

Two Bestowals of the Spirit? AUGUSTINE: For the Lord has transacted even this explicit imparting of the Holy Spirit not once but twice. For later when he arose from the dead, breathing on them, he said, "Receive the Holy Spirit." Then because he gave him at that time, did he therefore not also later send him whom he promised? Or is this not the same Holy Spirit who was both breathed by him then and later sent by him from heaven? Therefore, why his giving, which clearly was done, was done twice is another question. Perhaps this double giving of him was done in manifestation of the two commandments of love, that is, of neighbor and of God, in order that love might be shown to belong to the Holy Spirit. And if another reason must be sought, this discourse must not now by an inquiry into it be expanded to greater length than it ought, yet let it be established that without the Holy Spirit we cannot love Christ and keep his commandments. We can and do keep his commandments less as we receive him less, but so much the more as we receive him more. *Tractates on the Gospel of John 74.2.2-3.*

The Speech of Babylon and Pentecost. CYRIL OF JERUSALEM: The Galilean Peter or Andrew spoke Persian or Median. John and the other apostles spoke all the tongues of various nations, for the thronging of multitudes of strangers from all parts is not something new in Jerusalem, but this was true in apostolic times. What teacher can be found so proficient as to teach people in a moment what they have not learned? So many years are required through grammar and other arts merely to speak Greek well; and all do not speak it equally well. . . . But the Spirit taught them at once many languages, which they do not know in a whole lifetime. This is truly lofty wisdom. This is divine power. What a contrast between their long ignorance in the past and this sudden, comprehensive, varied and unaccustomed use of languages. *Catechetical Lecture 17.16-17.*

⊰ **PSALM OF RESPONSE:** *Psalm 104:24-34, 35b*

⊰ **NEW TESTAMENT READING:** *1 Corinthians 12:3b-13*

REFLECTIONS FROM THE CHURCH FATHERS

The Speaker of Truth. AMBROSIASTER: Any truth spoken by anyone is spoken by the Holy Spirit. *The Holy Spirit 1.11.124.*

Varieties of Gifts. CHRYSOSTOM: Even if the gift bestowed on you is less than the gift bestowed on someone else, the Giver is the same, and therefore you have equal honor with him. It is the same fountain from which you draw refreshment. *Homilies on the Epistles of Paul to the Corinthians 29.4.*

Adapting to Each. CYRIL OF JERUSALEM: The Holy Spirit adapts himself to each person. He sees the disposition of each. He sees into our reasoning and our conscience, what we say, what we think, what we believe. *Catechesis 14.22.*

The Faculties of Body and Soul Compared. HILARY OF POITIERS: If the soul has not breathed in the gift of the Spirit through faith, even though it will continue to possess the faculty for understanding, it will not have the light of knowledge. The one gift, which is in Christ, is available to everyone in its entirety. What is present in every place is given insofar as we desire to become worthy of it. This gift is with us even to the consummation of the world. This is the consolation of our expectation. This, through the efficacy of the gifts, is the pledge of our future hope. This is the light of the mind, the splendor of the soul. For this reason we must pray for this Holy Spirit. *Trinity 2.35.*

Wisdom and Knowledge. AMBROSIASTER: In other words, he is given knowledge not by book learning but by the enlightenment of the Holy Spirit. *Commentary on Paul's Epistles.*

Surpassing Human Nature. CYRIL OF JERUSALEM: This faith which is given by the Spirit as a grace is not just doctrinal faith but a faith which empowers activities surpassing human nature, a faith which moves mountains. . . . For just as a grain of mustard seed is of little bulk but of explosive energy, taking a trifling space for its planting and then sending out great branches all around, so that when it is grown it can give shelter to the birds, so in like manner the faith present

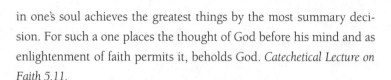

in one's soul achieves the greatest things by the most summary decision. For such a one places the thought of God before his mind and as enlightenment of faith permits it, beholds God. *Catechetical Lecture on Faith 5.11.*

The One Spirit Adapts to Personal Diversity. CYRIL OF JERUSALEM: One and the same rain comes down on all the world, yet it becomes white in the lily, red in the rose, purple in the violets and the hyacinths, different and many-colored in manifold species. Thus it is one in the palm tree and another in the vine, and all in all things, though it is uniform and does not vary in itself. For the rain does not change, coming down now as one thing and now as another, but it adapts itself to the thing receiving it and becomes what is suitable to each. Similarly the Holy Spirit, being One and of one nature and indivisible, imparts to each one his grace "according as he will." The dry tree when watered brings forth shoots. So too does the soul in sin, once made worthy through repentance of the grace of the Holy Spirit, flower into justice. *Catechesis 14.12.*

⚜ **GOSPEL READING:** *John 7:37-39*

REFLECTIONS FROM THE CHURCH FATHERS

The Spirit Flow in All of Us. IRENAEUS: The Spirit is in us all and he is the living water which the Lord supplies to those who rightly believe in him and love him. *Against Heresies 5.18.2.*

The Gift of the Holy Spirit. CYRIL OF ALEXANDRIA: The Spirit came to be in the prophets so that they could prophecy, and now the Spirit dwells in believers through Christ, having first dwelled in Christ when he was made man. For as God, Christ has the Spirit unceasingly, since the Spirit is essentially of Christ's nature: the Spirit is his own. Christ is anointed and is said to receive the Spirit as a man, not so that he could participate in the divine good things, but rather for our sake and for the sake of human nature as we have been taught. When the Evangelist says to us, "the Spirit had not been given, because Jesus was not yet glorified," let us understand him to mean the full and complete indwelling of the Holy Spirit in humankind. *Commentary on the Gospel of St. John 5.2.*

CLOSING PRAYER

Grant, we ask you, almighty God, that the splendor of your brightness may shine on us and the light of your Light confirm with the illumination of the Holy Spirit the hearts of those who have been born again through your grace: for the sake of Jesus Christ our Lord. [Amen.] *The Gregorian Sacramentary*

God the Creator

⸭ THEME

God is the Creator (Gen 1:1-2:4a), and we look at the glorious infinity and glittering magnificence of the night sky and cannot help but give him gratitude and praise (Ps 8). We are called by God to live in peace (2 Cor 13:11-13), mending our ways to conform to a godly life and telling everyone of Christ's resurrection and glory. Christ promises he will never leave us (Mt 28:16-20).

⸭ OPENING PRAYER: *Trinity Sunday: First Sunday After Pentecost*

Keep us, O Lord, from the vain strife of words, and grant to us a constant profession of the truth. Preserve us in the faith, true and undefiled, so that we may ever hold fast that which we professed when we were baptized into the name of the Father, and of the Son and of the Holy Spirit; that we may have you for our Father, that we abide in your Son and in the fellowship of the Holy Spirit; through the same Jesus Christ our Lord. Amen. *Hilary of Poitiers*

⸭ OLD TESTAMENT READING: *Genesis 1:1-2:4a*

REFLECTIONS FROM THE CHURCH FATHERS

Heaven and Earth Were Created Through the Word. ORIGEN: What is the beginning of all things except our Lord and "Savior of all" Jesus

Christ "the firstborn of every creature?" In this beginning, therefore, that is, in his Word, "God made heaven and earth" as the Evangelist John also says in the beginning of his Gospel: "In the beginning was the Word, and the Word was with God, and the Word was God. The same was in the beginning with God. All things were made by him, and without him nothing was made." *Homilies on Genesis 1.1.*

Heaven and Earth. CHRYSOSTOM: God is the creator and master technician of nature, and art, and everything made or imagined. *Sermon 1.3.*

A Symbol of Baptism. JEROME: In the beginning of Genesis, it is written: "And the Spirit was stirring above the waters." You see, then, what it says in the beginning of Genesis. Now for its mystical meaning— "The Spirit was stirring above the waters"—already at that time baptism was being foreshadowed. It could not be true baptism, to be sure, without the Spirit. *Homilies 10.*

The Spirit Hovered. EPHREM THE SYRIAN: It was appropriate to reveal here that the Spirit hovered in order for us to learn that the work of creation was held in common by the Spirit with the Father and the Son. The Father spoke. The Son created. And so it was also right that the Spirit offer its work, clearly shown through its hovering, in order to demonstrate its unity with the other persons. Thus we learn that all was brought to perfection and accomplished by the Trinity. *Commentary on Genesis 1.*

The Author of Light. AMBROSE: God is the author of light, and the place and cause of darkness is the world. But the good Author uttered the word *light* so that he might reveal the world by infusing brightness therein and thus make its aspect beautiful. Suddenly then, the air became bright and darkness shrank in terror from the brilliance of the novel brightness. *Hexaemeron 1.9.*

God Approves His Work. AUGUSTINE: "God saw that the light was good," and these words do not mean that God found before him a good that he had not known but that he was pleased by one that was finished. *Two Books on Genesis Against the Manichaeans 1.8.13.*

⹎ PSALM OF RESPONSE: *Psalm 8*

⹎ NEW TESTAMENT READING: *2 Corinthians 13:11-13*

REFLECTIONS FROM THE CHURCH FATHERS

Mending Their Ways. **AMBROSIASTER:** The joy referred to here will come when the Corinthians mend their ways, after which it will be possible for them to mature in faith. But before that there will be consolation, enabling them to abandon the pleasure of the present in favor of hope for things to come. The peace of God is one thing, but the peace of the world is another. People in the world have [a kind of] peace, but it works to their damnation. The peace of Christ is free from sins, and therefore it is pleasing to God. A person who has peace will also have love, and the God of both will protect him forever. *Commentary on Paul's Epistles.*

Following Paul's Commands. **CHRYSOSTOM:** How can Paul expect them to rejoice after he has said this kind of thing to them? It is for this very reason that he says it. For it they follow what he commands, there will be nothing to prevent them from rejoicing. Nothing is more comforting than a pure conscience. *Homilies on the Epistles of Paul to the Corinthians 30.1.*

⹎ GOSPEL READING: *Matthew 28:16-20*

REFLECTIONS FROM THE CHURCH FATHERS

As If to One Body. **CHRYSOSTOM:** After that, because he had enjoined on them great things, to raise their courage he reassures them that he will be with them always, "even to the end of the world." Now do you see the relation of his glory to his previous condescension? His own proper power is again restored. What he had said previously was spoken during the time of his humiliation. He promised to be not only with these disciples but also with all who would subsequently believe after them. Jesus speaks to all believers as if to one body. Do not speak to me, he says, of the difficulties you will face, for "I am with you," as the one who makes all things easy. Remember that this is also said repeatedly to the prophets in the Old Testament. Recall Jeremiah objecting that he is too young and Moses and Ezekiel shrinking from the prophet's office. "I am with you" is spoken to all these people. *The Gospel of Matthew, Homily 90.2.*

To the Close of the Age. CHRYSOSTOM: Observe the excellence of those who were sent out into the whole world. Others who were called found ways of excusing themselves. But these did not beg off. Jesus reminds his disciples of the consummation of all things. He seeks to draw them further on, that they may not look at the present dangers only but also at the good things to come that last forever. He is in effect saying, "These difficult things that you will undergo are soon to be finished with this present life. For this world will come to an end. But the good things you are to enjoy are immortal, as I have often told you before." Having invigorated and roused their minds by the remembrance of that coming day, he sent them out. Those who live faithfully, with good works, should strangely desire that day even as those who lack good works should fear it. So let us not fear and shudder. Let us repent while there is opportunity. Let us rise out of our sins. We can by grace, if we are willing. *The Gospel of Matthew, Homily 90.2.*

CLOSING PRAYER

Grant, O God, of your mercy, that we may come to everlasting life, and there beholding thy glory as it is, may equally say:

Glory to the Father who created us,

Glory to the Son who redeemed us,

Glory to the Holy Spirit who sanctified us.

Glory to the most high and undivided Trinity, whose works are insep-arable, whose kingdom without end abides, from age to age forever. Amen. *Augustine*

Sharing God's Grace

THEME

Abraham was quick to recognize God, to be obedient to him and to believe his promises (Gen 18:1-15; 21:1-7). We rejoice that through Christ's death for our sins we have lasting peace with God (Rom 5:1-8). God's goodness and love cause us to sing his praises (Ps 100), and in gratitude, we therefore share the good news of God's grace with others (Mt 9:35—10:8).

OPENING PRAYER: *Proper Six*

O God the Father, origin of divinity, good beyond all that is good, fair beyond all that is fair, in whom is calmness, peace and concord; make up the dissensions which divide us from each other and bring us back into a unity of love, which may bear some likeness to your sublime nature. And as you are above all things, make us one by the unanimity of a good mind, that through the embrace of charity and the bonds of affection we may be spiritually one, as well in ourselves as in each other, through that peace of yours which makes all things peaceful, and through the grace, mercy and tenderness of your only-begotten Son. [Amen.] *Jacobite Liturgy of Dionysius*

OLD TESTAMENT READING: *Genesis 18:1-15; 21:1-7*

REFLECTIONS FROM THE CHURCH FATHERS

Abraham Adored One. AMBROSE: Abraham who was glad to receive strangers, faithful to God and tireless in his service and prompt in fulfilling his duty, saw the Trinity typified. He added religious devotion to hospitality, for although he beheld three, he adored one, and yet while keeping a distinction of the persons, yet he called one Lord, thus giving honor to the three but signifying one power. For not knowledge but grace spoke in him. And he believed better what he had not learned than we who have been taught. No one had falsified the type of truth, and therefore he saw three but worshiped their unity. He brought out three measures of meal but slaughtered one calf, believing one sacrifice was sufficient, but a threefold offering; one victim, but a threefold gift. *On His Brother Satyrus 2.96.*

Hospitality Has Its Recompense. AMBROSE: Hospitality is a good thing, and it has its recompense: first of all the recompense of human gratitude and then, more importantly, the divine reward. In this earthly abode we are all guests. Here we have only a temporary dwelling place. We depart from it in haste. Let us be careful not to be discourteous or neglectful in receiving guests, lest we be denied entrance into the dwelling place of the saints at the end of our life. *On Abraham 1.5.34.*

The Mystery of the Trinity. CAESARIUS OF ARLES: He received the three men and served them loaves out of three measures. Why is this, brothers, unless it means the mystery of the Trinity? He also served a calf; not a tough one, but a "good, tender one." Now was it so good and tender as he who humbled himself for us even unto death? He himself is that fatted calf which the father killed upon receiving his repentant son. "For God so loved the world that he gave his only begotten Son." For this reason Abraham went to meet the three men and adored them as one. In the fact that he saw three, as was already said, he understood the mystery of the Trinity; but since he adored them as one, he recognized that there is one God in the three persons. *Sermon 83.4.*

PSALM OF RESPONSE: *Psalm 100*

NEW TESTAMENT READING: *Romans 5:1-8*

REFLECTIONS FROM THE CHURCH FATHERS

The Guarantee of Peace. ORIGEN: It is obvious from this that the apostle is inviting everyone who has understood that he is justified by faith and not by works to that "peace which passes all understanding," in which the height of perfection consists. But let us investigate further in order to see what the apostle means when he talks about peace, and especially about that peace which is through our Lord Jesus Christ. Peace reigns when nobody complains, nobody disagrees, nobody is hostile and nobody misbehaves. Therefore, we who once were enemies of God, following the devil, that great enemy and tyrant, now have peace with God, if we have thrown down his weapons and in their place taken up the sign of Christ and the standard of his cross. But this is through our Lord Jesus Christ, who has reconciled us to God through the offering of his blood.

Let us therefore have peace, so that the flesh will no longer war with the spirit, nor will the law of God be opposed by the law of our members. *Commentary on the Epistle to the Romans*

Access to Grace. CHRYSOSTOM: If God brought us near to himself when we were off, how much more will he keep us now that we are near! . . . What grace is it to which we now have access? It is being counted worthy of the knowledge of God, being forced to abandon error, coming to a knowledge of the truth, obtaining all the blessings which come through baptism. For the reason he brought us near in the first place was that we might receive these gifts. For we were not reconciled merely in order to receive forgiveness of sins; we were meant to

receive countless additional benefits as well. *Homilies on Romans 9.*

GOSPEL READING: *Matthew 9:35—10:8*

REFLECTIONS FROM THE CHURCH FATHERS

In All the Cities and Villages. CHRYSOSTOM: So do good to your companions not for their sake alone but for God's sake. Whatever they may do, do not cease doing them good. Your reward will be greater. When you are vilified, if you quit doing good, you signify that you are seeking the praise of others, not the praise of God. *The Gospel of Matthew, Homily 32.3.*

Preparing Disciples for Future Dangers. CHRYSOSTOM: Note the careful timing of their mission. They were not sent out at the beginning of their walk with him. They were not sent out until they had sufficiently benefited by following him daily. It was only after they had seen the dead raised, the sea rebuked, devils expelled, the legs of a paralytic brought to life, sins remitted, lepers cleansed, and had received a sufficient proof of his power both by deeds and words—only then did he send them out. And he did not send them out unprepared to do dangerous deeds, for as yet there was no danger in Palestine. They had only to stand against verbal abuse. However, Jesus still warned them of larger perils to come, preparing them for what was future. *The Gospel of Matthew, Homily 32.3.*

The House of Israel. GREGORY THE GREAT: Isn't it clear to all, dearly beloved, that our Redeemer came into the world for the salvation of the Gentiles? Yet when we behold Samaritans called daily to the faith, what did he mean when he sent his disciples to preach and said, "Go nowhere among the Gentiles, and enter no town of the Samaritans, but go rather to the lost sheep of the house of Israel"? He wished that the proclamation be offered first to the Jews alone. Then it would be offered to the Gentiles. *Forty Gospel Homilies 4.1.*

The Kingdom of Heaven Is at Hand. GREGORY THE GREAT: If someone's house were shaken and threatened with ruin, whoever lived in it would flee. The one who loved it when it was standing would hasten to leave it as soon as possible when it was falling. Therefore if the world is falling, and we embrace it by loving it, we are choosing rather to be overwhelmed than to live in it. Nothing separates us from its ruin insofar as our love binds us by our attachment to it. *Forty Gospel Homilies 4.2.*

CLOSING PRAYER

In peace, let us pray to the Lord.

Lord, have mercy upon us.

For peace from on high, and for the salvation of our souls, let us pray to the Lord.

Lord, have mercy upon us.

For the peace of the whole world, for the good estate of the holy churches of God, and for the union of all, let us pray to the Lord.

Lord, have mercy upon us.

For this holy house, and for those who with faith, reverence and godly fear enter therein, let us pray to the Lord.

Lord, have mercy upon us.

For our [bishops and other] clergy, and for the congregations committed to their charge, let us pray to the Lord.

Lord, have mercy upon us.

For our country, for all its people, and for those who are entrusted with civil authority, let us pray to the Lord.

Lord, have mercy upon us.

For this city, and for all the cities and countries, and for those who in faith dwell therein, let us pray to the Lord.

Lord, have mercy upon us.

[Amen.] *Slavonic Liturgy of John Chrysostom*

Precious to God

❧ THEME

We are offered living water and the assurance of God's continuing love and protection (Gen 21:8-21). Through baptism we are crucified with Jesus and die to sin, resurrected to a new life (Rom 6:1b-11). We need not fear anything, for we are precious to God (Mt 10:24-39). We continue to ask him for help, guidance and direction and pray he will preserve us from our enemies (Ps 86:1-10, 16-17).

❧ OPENING PRAYER: *Proper Seven*

O God, the author of love and the lover of pure peace and affection: let all who are terrified with fears, afflicted by poverty, harassed by tribulation, worn down by illness, be set free by your indulgent tenderness, raised up by amendment of life and cherished by your daily compassion. *The Gallican Sacramentary*

❧ OLD TESTAMENT READING: *Genesis 21:8-21*

REFLECTIONS FROM THE CHURCH FATHERS

Hagar Sees a Well of Living Water. ORIGEN: After this, when already he had been abandoned as dead and had wept, the angel of the Lord is present with him "and opened Hagar's eyes, and she saw a well of living water." . . . Frequently we also lie around the well "of living water," that is, around the divine Scriptures, and err in them. We hold the books and we read them, but we do not touch upon the spiritual sense. And therefore there is need for tears and incessant prayer that the Lord may open our eyes, because even the eyes of those blind men who were sitting in Jericho would not have been opened unless they had cried out to the Lord. And what am I saying? That our eyes, which are already opened, might be opened? For Jesus came to open the eyes of the blind. Our eyes therefore are opened, and the veil of the letter of the law is removed. But I fear that we ourselves may close them again in a deeper sleep while we are not watchful in the spiritual meaning. *Homilies on Genesis 7.6.*

God's Grace Is all We Require. CHRYSOSTOM: In her neediness the Lord granted her means, and when she found herself so much at a loss and lacking all hope of survival, he gave evidence in her case of his characteristic generosity by consoling her and at the same time exercising care for the child. In like manner, whenever God wishes, even if we are utterly alone, even if we are in desperate trouble, even if we have no hope of survival, we need no other assistance, since God's grace is all we require. You see, if we win favor from him, no one will get the better of us, but rather we will prevail against anyone. "God was with the boy," the text goes on; "he grew up and lived in the desert." In similar fashion, whenever we have God on our side, even if we are utterly alone, we will live more securely than those who dwell in the cities. After all, the grace of God is the greatest security and the most impregnable fortification. *Homilies on Genesis 46.7-8.*

PSALM OF RESPONSE: *Psalm 86:1-10, 16-17*

NEW TESTAMENT READING: *Romans 6:1b-11*

REFLECTIONS FROM THE CHURCH FATHERS

What It Means to Be Dead to Sin in Baptism. CHRYSOSTOM: Being dead to sin means not obeying it any more. Baptism has made us dead to sin once and for all, but we must strive to maintain this state of affairs, so that however many commands sin may give us, we no longer obey it but remain unmoved by it. *Homilies on Romans 10.*

When We Become an Obstacle to Grace. AUGUSTINE: Here Paul makes the point that past sins have been forgiven and that in this pardon grace so superabounded that earlier sins were remitted as well. Thus whoever tries to increase sin in order to feel an increase of grace does not understand that he is behaving in such a way that grace can do nothing in him. For the work of grace is that we should die to sin. *Augustine on Romans 31.*

Whether Baptism Is the Death of Sin. AMBROSIASTER: Paul says this so that we might know that once we have been baptized we should no longer sin, since when we are baptized we die with Christ. This is what it means to be baptized into his death. For there all our sins die, so that, renewed by the death we have cast off, we might be seen to rise as those who have been born again to new life, so that just as Christ died to sin and rose again, so through baptism we might also have the hope of resurrection. Therefore, baptism is the death of sin so that a new birth might follow, which, although the body remains, nevertheless renews us in our mind and buries all our old evil deeds. *Commentary on Paul's Epistles.*

Dead to Sin. AUGUSTINE: To be baptized into the death of Christ is nothing else but to die to sin, just as he died in the flesh. *Against Julian 1.7.33.*

Metaphor or Reality? OECUMENIUS: See the goodness of God. We have died Christ's death metaphorically, but we shall share his resurrection truly. *Pauline Commentary from the Greek Church.*

Set Free. BASIL THE GREAT: He is set free, he is delivered, he is cleansed of all sin, and not sin in word and deed only but also of all irrational movements of the mind. *Concerning Baptism 1.2.*

Freedom from Sin Not Yet Complete. CHRYSOSTOM: Paul says: "Consider yourselves" . . . because complete freedom from sin is not a reality as yet. . . . We are told to live for God in Jesus Christ our Lord and to lay hold of every virtue, having Jesus as our ally in the struggle. *Homilies on Romans 11.*

GOSPEL READING: *Matthew 10:24-39*

REFLECTIONS FROM THE CHURCH FATHERS

Calling the Master Beelzebul. CHRYSOSTOM: What Christ is saying to the faithful is, I am now already sharing with you the same stigma you are presently suffering. That is sufficient for your encouragement. . . . For why do you now grieve? Are you troubled that someone is calling you a deceiver or a liar? So what? Wait a little while. In time you will be seen as benefactors of the world and champions of faith. . . . With time lengthening to reveal and proclaim your innocence, you will shine brighter than the sun. . . . So do not let what is now being said demoralize you. Rather, let the hope of the good things to come raise you up. For the true story of your testimony cannot be suppressed forever. *The Gospel of Matthew, Homily 34.1.*

Do Not Fear Those Who Kill the Body. ANONYMOUS: The essence of the human is not the body, but the soul. It is the soul alone that God made in his own image and the soul that he loves. . . . For the sake of the soul even the Son of God came into the world. *Incomplete Work on Matthew, Homily 25.*

Fear Not. CHRYSOSTOM: If then God is not ignorant of anything that happens in creation, and if God loves us more truly than the best human father, and if God loves us so as to have numbered our very hairs, then we need not be afraid. . . . Don't you see that God views your fear with more concern than the lives of many sparrows? He already knows the secrets of your heart. *The Gospel of Matthew, Homily 34.2-3.*

How Peace Requires a Sword. CHRYSOSTOM: This more than anything is peace: when the cancer is cut away. Only with such radical surgery is it possible for heaven to be reunited to earth. Only in this way does the physician preserve the healthy tissue of the body. The incurable part must be amputated. Only in this way does the military commander preserve the peace: by cutting off those in rebellion. *The Gospel of Matthew, Homily 35.1.*

One Who Loses Life Will Find It. HILARY OF POITIERS: After he commands us to abandon everything that is most valuable in earthly life, he adds, "He who does not take up his cross and follow me is not worthy of me." This is because those who belong to Christ have crucified their bodies with their sinful practices and pleasures. We are unworthy of Christ if we do not take up our own cross, by which we suffer, die and are buried and resurrected together with him. Only by this pledge of faith in the Spirit will he triumph in new life in us. *On Matthew 10.25-26.*

⸎ CLOSING PRAYER

O heavenly Father, in whom we live and move and have our being, we humbly pray to you so to guide and govern us by your Holy Spirit that in all the cares and occupations of our daily life we may never forget you but remember that we are ever walking in your sight; for your own name's sake. Amen. *Anonymous*

God's Promises

⫶ THEME

Abraham's willingness to sacrifice Isaac shows his complete confidence in God's promises (Gen 22:1-14). Although we sometimes question how long we will have to endure certain trials, we trust God to see us through them (Ps 13). Therefore, we need to yield to God, who offers us eternal life, not giving in to sin (Rom 6:12-23) and offering hospitality in God's name to others (Mt 10:40-42).

⫶ OPENING PRAYER: *Proper 8*

Confirm, O Lord, we pray you, the hearts of your children, and strengthen them with the power of your grace; that they may both be devout in prayer to you and sincere in love for each other; through Jesus Christ our Lord. [Amen.] *The Leonine Sacramentary*

⫶ OLD TESTAMENT READING: *Genesis 22:1-14*

REFLECTIONS FROM THE CHURCH FATHERS

Future Truth. ORIGEN: What do you say to these things, Abraham? What kind of thoughts are stirring in your heart? A word has been uttered by God that is such as to shatter and try your faith. What do you say to these things? What are you thinking? What are you reconsidering? Are you thinking, are you turning over in your heart that if the promise has been given to me in Isaac but I offer him for a burnt offering, it remains that the promise holds no hope? Or rather do you think of those well-known words and say that it is impossible for him who promised to lie; be that as it may, the promise shall remain? . . . Abraham knew himself to prefigure the image of future truth. He knew the Christ was to be born from his seed, who also was to be offered as a truer victim for the whole world and was to be raised from the dead. *Homilies on Genesis 8.1.*

Symbolic Meaning. CAESARIUS OF ARLES: When Isaac carried the wood for the sacrifice of himself, in this too he prefigured Christ our Lord, who carried his own cross to the place of his passion. *Sermon 84.3.*

Abraham Speaks About the Future. ORIGEN: Abraham's response, sufficiently accurate and cautious, moves me. I do not know what he saw in his spirit, for he does not speak about the present but about the future: "God himself will provide himself a sheep." He responded to his son's inquiry about present things with future things. For "the Lord himself will provide himself a sheep" in Christ, because also, "Wisdom herself has built herself a house," and "He himself humbled himself unto death." *Homilies on Genesis 8.6.*

PSALM OF RESPONSE: *Psalm 13*

NEW TESTAMENT READING: *Romans 6:12-23*

REFLECTIONS FROM THE CHURCH FATHERS

Withholding Consent to the Reign of Sin. CAESARIUS OF ARLES: Paul did not say: "Let sin not exist," but "Let it not reign." Sin is within you if you take delight in it; it reigns if you consent to it. *Sermon 134.3.*

Sustaining a Disposition of Urgency. BASIL THE GREAT: This injunction would be successfully carried out, I believe, if we were willing always to keep the same disposition of mind as we had at the time of danger. For surely we realized to some degree the vanity of life, as well as the unreliability and instability of human affairs, which change so easily. And in all likelihood we felt contrition for our past faults and promised that for the future, if we were saved we would serve God with watchful exactitude. *Letter 26.*

Grace Enables Action. AUGUSTINE: It is not that the law is evil but what it makes those under it guilty by giving commands without providing help to fulfill them. In fact, grace helps one to become a doer of the law, for without such grace one living under the law will be no more than a hearer of the law. *Grace and Free Will 12.24.*

Aided by the Spirit. THEODORET OF CYR: In other words, nature is no longer struggling on its own but has the Holy Spirit to help it. *Interpretation of the Letter to the Romans.*

No Longer Under Law. AMBROSIASTER: Although it was right for the law to be given—for it was given in order to show that those who sinned against it were guilty before God and in order to dissuade people from continuing to sin—yet because of the weakness of its infirmity the human race was unable to restrain itself from sin and had become subject to the death of hell. God was moved by the righteousness of his mercy, by which he always comes to the aid of the human race, and through Christ he provided a way by which he could reward those who were without hope. By forgiving their sins he released them from the law which had held them subject. Restored and made whole again by the help of God, they could reject the sins by which they had previously been held down. Therefore we did not sin in rejecting the law but rather we followed the providence of God himself through Christ. *Commentary on Paul's Epistles.*

Recognizing Your Past Life for What It Was. CHRYSOSTOM: If even the recollection of your former slavery makes you ashamed, think how much more the reality of it would do so. You have gained in two ways—by being set free from your former shame and by having come to recognize your past life for what it was. *Homilies on Romans 12.*

King Sin's Wages. ORIGEN: The death being referred to here is not the death which separates the body from the soul but the death by which because of sin the soul is separated from God. *Commentary on the Epistle to the Romans.*

GOSPEL READING: *Matthew 10:40-42*

REFLECTIONS FROM THE CHURCH FATHERS

Giving a Cup of Cold Water. HILARY OF POITIERS: He teaches that no deed of a good conscience is useless. It is no crime for a believer to have hope that transcends another's unbelief. For he foresaw that there would be many who glory merely in the name of apostleship but whose every action proves they are unworthy. They deceive and lie perpetually. And yet when we grant these people the favors that are due them because of their mere appearance of religiosity, he does not withhold from us the reward of doing his work and of hope. For even if they are the very least, that is, the worst sinners of all—for nothing is smaller than the "least"—nonetheless she decrees that we have duties toward them. These duties are light but not useless. They are represented by the phrase "cold water." For honor is to be paid not to the sins of the individual but to his status as a disciple. He grants his reward to the faith of the one who gives, not to the deceitfulness of the one who receives. *On Matthew 10.29.*

Overcoming Evasions. JEROME: Jesus said, "He who receives you receives me." But there are many false prophets and false preachers who perhaps make this doctrine difficult. He has also cured this stumbling block by saying, "He who receives a righteous man because he is a righteous man will receive a righteous man's reward." Then again, someone may object and say, "I am prevented by poverty. My own lack prevents me from acting as a host." Jesus eliminated this excuse, too, by the easily fulfilled command that we should offer a cup of cold water with our whole heart. He said "cold water" rather than "hot water" so that we could not object because of our poverty or lack of fuel for hot water. *Commentary on Matthew 1.10.40-42.*

CLOSING PRAYER

O Lord Jesus Christ, Good Shepherd of the sheep, who came to seek the lost and to gather them to your fold, have compassion on those who have wandered from you; feed those who hunger, cause the weary to lie down in your pastures, bind up those who are broken in heart and strengthen those who are weak, that we, relying on your care and being comforted by your love, may abide in your guidance to our lives' end; for your name's sake. Amen. *Anonymous*

Rest in God

⫞ THEME

Almighty God is faithful to care for us (Ps 145:8-14) and is actively involved in our lives (Gen 24:34-38, 42-29). We long to live sinless lives,
but we struggle: we seem to do the very things we do not want to do
(Rom 7:15-25a). Jesus invites us to come to him when we are weary
and discouraged, and he will give us rest (Mt 11:16-19, 25-30).

⫞ OPENING PRAYER: *Proper 9*

O God, the unsearchable abyss of peace, the ineffable sea of love, the
fountain of blessings and the bestower of affection, who sends peace to
those who receive it, open to us this day the sea of your love, and water
us with plenteous streams from the riches of your grace and from the
most sweet springs of your benignity. Make us children of quietness
and heirs of peace. Enkindle in us the fire of your love; sow in us your
fear; strengthen our weakness by your power; bind us closely to you
and to each other in one firm and indissoluble bond of unity. [Amen.]
Syrian Clementine Liturgy

⫞ OLD TESTAMENT READING: *Genesis 24:34-67*

REFLECTIONS FROM THE CHURCH FATHERS

The Union of the Soul with the Word of God. ORIGEN: Do you think
these are the only words related about wells? Jacob also goes to a well

and finds Rachel there. . . . But also Moses finds Zipporah, the daughter of Reuel, at a well. . . . But let us come also to the Gospels. Let us see where the Lord seeks rest when he was "wearied from the journey." "He came," Scripture says, "to the well and sat upon it." You see that everywhere the mysteries are in agreement. You see the patterns of the New and Old Testament to be harmonious. There one comes to the wells and the waters that brides may be found; and the church is united to Christ in the bath of water. You see how great a heap of mysteries presses upon us. We cannot treat all the things that present themselves. These things at least ought to stimulate you to listen, to assemble. Even if we hurry over some things for the sake of brevity, you yourself even, when you read the text again and inquire into it, may dispel the mystery and discover . . . that the Word of God, finding you also at the waters, may take you up and unite you with himself, that you may be made "one spirit" with him in Christ Jesus our Lord. "To him belongs glory and sovereignty forever and ever. Amen." *Homilies on Genesis 10.5.*

Christ Established the Church. CAESARIUS OF ARLES: Therefore Isaac took Rebekah "and led her into the tent of his mother." Christ also took the church and established it in place of the synagogue. . . . As the apostle says, by pride "the branches" of the olive tree "have been broken off," in order that the lowly wild olive may be engrafted. For this reason Isaac took Rebekah, "and because he loved her he was consoled for the loss of his mother." Christ took the church and loved it so much that by this very love he tempered the grief that was occasioned by the death of his mother, the synagogue. Indeed, just as the synagogue's lack of faith caused Christ sorrow, so the church's faith produced joy in him. *Sermon 85.5.*

PSALM OF RESPONSE: *Psalm 145:8-14*

NEW TESTAMENT READING: *Romans 7:15-25a*

REFLECTIONS FROM THE CHURCH FATHERS

Nothing Good Dwells Within Me. AMBROSIASTER: Man can agree that what the law commands is good; he can say that it naturally pleases him and that he wants to do it. But in spite of all that, the power and the strength to carry out his wishes is lacking because he is so oppressed by the power of sin that he cannot go where he wants nor can he make contrary decisions, because another power is in control of him. For man is burdened by his habit of sinning and succumbs to sin more readily than to the law, which he knows teaches what is good. For if he wants to do what is good, habit backed by the enemy prevents him. *Commentary on Paul's Epistles.*

By His Own Fault. AMBROSIASTER: Is the sinner compelled to sin by a power outside himself? Not at all. For it was by his own fault that these evil things began, for whoever binds himself to sin voluntarily is ruled by its law. Sin persuades him first, and when it has conquered him it takes control. *Commentary on Paul's Epistles.*

The Common Lot of Humanity, Excepting the Faithful. DIODORE: Here Paul is describing the common lot of man. For the ordinary person can see in his mind what ought to be done but cannot achieve it. But the man who has believed in Christ with his mind can achieve it with the help of the Holy Spirit. Such a person is therefore called "spiritual." *Pauline Commentary from the Greek Church.*

Who Will Deliver Me? GENNADIUS OF CONSTANTINOPLE: Paul did not say "bad" or "evil man" but rather "wretched man" . . . for having shown that this person contemplated the good with his mind but was drawn toward evil by the passion of the flesh, he presents him as more deserving of mercy than of punishment. *Pauline Commentary from the Greek Church.*

Equipped for Struggles. CHRYSOSTOM: Christ not only set us free without demanding any payment for his services; he also equipped us for greater struggles in the future. *Homilies on Romans 13.*

GOSPEL READING: *Matthew 11:16-19, 25-30*

REFLECTIONS FROM THE CHURCH FATHERS

John Came, and the Son Came. THEODORE OF MOPSUESTIA: Those who were looking for the truth, he says, accepted the leadership of John and of Christ. It changed their lives. . . . Still, he who fulfilled everything wisely by neglecting none of these things that contributed to their profit and salvation was judged harshly by them. And no longer hereafter could they accuse him, because Jesus fulfilled all his promises and did not leave behind for them a shadow either of unkindness or of ingratitude. *Fragment 62.*

Everything Handed Down from the Father. CYRIL OF ALEXANDRIA: The one who sees the Son, who has the image of the Father in himself, sees the Father himself. . . . These things are to be understood in a manner befitting to God. He said, "Everything has been handed down to me" so that he might not seem to be a member of a different species or inferior to the Father. Jesus added this in order to show that his nature is ineffable and inconceivable, like the Father's. For only the divine nature of the Trinity comprehends itself. Only the Father knows his own Son, the fruit of his own substance. Only the divine Son recognizes the One by whom he has been begotten. Only the Holy Spirit knows the deep things of God, the thought of the Father and the Son. *Fragment 14.8.*

You Will Find Rest. CYRIL OF ALEXANDRIA: Stand apart from the inclination to love sin and to love the flesh. Turn to deeds worthy of praise. Draw near to me, so that you may become sharers of the divine nature and partakers of the Holy Spirit. Jesus called everyone, not only the people of Israel. As the Maker and Lord of all, he spoke to the weary Jews who did not have the strength to bear the yoke of the law. He spoke to idolaters heavy laden and oppressed by the devil and weighted down by the multitude of their sins. To Jews he said, "Obtain the profit of my coming to you. Bow down to the truth. Acknowledge your Advocate and Lord. I set you free from bondage under the law, bondage in which you endured a great deal of toil and hardship, unable to accomplish it easily and accumulating for yourselves a very great burden of sins." *Fragment 149.*

CLOSING PRAYER

In your mercy, Lord my God, tell me what you are to me. "Say to my soul, I am your salvation." So speak that I may hear you. The ears of my heart are turned to you, Lord; open them and say to my soul: "I am your salvation." I will run after your voice, and I will lay hold of you. Do not hide your face from me. Let me see your face even if I die, for if I see it not, I shall die of longing. [Amen.] *Augustine*

Asking God for Help

THEME

Just as Esau did with his birthright, we treat with indifference that which is most important (Gen 25:19-34). If God lives in us, we are no longer controlled by our sinful nature (Rom 8:1-11). We need to put down deep roots in our faith, letting the word of God fall on fertile soil (Mt 13:1-9, 18-23). Desiring this, we pray to God for help and direction (Ps 119:105-112).

OPENING PRAYER: *Proper 10*

By the power of the Holy Spirit enable us, whom you have appointed to this ministry of yours at all times and in all places to call on you without condemnation and without offense, with the testimony of a pure conscience; that you may hear us and be merciful to us, after the multitude of thy great goodness, for all glory, honor and worship befits you, the Father, the Son and your Holy Spirit, now and for ever, and world without end. [Amen.] *The Liturgy of John Chrysostom*

OLD TESTAMENT READING: *Genesis 25:19-34*

REFLECTIONS FROM THE CHURCH FATHERS

The Struggle Within Rebekah. CAESARIUS OF ARLES: Almost everyone accepts the fact that the blessed Isaac represented a type of the Lord our Savior. Therefore Isaac prefigured Christ and blessed

Rebekah the church, because although like the church she remained sterile for a long time, she conceived through the prayers of blessed Isaac and the Lord's gift. Now the children struggled in her womb, and not tolerating this annoyance, she said, "If this be so, why am I pregnant?" Then the Lord replied to her, "Two nations are in your womb; two peoples shall stem from your body. One people shall be stronger than the other and the elder shall serve the younger." Indeed, as the apostle says, dearly beloved, "All these things happened to them as a type, and they were written for us." Therefore Rebekah corporally conceived of blessed Isaac, because the church was going to conceive spiritually of Christ. Moreover, just as the two children struggled in Rebekah's womb, so two peoples continually oppose each other in the church's womb. If there were only wicked or only good persons, there would be just one people. In the church, so much the worse, good and bad people are found, two peoples struggling as in the womb of the spiritual Rebekah—the humble, indeed, and the proud, chaste and adulterous, meek and irascible, kind and envious, merciful and avaricious. *Sermon 86.2.*

Two Nations Within You. ORIGEN: I think that this can be said also of each of us as individuals that "two nations and two peoples are within you." For there is a people of virtue within us, and there is no less a people of vice within us. "For from our heart proceed evil thoughts, adulteries, thefts, false testimonies" but also "deceits, contentions, heresies, jealousies, revelings and such like." Do you see how great a people of evil is within us? . . . But . . . the flesh shall serve the Spirit, and vices shall yield to virtues. *Homilies on Genesis 12.3.*

Recognize the Dangers of Wealth. CHRYSOSTOM: Let us learn the lesson never to neglect the gifts from God or forfeit important things for worthless trifles. I mean, why, tell me, should we be obsessed with a desire for money when the kingdom of heaven and those effable blessings are within our grasp, and why prefer blessings that endure forever and ever to those that are passing and scarcely last until evening? What could be worse than the folly of being deprived of the former through lust after the latter and never being able to enjoy them in a pure fashion? What good, after all, tell me, is such wealth? Are you not aware that acquisition of great wealth brings us nothing else than an increase in worry, anxiety and sleeplessness? Do you not see that these people (in particular those possessing great wealth) are, so to say, everyone's slaves, and day in and day out are in fear even of shadows? This, you see, is the source of plotting, envy, deep hatred and countless other evils. Often you would see the person with ten thousand talents of gold hidden away calling blessed the one behind the shop counter who prepares his own meals by hand. *Homilies on Genesis 50.7.*

PSALM OF RESPONSE: *Psalm 119:105-112*

NEW TESTAMENT READING: *Romans 8:1-11*

REFLECTIONS FROM THE CHURCH FATHERS

In Christ We Have the Power to Avoid Postbaptismal Sin. GENNA-DIUS OF CONSTANTINOPLE: Look how great Christ's grace is in that he has set us free from condemnation. *Pauline Commentary from the Greek Church.*

Distinguishing Sinful Flesh and the Likeness of Sinful Flesh. AUGUS-TINE: What does sinful flesh have? Death and sin. What does the likeness of sinful flesh have? Death without sin. If it had sin it would be sinful flesh; if it did not have death it would not be the likeness of sinful flesh. As such he came—he came as Savior. He died but he vanquished death. In himself he put an end to what we feared; he took it upon himself and he vanquished it—as a mighty hunter he captured and slew the lion. *Sermons for Easter Season, Homily 233.3.*

Remaining Without Sin. BEDE: He who came in the likeness of sinful flesh—not in sinful flesh—did not turn away from the remedy by which sinful flesh was ordinarily made clean. . . . Not from necessity but by way of example he submitted to the water of baptism, by which he wanted the people of the new law of grace to be washed from the stain of sin. *Homilies on the Gospel. 1.1.*

GOSPEL READING: *Matthew 13:1-9, 18-23*

REFLECTIONS FROM THE CHURCH FATHERS

Different Parables for Different Hearers. JEROME: The crowd is not of a single mentality, for each person has a different frame of mind. He therefore speaks to them in many parables so they may receive different teachings depending on their frame of mind. *Commentary on Matthew 2.13.3.*

The Birds Came and Devoured Them. CYRIL OF ALEXANDRIA: Then what are those upon the rock? They are those people who do not take much care of the faith they have in themselves. They have not set their minds to understand the touchstone of the mystery. The reverence these people have toward God is shallow and rootless. It is in times of ease and fair weather that they practice Christianity, when it involves none of the painful trials of winter. They will not preserve their faith in this way, if in times of tumultuous persecution their soul is not prepared for the struggle. *Fragment 168.*

Receptivity of the Soil Varies. CHRYSOSTOM: But mark this carefully: there is more than one road to destruction. There are differing ones, and wide apart from one another. For they who are like the wayside are the coarse-minded and indifferent and careless; but those on the rock such as fail from willed weakness only. *The Gospel of Matthew, Homily 44.4-5.*

CLOSING PRAYER

O God, who in your loving-kindness both begins and finishes all good things: grant that as we now glory in the beginnings of your grace, so we may hereafter rejoice in its completion; through Jesus Christ our Lord. Amen. *The Leonine Sacramentary*

God Keeps Promises

⊰ THEME

God keeps his promises (Gen 28:10-19a). We praise God for his greatness and ask him for help with difficult situations and in dealing with
those who wrong us (Ps 86:11-17). We are the children of God (Rom
8:12-25) and have the promise that at the end of the age, evil will be
defeated and we will have eternal salvation (Mt 13:24-30, 36-43).

⊰ OPENING PRAYER: *Proper 11*

Beloved, let us arm ourselves with all our might, let us prepare ourselves for the struggle by innocence of heart, integrity of faith, dedica-
tion to virtue. [Amen.] *Cyprian*

⊰ OLD TESTAMENT READING: *Genesis 28:10-19a*

REFLECTIONS FROM THE CHURCH FATHERS

The Ladder Is the Cross of Christ. CHROMATIUS OF AQUILEIA:
Through the resurrection of Christ the way was opened. Therefore with
good reason the patriarch Jacob relates that he had seen in that place a
ladder whose end reached heaven and that the Lord leaned on it. The
ladder fixed to the ground and reaching heaven is the cross of Christ,
through which the access to heaven is granted to us, because it actually
leads us to heaven. On this ladder different steps of virtue are set
through which we rise toward heaven: faith, justice, chastity, holiness,

patience, piety and all the other virtues are the steps of this ladder. If we faithfully climb them, we will undoubtedly reach heaven. And therefore we know well that the ladder is the symbol of the cross of Christ. As, in fact, the steps are set between two uprights, so the cross of Christ is placed between the two Testaments and keeps in itself the steps of the heavenly precepts, through which we climb to heaven. *Sermon 1.6.*

The Ladder Is the Church. BEDE: The Lord made mention of this place and most clearly bore witness in a figurative way concerning himself and his faithful ones. The ladder which he saw is the church, which has its birth from the earth but its "way of life in heaven." And by it angels ascend and descend, when evangelists announce at one time to perfect hearers the preeminent hidden mysteries of [Christ's] divinity and at another time announce to those still untaught the weaknesses of his humanity. Or they ascend when [in their teaching] they pass to heavenly things to be contemplated by the mind, and they descend when they educate their listeners as to how they ought to live on earth. *Homilies on the Gospels 1.17.*

Prefiguration and Fulfillment. CAESARIUS OF ARLES: Blessed Isaac, as we said, sending his son away was a type of God the Father; Jacob who was sent signified Christ our Lord. The stone that he had at his head and anointed with oil also represented the Lord our Savior. The ladder touching heaven prefigured the cross; the Lord leaning on the ladder is shown to be Christ fastened to the cross. The angels ascending and descending on it are understood to be the apostles, apostolic men and all doctors of the church. They ascend by preaching perfect truths to the just; they descend by telling the young and ignorant what they can understand. For our part, brothers, we who see fulfilled in the New Testament all the truths which were prefigured in the Old should thank God as well as we can because he has deigned to give us such great gifts without any preceding merits on our part. *Sermon 87.6.*

PSALM OF RESPONSE: *Psalm 86:11-17*

NEW TESTAMENT READING: *Romans 8:12-25*

REFLECTIONS FROM THE CHURCH FATHERS

The Assurance That Dares to Say "Abba, Father." AMBROASI-
ASTER: Set free by the grace of God from fear, we have received the
Spirit of sonship so that, considering what we were and what we have
become by the gift of God, we might govern our life with great care lest
the name of God the Father be disgraced by us and we incur all the
things we have escaped from. . . . We have received such grace that we
can dare to say to God: "Abba! Father!" For this reason, Paul warns us
not to let our trust degenerate into pride. For if our behavior does not
correspond to our voice when we cry, "Abba! Father!" we insult God by
calling him Father. Indeed, God in his goodness has indulged us with
what is beyond our natural capacity. *Commentary on Paul's Epistles.*

His Spirit and Ours. THEODORET OF CYR: Paul uses the word
spirit in two senses. The first is the Spirit of God, the second is our
spirit, that is, through the grace which we have been given. *Interpretation of the Letter to the Romans.*

Incomparability. ORIGEN: There is nothing which is worthy of comparison with the future glory. For how can what is mortal be compared
to what is immortal, what is visible to what is invisible, what is temporal to what is eternal or what is perishable to what is everlasting? *Commentary on the Epistle to the Romans.*

Not Worth Comparing. JEROME: Do you dread poverty? Christ calls
the poor blessed. Does toil frighten you? No athlete is crowned but in
the sweat of his brow. Are you anxious as regards food? Faith fears no
famine. Do you dread the bare ground for limbs wasted with fasting?
The Lord lies there beside you. . . . Does the boundless solitude of the

desert terrify you? In the Spirit you may walk always in paradise. Do but turn your thoughts there and you will be no more in the desert. *Letter 14.10.*

Subjected to Futility. AMBROSE: Creation itself will also be delivered from its slavery to corruption when the grace of divine reward shines forth. *Six Days of Creation 1.6.22.*

Hope Distinguished from Patience. AUGUSTINE: Patience trains up the longing. Wait, for he waits. Walk on steadfastly that you may reach the end. He will not leave that place to which you are moving. *Homilies on 1 John 4.7.*

GOSPEL READING: *Matthew 13:24-30, 36-43*

REFLECTIONS FROM THE CHURCH FATHERS

The Sower of Good Seeds. CHROMATIUS OF AQUILEIA: The Lord clearly points out that he is the sower of good seeds. He does not cease to sow in this world as in a field. God's word is like good seed in the hearts of people, so that each of us according to the seeds sown in us by God may bear spiritual and heavenly fruit. *Tractate on Matthew 51.1.*

Until the Harvest. JEROME: The words the Lord spoke—"Lest gathering the weeds you root up the wheat along with them"—leave room for repentance. We are advised not to be quick in cutting off a fellow believer, for it may happen that one who has been corrupted today by evil may recover his senses tomorrow by sound teaching and abide by the truth. . . . Between wheat and weeds there is something called darnel, when the plant is in its early growth and there is no stalk yet. It looks like an ear of corn, and the difference between them is hardly noticeable. The Lord therefore advises us that we should not be quick to judge what is doubtful but should leave judgment up to God. *Commentary on Matthew 2.13.29-30.*

CLOSING PRAYER

O you who are faithful and true, reject us not utterly though we are often lukewarm in your service. Save us from thinking that we are rich in good works; show us where we are poor and blind and naked; and as you chasten those whom you love, incline us to lay to heart the reproofs of your Spirit and to be zealous and to repent. Let your people, O Lord, hear your voice and open to you, that in the power of so holy and mighty an Indweller your church may conquer, and we finally may be enthroned with you in your kingdom. [Amen.] *The Gelasian Sacramentary*

The Spirit Intercedes

 THEME

Jacob was willing to work hard for what he desired, even when obstacles stood in his way (Gen 29:15-28). We desire to keep God's laws and pray for deliverance from our enemies who reject God (Ps 119:129-136). Nothing can separate us from the love of God. When we have no words to approach him, the Holy Spirit will intercede for us (Rom 8:26-39). No one is too small for God to use for his glory (Mt 13:31-33, 44-52).

OPENING PRAYER: *Proper 12*

That it may please you to defend us from dangerous enemies;

That it may please you to make us persevere in good works;

That it may please you to give us celestial armor against the devil;

That your mercy and pity may keep us safe;

That you would give us the will and the power to repent in earnest;

That it may please you to give us pardon of all sins;

That it may please you to give us right faith, firm hope in your goodness
   and perfect love, and constant fear of you;

That it may please you to remove evil thoughts from us;

That it may please you to pour into our souls the grace of the
   Holy Spirit;

That it may please you to give us perpetual light;

That it may please you to give us a happy end;

That it may please you to bring us to everlasting joys;

That it may please you to hear us;

Son of God;

O Lamb of God, who takes away the sins of the world; *Spare us.*

O Lamb of God, who takes away the sins of the world; *Give us pardon.*

O Lamb of God, you takes away the sins of the world; *Hear us.*

[Amen.] *From various Gallican Litanies*

⌁ OLD TESTAMENT READING: *Genesis 29:15-28*

REFLECTIONS FROM THE CHURCH FATHERS

Love Reduces Work and Time. CHRYSOSTOM: Why are you surprised, dearly beloved, that he promised to serve seven years for the maiden he loved? To show, in fact, how his great love reduced the labor and the period of time, sacred Scripture says, "Jacob served seven years for Rachel, and in his eyes they were but a few days when measured against his love for her." The period of seven years, it is saying, was counted but a few days because of his surpassing love for the maiden. You see, when someone is smitten with love's desire, far from seeing any problem, he easily puts up with everything, albeit fraught with danger and much difficulty besides, having in view one thing only—obtaining the object of his desire. *Homilies on Genesis 55.7.*

In Everything God Works for Good. CHRYSOSTOM: Even opposition and disappointment are turned into good, which is exactly what happened with this remarkable man, the apostle Paul. *Homilies on Genesis 67.19.*

⌁ PSALM OF RESPONSE: *Psalm 119:129-136*

¶ NEW TESTAMENT READING: *Romans 8:26-39*

REFLECTIONS FROM THE CHURCH FATHERS

The Spirit Importunes. NOVATIAN: The Holy Spirit importunes the divine ears on our behalf "with sighs too deep for words," thereby discharging his duties as advocate and rendering his services in our defense. He has been given to dwell in our bodies and to bring about our sanctification. *The Trinity 29.16.*

The Spirit Himself Intercedes. [PSEUDO-]CONSTANTIUS: We find it difficult to express in words the desire of our prayer, which we have conceived in the heart. That is why Paul adds that the Spirit prays for us with sighs which cannot be uttered. Therefore God, who tries the hearts, knows how much we desire to believe, even if we cannot comprehend it in words. Furthermore, he knows that we ask him for holy things and not for things of this world, according to his will. *The Holy Letter of St. Paul to the Romans.*

He Who Searches the Heart. ORIGEN: Paul shows here that God pays less attention to the words we use in prayer than he does to what is in our heart and mind. *Commentary on the Epistle to the Romans.*

For Those Who Love God. THEODORE OF MOPSUESTIA: We must not worry if we find that things which we expect to turn out for our good are unexpectedly evil in the present life, because we know that in the end everything works together for good for those who love God. *Pauline Commentary from the Greek Church.*

Whom He Foreknew He Predestined. DIODORE: This text does not take away our free will. It uses the word foreknew before predestined. Now it is clear that "foreknowledge" does not by itself impose any particular kind of behavior. What is said here would be clearer if we started from the end and worked backwards. Whom did God glorify? Those whom he justified. Whom did he predestine? Those whom he foreknew, who were called according to his plan, that is, who demonstrated that they were worthy to be called by his plan and made conformable to Christ. *Pauline Commentary from the Greek Church.*

Firstborn, Only Begotten. AUGUSTINE: Not all who are called are called according to God's purpose, for the purpose relates to God's foreknowledge and predestination. God only predestined those whom he knew would believe and follow the call. Paul refers to them as the "elect." For many do not come, even though they have been called, but no one comes who has not been called. *Augustine on Romans 55.*

Distinguishing Many Called from Some Called According to His Purpose. AMBROSIASTER: To "call" is to help somebody who is already thinking about faith or else to address him firmly in the knowledge that he will listen. *Commentary on Paul's Epistles.*

God's Foreknowing Does Not Imply Direct Causing. THEODORET OF CYR: Those whose intention God foreknew he predestined from the beginning. Those who are predestined, he called, and those who were called, he justified by baptism. Those who were justified, he glorified, calling them children: "To all who received him, who believed in his name, he gave power to become children of God." Let no one say that God's foreknowledge was the unilateral cause of these things. For it was not foreknowledge which justified people, but God knew what would happen to them, because he is God. *Interpretation of the Letter to the Romans.*

⌐ GOSPEL READING: *Matthew 13:31-33, 44-52*

REFLECTIONS FROM THE CHURCH FATHERS

The Seed Sowed and Buried. HILARY OF POITIERS: The Lord compared his reign with a grain of mustard seed, which is very pungent and the smallest of all seeds. Its inherent potency is heightened under stress and pressure. Therefore, after this grain is sown in the field—that is, when it has been seized by someone and delivered up to death as though buried in the field by a sowing of its body—it grows up to become larger than any herb and surpasses all the glory of the prophets. *On Matthew 13.4.*

Hid Until It Was All Leavened. CHRYSOSTOM: For as leaven converts the large quanity of meal into its own quality, even so shall you convert the whole world. *The Gospel of Matthew, Homily 46.2.*

Selling Everything to Buy That Field. GREGORY THE GREAT: One who renounces the pleasures of the body and conquers all earthly desires by observing the heavenly discipline, so that nothing his body favors is compelling any longer and his spirit no longer fears anything that might destroy his bodily life, is truly one who sells everything and buys the field. *Forty Gospel Homilies 11.1.*

Both Old and New Testaments. AUGUSTINE: And now the voice of Christ speaks to Jews through the voice of the old Scriptures. They hear the voice of those Scriptures but do not see the face of the one who speaks. . . . We then say, Those things which are brought forth from the old are enlightened through the new. We therefore come to the Lord that the veil may be removed. *Sermon 74.5.*

CLOSING PRAYER

May the power of God preserve us. May the wisdom of God instruct us and the way of God direct us. May the hand of God protect us and the host of God guard us against the snares of evil and the temptations of the world. *Patrick*

God's Mercy

THEME

Jacob deeply desired that God bless him (Gen 32:22-32). We can count
on God to watch over those who love him with compassion and mercy
(Ps 145:8-9, 14-21); Paul mourned that so many of the Jews did not
acknowledge Christ (Rom 9:1-5). Jesus cares for our earthly needs and
has power over all things, as evinced in the feeding of the five thousand
(Mt 14:13-21).

OPENING PRAYER: *Proper 13*

Let us, therefore, not cling to fleeting things, which slip away and depart, but to those which are enduring and immovable. May we all attain
them through the grace and loving-kindness of our Lord Jesus Christ,
through whom and with whom be glory to the Father and the Holy
Spirit, now and always, for ever and ever. *Chrysostom*

OLD TESTAMENT READING: *Genesis 32:22-32*

REFLECTIONS FROM THE CHURCH FATHERS

The Struggle for Virtue. AMBROSE: Therefore Jacob, who had purified his heart of all pretenses and was manifesting a peaceable disposition, first cast off all that was his, then remained behind alone and
wrestled with God. For whoever forsakes worldly things comes nearer
to the image and likeness of God. What is it to wrestle with God other

than to enter upon the struggle for virtue, to contend with one who is stronger and to become a better imitator of God than the others are? *Jacob and the Happy Life 7.30.*

The Angel Typified Our Lord and Savior. CAESARIUS OF ARLES: Now as to the fact that Jacob came to the Jordan and after sending over all his possessions remained alone and wrestled with a man until the break of day. In that struggle Jacob prefigured the people of the Jews: the angel with whom he wrestled typified our Lord and Savior. Jacob wrestled with the angel because the Jewish people were to wrestle with Christ even to death. However, not all the Jews were unfaithful to Christ, as we said above, but a considerable number of them are read to have believed in his name, and for this reason the angel touched Jacob's thigh, which began to be lame. That foot with which he limped typified the Jews who did not believe in Christ; the one that remained uninjured signified those who received Christ the Lord. *Sermon 88.5.*

The Lord's Consideration for Our Limitations. CHRYSOSTOM: Do you see how much confidence Jacob gained from the vision he had? That is to say, "my spirit survived," he is saying, "which had almost perished from fear. Since I was privileged to see God face to face 'my spirit survived.'" Now the sun rose on him as he passed the sight of God. Do you see how the Lord shows considerateness for our human limitations in all he does and in arranging everything in a way that gives evidence of his characteristic love? Don't be surprised, dearly beloved, at the extent of his considerateness; rather, remember that with the patriarch as well, when Abraham was sitting by the oak tree, God came in human form as the good man's guest in the company of the angels, giving us a premonition from on high at the beginning that he would one day take human form to liberate all human nature by this means from the tyranny of the devil and lead us to salvation. *Homilies on Genesis 58.11-12.*

PSALM OF RESPONSE: *Psalm 145:8-9, 14-21*

⚜ NEW TESTAMENT READING: *Romans 9:1-5*

REFLECTIONS FROM THE CHURCH FATHERS

Accursed for the Sake of My Brethren. ORIGEN: Why be surprised that the apostle desires to be cursed for his brethren's sake, when he who is in the form of God emptied himself and took on the form of a servant and was made a curse for us? Why be surprised if, when Christ became a curse for his servants, one of his servants should become a curse for his brethren? *Commentary on the Epistle to the Romans.*

To Them Belongs the Sonship. ORIGEN: Israel was adopted by God and given the sonship. . . . "The worship" refers to the priestly sacrifices. "The promises" are those which were made to the patriarchs and which are given to all who are called children of Abraham. *Commentary on The Epistle to the Romans.*

Of Their Flesh Is the Christ. AMBROSIASTER: Paul lists so many indications of the nobility and dignity of the Jewish people and of the promises they received in order to deepen his grief for all these things, because by not accepting the Savior they lost the privilege of their fathers and the merit of the promises, and they became worse in faith than the non-Jewss, whom they had previously detested when they were without God. For it is a worse evil to lose a dignity than never to have had it. As there is no mention of the Father's name in this verse and Paul is talking about Christ, it can not be disputed that he is called God here. For, if Scripture is speaking about God the Father and adds the Son, it often calls the Father God and the Son Lord. If someone does not think that it is said here about Christ that he is God, then let him name the person about whom he thinks it is said, for there is no mention of God the Father in this verse. *Commentary on Paul's Epistles.*

⚜ GOSPEL READING: *Matthew 14:13-21*

REFLECTIONS FROM THE CHURCH FATHERS

To a Lonely Place Apart. CHRYSOSTOM: We see him on many occasions "departing." We see this when John was imprisoned and killed and when the Jews heard that he was making more disciples. For it was his will to live his life in an ordinary rhythm of interaction and solitude. The time had not yet come for him to reveal his divine glory plainly. This is why Jesus told his disciples to "tell no one that he is the Christ." His will was that this should be better known after his resurrection. During this time he was not very severe with those who were obstinate in their unbelief. Rather, he was prone to be indulgent with them. *The Gospel of Matthew, Homily 49.*

The Five Loaves of the Five Books of the Law. HILARY OF POITIERS: But was Jesus unaware there was nothing to give? Did he not know the disciples possessed a limited amount of food? He could read their minds, so he knew. We are invited to explain things by reasoning according to types. It was not yet granted to the apostles to make and administer heavenly bread for the food of eternal life. Yet their response reflected an ordered reasoning about types; they had only five loaves, and two fish. This means that up to then they depended on five loaves—that is, the five books of the law. And two fish nourished them—that is, the preaching of the prophets and of John. For in the works of the law there was life just as there is life from bread, but the preaching of John and the prophets restored hope to human life by virtue of water. Therefore the apostles offered these things first, because that was the level of their understanding at the time. From these modest beginnings the preaching of the gospel has proceeded from them, from these same apostles, until it has grown into an immense power. *On Matthew 14.10.*

He Looked to Heaven. JEROME: He looked up to heaven that he might teach them to keep their eyes focused there. He then took in hand five loaves of bread and two fish; he broke the loaves and gave the food to the disciples. By the breaking of the bread, he makes it into a seedbed of food—for it the bread had been left intact and not pulled apart and broken into pieces, they would have been unable to feed the great crowds of men, women and children. The law with the prophets are therefore pulled apart and broken into pieces. Mysteries are made manifest, so that what did not feed the multitude of people in its original whole and unbroken state now feeds them in its divided state. *Commentary on Matthew 2.14-19.*

CLOSING PRAYER

Lord Jesus, think on me,
Nor let me go astray
Through darkness and perplexity
You point the heavenly way.
Lord Jesus, think on me,
That when the flood is past,
I may the eternal brightness see,
And share your joy at last. [Amen.] *Synesius of Cyrene*

Peace and Justice

THEME

The story of Joseph is also a story of envy, betrayal and forgiveness, as well as having many symbols of the life of Christ (Gen 37:1-4, 12-28). Because Christ gave his life for us, we tell others the good news (Rom 10:5-15). God offers peace, salvation, love and justice for his people (Ps 85:8-13). We spend time in solitude, as Jesus modeled for us in the Scriptures. Because Jesus is ruler over everything, we need not fear; rather, we need to have faith (Mt 14:22-33).

OPENING PRAYER: *Proper 14*

Lord our God, great, eternal, wonderful in glory, who keeps covenant and promises for those who love you with their whole heart; who are the life of all, the help of those who flee to you, the hope of those who cry to you; cleanse us from our sins, secret and open, and from every thought displeasing to your goodness. Cleanse our bodies and souls, our hearts and consciences, that with a pure heart and a clear soul, with perfect love and calm hope, we may venture confidently and fearlessly to pray to you. *Coptic Liturgy of Basil*

OLD TESTAMENT READING: *Genesis 37:1-4, 12-28*

REFLECTIONS FROM THE CHURCH FATHERS

Envy Damages the Soul. CHRYSOSTOM: Envy is a terrible passion, you see, and when it affects the soul, it does not leave it before bringing it to an extremely sorry state. [It damages] the soul that gives it birth and affect[s] the object of its envy in the opposite way to that intended, rendering him more conspicuous, more esteemed, more famous—which in turn proves another severe blow to the envious person. *Homilies on Genesis 61.4.*

The Prefigurement of the Cross. AMBROSE: Accordingly, even at that time, the cross that was to come was prefigured in sign; and at the same time that he was stripped of his tunic, that is, of the flesh he took on, he was stripped of the handsome diversity of colors that represented the virtues. Therefore his tunic, that is, his flesh, was stained with blood, but not his divinity; and his enemies were able to take from him his covering of flesh but not his immortal life. *On Joseph 3.15.*

They Were Unconcerned That He Was Their Brother. CHRYSOSTOM: What an unlawful contract! What baleful profit! What illicit sale! The one who caused the same birth pangs as yourselves, the one so dear to your father, the one who came to see you, who never did you the slightest wrong, you endeavored to sell—and sell to savage people traveling down to Egypt. What unlawful frenzy! What dreadful malice! I mean, even if you did this out of fear of the dreams, convinced that they would certainly come to pass in every detail, why did you attempt the impossible and give evidence by what you did of your hostility toward God, who had foretold this to Joseph? If, on the contrary, you give no credence to the dreams but consider them nonsense, why did you do what brought you everlasting defilement and caused your father irreparable grief? . . . They abandoned every sane consideration and had one thing on their minds, allowing their envy to have (as they thought) an immediate effect. *Homilies on Genesis 61.15-16.*

PSALM OF RESPONSE: *Psalm 85:8-13*

NEW TESTAMENT READING: *Romans 10:5-15*

REFLECTIONS FROM THE CHURCH FATHERS

Descent and Ascent. DIODORE: The Word of God leaves believers in no doubt either about the descent of the Lord from heaven for our sake or about the resurrection from the dead and the ascent into heaven. *Pauline Commentary from the Greek Church.*

The Creed. AUGUSTINE: The creed builds up in you what you ought to believe and confess in order to be saved. *Sermons for the Recent Converts, Homily 214.1.*

Consistency Needed. IGNATIUS: Men believe with the heart and confess with the mouth, the one unto righteousness, the other unto salvation. It is good to teach, if the teacher also does what he says. *Epistle to the Ephesians 15.*

GOSPEL READING: *Matthew 14:22-33*

REFLECTIONS FROM THE CHURCH FATHERS

The Plain and Spiritual Meaning. HILARY OF POITIERS: The spiritual significance of this must be discerned, comparing the temporal order with the coming revelation. The historical event of his solitude in the evening anticipates a future event; his solitude at the time of the Passion, when everyone else had fled in fear. He then orders his disciples to get into the boat and cross the sea while he dismissed the crowds. Once they are dismissed, he goes up on the mountain. This prefigures that he is on the sea and within the church. He orders that he be carried throughout the world until he returns in a dazzling second advent to all who are left from the house of Israel, when he will bring salvation and forgive sins. Finally, in dismissing the crowds, the Lord is symbolically permitting them to enter into the kingdom of heaven. Then he proceeds to give thanks to God the Father, which anticipates his taking place in glory and in majesty. *On Matthew 14.13.*

Into the Hills. CHRYSOSTOM: For what purpose does he go up into the hills on the mountain? To teach us that solitude and seclusion are good, when we are to pray to God. With this in view, you see, we find him continually withdrawing into the wilderness. There he often spends the whole night in prayer. This teaches us earnestly to seek such quietness in our prayers as the time and place may afford. For the wilderness is the mother of silence; it is a calm and a harbor, delivering us from all turmoils. *The Gospel of Matthew, Homily 50.1.*

It Is a Ghost! CHRYSOSTOM: Note that he did not too easily remove the darkness. He did not come quickly to their rescue. He was training them, as I said, by the continuance of these fears and instructing them to be ready to endure. *The Gospel of Matthew, Homily 50.1.*

CLOSING PRAYER

O Lord, holy and true, who opens and none can shut; as you have set before your church an open door, strengthen your servants boldly to enter in and to declare your name, that they who oppose may yet come to worship and may know that you love your church. Grant to your people patience to keep your Word, and keep them from the hour of trial which is coming upon the whole world to try them who dwell on the earth. And encourage all Christians in every land to hold fast that which you have given, that their crown of glory be not taken away but that, having overcome, they may stand before you as pillars in the temple of God and bear the name of the heavenly city and your own new name, O Christ our God. Father, we commend to you all who are joined to us by natural ties and bonds of love; the little children dear to our hearts, and all who for our sakes daily deny themselves. May all our kindred, having your Holy Spirit as their helper, be at peace and have unfeigned charity among themselves. And grant them, O Lord, not only sufficient to supply the wants of this present life but also the good and eternal gifts that are laid up for them who do your commandments. *Columba*

Forgiveness

THEME

Joseph's forgiveness of his brothers prefigures Christ's forgiveness on
the cross (Gen 45:1-15). We are grateful for God's gifts, and we pray for
his continued blessings (Ps 67), clean hearts and a strong faith (Mt
15:10-20, 21-28) while thanking God for his generous mercy toward
us (Rom 11:1-2a, 29-32).

OPENING PRAYER: *Proper 15*

O Lord, we draw near to you, acknowledging our unworthiness, and
we ask you that all the sins and defects of our past services may be
freely pardoned and entirely done away, through the precious blood of
your dear Son Jesus Christ our Lord. Amen. *Anonymous*

OLD TESTAMENT READING: *Genesis 45:1-15*

REFLECTIONS FROM THE CHURCH FATHERS

They Were Dumbfounded. **CHRYSOSTOM:** I cannot but be amazed
here at this blessed man's remarkable fortitude in putting up with the
strain of concealing his identity to this point and not letting on. And [I]
am particularly surprised at the way they could stand there and gape
without their soul parting company with their body, without their going out of their mind or hiding themselves in the ground. "His brothers
were unable to say anything to him in reply. They were dumbfounded."

No wonder! Aware of the way they had treated Joseph, of his position in comparison with theirs and realizing the high office he had attained, they feared for their very lives, so to say. *Homilies on Genesis 64.27.*

Tears of Charity Wash Away Former Enmity. CAESARIUS OF ARLES: You have admired the chastity of Joseph; now behold his generosity. He repays hatred with charity. When he saw his brothers, or rather enemies in his brothers, he gave evidence of the affection of his love by his pious grief when he wanted to be recognized by them. He tenderly kissed each one of them and wept over them individually. As Joseph moistened the necks of his frightened brothers with his refreshing tears, he washed away their hatred with the tears of his charity. He loved them always as with the love of their living father and dead brother. He did not recall that pit into which he had been thrown to be murdered; he did not think of himself, a brother, sold for a price. Instead, by returning good for evil, even then he fulfilled the precepts of the apostles that were not yet given. Therefore, by considering the sweetness of true charity, blessed Joseph, with God's help, was eager to repel from his heart the poison of envy with which he knew his brothers had been struck. *Sermon 90.4.*

PSALM OF RESPONSE: *Psalm 67*

NEW TESTAMENT READING: *Romans 11:1-2a, 29-32*

REFLECTIONS FROM THE CHURCH FATHERS

Has God Rejected His People? CHRYSOSTOM: God has not rejected his people, because Paul himself was one of them. If God had cast them off, he would not have chosen one of them as the one to whom he entrusted all his preaching, the affairs of the world, all the mysteries and the whole message of salvation. *Homilies on Romans 18.*

Cleansed by the Same Grace. CYRIL OF ALEXANDRIA: Paul shows that both Jews and Gentiles were guilty of the same thing and that they were likewise cleansed by one and the same grace. *Explanation of the Letter to the Romans.*

Consigned All to Disobedience. AUGUSTINE: The apostle did not mean by these words that God would not condemn anybody. What he meant is made clear by the context. Paul was speaking about those Jews who would one day believe. *The City of God 21.24.*

Consigned by Divine Permission, Not by Divine Action. JOHN OF DAMASCUS: This is not to be taken in the sense of God acting but in the sense of God permitting, because of free will and because virtue is not forced. *Orthodox Faith 4.19.*

GOSPEL READING: *Matthew 15:10-20, 21-28*

REFLECTIONS FROM THE CHURCH FATHERS

Food as Such Does Not Defile. CHROMATIUS OF AQUILEIA: The Lord wanted to show up the uncalled for offense taken by the scribes and the Pharisees about unwashed hands. So he beckoned the crowd to him and said, "What goes into the mouth does not defile a man; but that which comes out of the mouth, that defiles a man." He explained that a man is defiled not from the food that enters his mouth but from the perverse thoughts of his mind, which proceed from his heart. For the food we receive for eating was created and blessed by God to sustain human life. So it cannot defile a man. Indeed, wicked and perverse thoughts that proceed from the heart, as the Lord himself noted— "murder, adultery, fornication, theft, false witness, blasphemy," the author of which is the devil—these are the things that really defile a man. *Tractate on Matthew 53.2.*

What Comes Out of One's Mouth Defiles, Not What Goes In. AUGUSTINE: At that time many people who were strong in their faith and who knew the Lord's teaching, that it is what comes out of the mouth which defiles a man, not what goes into it, were eating whatever they liked with a clear conscience. But some weaker ones abstained from meat and wine, so as to avoid unknowingly eating foods which had been sacrificed to idols. At that time the Gentiles sold all sacrificed meat to the butcher shops, poured out the first fruits of the wine as a libation to their idols and even made some offerings in the wine presses. *Augustine on Romans 78.*

Great Is Your Faith. THEODORE OF MOPSUESTIA: He uses the term dog on account of the Gentiles' unclean lifestyle and proneness to idolatry, while he calls the Jews children on account of the fact that they appeared to be devoted to God. . . . The woman does not complain even when insulted. What does the Savior do? By his answer, he showed what he had premeditated from the outset. For it was for this reason that he postponed giving a reply: that the woman might cry aloud with this word. Thereby he would show her to be worthy of a thousand crowns. For it was not because he did not want to give her the gift that he delayed but because he sought and took care beforehand to reveal her faith. With his accolades he honors her as presenting a type of the church that is from the Gentiles. Note that he did not say, "Let your child be healed," but "Be it done for you as you desire," in order to show that it was the power of her faith that elicited the healing. Even if she were worthy of even greater things, nevertheless that which she wanted was what was given to her. *Fragment 83.*

CLOSING PRAYER

Rouse us, O Lord, from the sleep of apathy and from tossing to and fro in our thoughts, that we may no longer live as in a troubled dream but as people awake and resolved to finish the work you have given them to do. By your humble birth root out of our hearts all pride and haughtiness, that humble ways may content us, if so be that we may serve the humble. By the life of compassion for those who labor and are heavy laden, teach us to be concerned one for another and to bear one another's burdens. By your hallowed and most bitter anguish on the cross, make us to fear you, and love you, and follow you, O Christ. [Amen.] *Brigid*

Protection and Help

⸙ THEME

God showed his care for the Israelites through raising up Moses to lead
them out of Egypt (Ex 1:8—2:10). We are grateful for God's protection
in the past and continuing help for the present and future (Ps 124). We
confess Christ, the Son of the living God and author of our salvation (Mt
16:13-20), and offer our bodies as a living sacrifice to God (Rom 12:1-8).

⸙ OPENING PRAYER: *Proper 16*

You, O Lord, who command us to ask, grant that we may receive. You
have put us on seeking; let us be happy in finding. You have bidden us
knock; we pray you open to us. Be graciously pleased to direct and govern all our thoughts and actions, that for the future we may serve you
and entirely devote ourselves to obeying you. Accept us, we ask you,
and draw us to yourself, that we may henceforth be yours by obedience
and love, who are already all your own as your creatures, even yours,
O Lord, who lives and reigns for ever and ever. Amen. *Augustine*

⸙ OLD TESTAMENT READING: *Exodus 1:8—2:10*

REFLECTIONS FROM THE CHURCH FATHERS

Irony in God's Providence. **EPHREM THE SYRIAN:** Just as Pharaoh
was drowned in those very waters in which he had drowned the in-
fants, so too David removed Goliath's head with that very sword with

which he had destroyed many. Moses divided the waters through the symbol of the cross, while David laid Goliath low through the symbol of the stone. *Commentary on Tatian's Diatessaron 12.*

A Hymn to Moses' Mother and the Midwife. PRUDENTIUS:

Thus Moses in a former age
Escaped proud Pharaoh's foolish law,
And as the savior of his race
Prefigured Christ who was to come.
A cruel edict had been passed
Forbidding Hebrew mothers all,
When sons were born to them, to rear
These virile pledges of their love.
Devoutly scornful of the king,
A zealous midwife found a way
To hide her charge and keep him safe
For future glory and renown. *Hymns for Every Day 12, 141-52.*

PSALM OF RESPONSE: *Psalm 124*

NEW TESTAMENT READING: *Romans 12:1-8*

REFLECTIONS FROM THE CHURCH FATHERS

How the Body Becomes a Sacrifice. CHRYSOSTOM: How is the body to become a sacrifice? Let the eye look on no evil thing, and it has already become a sacrifice. Let the tongue say nothing filthy, and it has become an offering. Let your hand do nothing evil, and it has become a whole burnt offering. But even this is not enough for we must have good works also. The hand must do alms, the mouth must bless those who curse it, and the ears must find time to listen to the reading of Scripture. Sacrifice allows of no unclean thing. It is the first fruits of all other actions. *Homilies on Romans 20.*

Aflame with Divine Love. AUGUSTINE: If the body, which is less than the soul and which the soul uses as a servant or a tool, is a sacrifice when it is used well and rightly for the service of God, how much more so is the soul when it offers itself to God? In this way, aflame in the fire of divine love and with the dross of worldly desire melted away, it is remolded into the unchangeable form of God and becomes beautiful in his sight by reason of the bounty of beauty which he has bestowed upon it. *The City of God 10.6.*

I Appeal to You. LUCULENTIUS: The difference between asking and appealing is that we ask about unimportant matters but appeal about important ones. . . . Our bodies are sacrifices because the flesh is put to death. They are living sacrifices, because the Spirit has given them life. *Commentary 3.*

Members Need Each Other. AMBROSIASTER: By using the example of the body, Paul teaches that it is impossible for any one of us to do everything on our own, for we are members of each other and need one another. For this reason we ought to behave toward one another with care, because we need each other's gifts. *Commentary on Paul's Epistles.*

Members One of Another. CLEMENT OF ROME: Why do we divide and tear to pieces the members of Christ and raise up strife against our own body, and why have we reached such a height of madness as to forget that "we are members one of another?" *The First Epistle of Clement 46.*

The Gift of Prophecy. DIODORE: "Prophecy" means primarily the explanation of things which are unclear, whether future or past, whether present or hidden. "Prophecy" may also refer to the interpretation of a prophet's words. *Pauline Commentary from the Greek Church.*

Liberality, Zeal, Cheerfulness. CHRYSOSTOM: Exhortation is a form of teaching. . . . In giving Paul looks for liberality; in showing mercy, for cheerfulness; in caregiving, for diligence. For it is not just with money that Paul wants us to help those in need but with words, deeds, in person and in every other way. *Homilies on Romans 21.*

GOSPEL READING: *Matthew 16:13-20*

REFLECTIONS FROM THE CHURCH FATHERS

Son of Man, Son of God. THEODORE OF HERACLEA: Jesus asks this in order that we might know what opinions about him were current among the Jews. [He also asks] so that we might learn to inquire intently into what people are saying about him, and if it is bad, to remove the causes, or if complimentary, to increase them. But he said "Son of man" in order to show that he himself not only appears to be but in fact unchangeably is man, and again, is true God. [It is] not as if he were divided into different species, one part God and one part man; rather one may address him as Son of man with no doubt that this very same one is also the Son of God. *Fragment 101.*

Upon This Rock. THEODORE OF MOPSUESTIA: This is not the property of Peter alone, but it came about on behalf of every human being. Having said that his confession is a rock, he stated that upon this rock I will build my church. This means he will build his church upon this same confession and faith. *Fragment 92.*

He Strictly Charged Them. CHRYSOSTOM: And why did he charge them? That when the things which offend are taken out of the way, the cross is accomplished and the rest of his sufferings fulfilled, and when there is nothing any more to interrupt and disturb the faith of the people in him, the right opinion concerning him may be engraven pure and immovable in the mind of the hearers. For in truth his power had not clearly shone forth. Accordingly it was his will then to be preached by them when both the plain truth of the facts and the power of his deeds were pleading in support of the assertions of the apostles. For it was by no means the same thing to see him in Palestine, now working miracles and now insulted and persecuted, especially when the very cross was presently to follow the miracles that were happening, and then to behold him everywhere in the world, adored and believed, and no more suffering anything such as he had suffered. *The Gospel of Matthew, Homily 54.4.*

CLOSING PRAYER

O gracious Light,
Pure brightness of the everlasting Father in heaven,
O Jesus Christ, holy and blessed!
Now as we come to the setting of the sun,
And our eyes behold the vesper light,
We sing praises, O God: Father, Son and Holy Spirit.
You are worthy at all times to be praised by happy voices,
O Son of God, O giver of life,
And to be glorified through all the worlds. [Amen.] *Phos Hilaron*

Walking in Truth

THEME

God is holy and unchanging (Ex 3:1-15). We trust him unreservedly. We walk in truth (Ps 26:1-8) as we take up our crosses, follow Christ (Mt 16:21-28), love one another and repay evil with good (Rom 12:9-21).

OPENING PRAYER: *Proper 17*

O God, whose ways are all mercy and truth, carry on your gracious work, and bestow, by your benefits, what human frailty cannot attain; that they who attend upon the heavenly mysteries may be grounded in perfect faith, and shine forth conspicuous by the purity of their souls; through Jesus Christ our Lord. Amen. *The Leonine Sacramentary*

OLD TESTAMENT READING: *Exodus 3:1-15*

REFLECTIONS FROM THE CHURCH FATHERS

God Is the Only Cause of Existence. EUSEBIUS OF CAESAREA: Everything that has ever existed or now exists derives its being from the One, the only existent and preexistent being, who also said, "I am the existent." . . . As the only being and the eternal being, he is himself the cause of existence to all those to whom he has imparted existence from himself by his will and his power and gives existence to all things and

their powers and forms, richly and ungrudgingly from himself. *Proof of the Gospel 4.1.*

To Be Is Most Characteristic of God. HILARY OF POITIERS: It is known that there is nothing more characteristic of God than to be, because that itself which is does not belong to those things which will one day end or to those which had a beginning. But that which combines eternity with the power of unending happiness could never not have been, nor is it possible that one day it will not be, because what is divine is not liable to destruction, nor does it have a beginning. And since the eternity of God will not be untrue to itself in anything, he has revealed to us in a fitting manner this fact alone, that he is, in order to render testimony to his everlasting eternity. *On the Trinity 1.5.*

Existence and Goodness Derive from God. AUGUSTINE: He is the first and greatest existence, who is utterly unchangeable and who could say most perfectly, "I am who I am, and you shall say to them, He who is has sent me to you." *On Christian Teaching 1.32.35.*

PSALM OF RESPONSE: *Psalm 26:1-8*

NEW TESTAMENT READING: *Romans 12:9-21*

REFLECTIONS FROM THE CHURCH FATHERS

Let Love Be Genuine; Hate What Is Evil. ORIGEN: I think that any love without God is artificial and not genuine. For God, the Creator of the soul, filled it with the feeling of love, along with the other virtues, so that it might love God and the things which God wants. But if the soul loves something other than God and what God wants, this love is said to be artificial and invented. And if someone loves his neighbor but does not warn him when he sees him going astray or correct him, such is only a pretense of love. *Commentary on the Epistle to the Romans.*

Hold Fast to What Is Good. **CHRYSOSTOM:** If you have love, you will not notice the loss of your money, the labor of your body, the toil of your words, your trouble or your ministering, but you will bear everything courageously. *Homilies on Romans 21.*

Christ Died for the Ungodly. **ORIGEN:** It happens that we hate things we ought not to, just as we love things we ought not to. We are ordered to love our brothers, not to hate them. If you think that someone is ungodly, remember that "Christ died for the ungodly." And if you think that because your brother is a sinner you do not have to love him, remember that "Christ Jesus came into this world to save sinners." But if he is righteous, then he is much more worthy of love, for "God loves the righteous." *Commentary on the Epistle to the Romans.*

Feeling Compassion. **CHRYSOSTOM:** Paul wants us to be penetrated with the warmth of friendship. This is why he goes on to say that we are not merely to bless but that we are to feel compassion for their pains and sufferings whenever we happen to see them fall into trouble. *Homilies on Romans 22.*

God Resists the Proud. **AMBROSIASTER:** To be haughty is pride, which is how the devil fell. . . . Solomon says that "God resists the proud." Put pride aside and make other people's cares your own so that you might be acceptable to God. *Commentary on Paul's Epistles.*

Never Avenge Yourselves. **AMBROSIASTER:** Paul warns us to avoid anger, especially because so often anger is the chief cause of sin. Someone who is motivated by wrath will demand more than the cause of the sin merits or will put himself out to do more harm while seeking revenge. . . . In the end he will destroy someone when he could have corrected and restored him instead. *Commentary on Paul's Epistles.*

Interior Freedom. **THEODORET OF CYR:** Revenge is mean-spirited. True victory is returning good for evil. *Interpretation of the Letter to the Romans.*

GOSPEL READING: *Matthew 16:21-28*

REFLECTIONS FROM THE CHURCH FATHERS

Get Behind Me, Satan! CHRYSOSTOM: Therefore, the rest being troubled and in perplexity, Peter again in his ardor alone ventures to discuss these things. And he does not discuss them openly but only when he had taken him aside. Having separated himself from the rest of the disciples, he says, "God forbid, Lord! This shall never happen to you." What is happening here? The very one who had obtained a revelation, who had been blessed, has now so soon fallen away, so as now to fear the passion of the Lord, and thereby his faith has been overthrown. It is remarkable that Peter, who had not yet been fully instructed in the course of revelation, should come up with these responses. The larger picture had not yet been revealed to Peter, and he was confused and overwhelmed. Peter had learned that Christ is the Son of God. But he had not learned of the mystery of the cross and the resurrection. . . . Do you see how correct Jesus was in forbidding them not to declare his identity publicly? For if it so confounded the disciples, who were being made aware of it, who knows what the response of others might have been. *The Gospel of Matthew, Homily 54.5-6.*

The Disciples' Human Weakness. CYRIL OF ALEXANDRIA: Since the disciples had not yet received power from on high, it was perhaps not unnatural that they should fall occasionally into human weaknesses and, thinking something of this sort, say "How shall someone deny himself? Or how can someone, by losing his own life, save it?" *Fragment 195.*

CLOSING PRAYER

God's might to uphold me
God's wisdom to guide me,
God's eye to look before me,

God's ear to hear me,
God's word to speak for me,
God's hand to guard me,
God's way to lie before me,
God's shield to protect me,
God's hosts to save me. *Patrick*

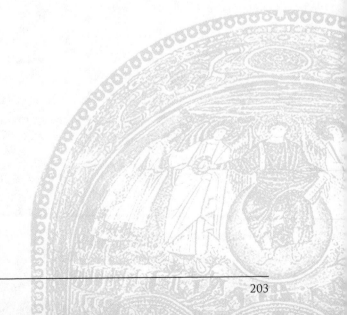

Right Paths

☙ THEME

The power of Christ's precious blood is seen in the Passover, as are other symbols of the faith (Ex 12:1-14). We pray for God to help us better understand his instructions so we can wholeheartedly walk in the right paths on our spiritual journey (Ps 119:33-40). We pledge to confront in love our fellow Christians who fall away from the faith in some way (Mt 18:15-20). We cast off the works of darkness to walk in the light of love (Rom 13:8-14).

☙ OPENING PRAYER: *Proper 18*

Light of Light, and God of God, who did bow your holy heavens and descend to earth for the salvation of the world, out of your love of humanity; extend your almighty right hand, and send out your blessings on us all. . . . Guide our steps into the paths of righteousness, that we may behave ourselves according to your will and observe your commandments and do them all the days of our life, and come to a blessed end and sing a ceaseless hymn with your saints to you, and your Father and your Holy Spirit. [Amen.] *Liturgy of Dioscorus*

☙ OLD TESTAMENT READING: *Exodus 12:1-14*

REFLECTIONS FROM THE CHURCH FATHERS

Marked with the Blood of the Lamb. AUGUSTINE: For why would the Lord instruct them to kill a sheep on this very feast day except that it was he about whom it was prophesied: "As a sheep is led to the slaughter." The doorposts of the Jews were marked with the blood of a slaughtered animal. Our foreheads are marked with the blood of Christ. And that sign, because it was a sign, was said to keep the destroyer away from the houses marked with the sign. The sign of Christ drives the destroyer away from us insofar as our heart receives the Savior. *Tractate on the Gospel of John 50.3.*

Bitter Herbs Are Grief or Trials. ORIGEN: But we eat the flesh of the lamb and the unleavened bread with bitter herbs either by being grieved with a godly grief because of repentance for our sins, a grief which produces in us a repentance unto salvation which brings no regret, or by seeking and being nurtured from the visions of the truth which we discover because of our trials. *Commentary on the Gospel of John 10.102.*

The Devil Lost What He Held. CAESARIUS OF ARLES: Original sin could not have easily been forgiven, if a victim had not been offered for it, if that sacred blood of propitiation had not been shed. Even then the words in Exodus were not vainly said of our Lord: "I shall see the blood and shall protect you." That figure of the lamb represented this passion of Christ our Lord. Blood is given for blood, death for death, a victim for sin, and thus the devil lost what he held. *Sermon 11.5.*

PSALM OF RESPONSE: *Psalm 119:33-40*

NEW TESTAMENT READING: *Romans 13:8-14*

REFLECTIONS FROM THE CHURCH FATHERS

Fulfill the Law. CHRYSOSTOM: Love is a debt which you owe to your brother because of your spiritual relationship to him. . . . If love departs from us, the whole body is torn in pieces. Therefore love your brother, for if you can fulfill the law by befriending him, then the benefit you receive puts you in his debt. *Homilies on Romans 23.*

Abstain from Evil, Do Good. THEODORE OF MOPSUESTIA: Every law either forbids evil or tells us to do good. Legislators pass the first kind of law in order that we should not harm one another and the second kind in order that we should help one another as far as possible. But they are all summed up in the one command that we should love our neighbor. *Pauline Commentary from the Greek Church.*

The Rule of Love. AUGUSTINE: The rule of love is that one should wish his friend to have all the good things he wants to have himself and should not wish the evils to befall his friend which he wishes to avoid himself. *Of True Religion 87.*

Love Is the Fulfilling of the Law. CAESARIUS OF ARLES: Therefore, whatever you do, do it for the love of Christ, and let the intention or end of all your actions look to him. Do nothing for the sake of human praises but everything for the love of God and the desire for eternal life. *Sermon 137.1.*

Restraint of Excess. CHRYSOSTOM: Paul does not forbid alcohol; he is opposed only to its excessive use. Nor does he prohibit sexual intercourse; rather he is against fornication. What he wants to do is get rid of the deadly passions of lust and anger. Therefore he does not merely attack them but goes to their source as well. *Homilies on Romans 24.*

GOSPEL READING: *Matthew 18:15-20*

REFLECTIONS FROM THE CHURCH FATHERS

The Art of Reconciliation. CHRYSOSTOM: He does not say "accuse him" or "punish him" or "take him to court." He says "correct him." For he is possessed, as it were, by some stupor, and drunk in his anger and disgrace. The one who is healthy must go to the one who is sick. You must conduct your judgment of him privately. Make your cure easy to accept. For the words "correct him" mean nothing other than help him see his indiscretion. Tell him what you have suffered from him. What then if he does not listen, if he stubbornly flares up? Call to your side someone else or even two others, so that two witnesses may corroborate all that's said. For the more shameless and boldfaced he is, so much the more must you be earnest toward his cure, not toward satisfying your anger and hurt feelings. For when a physician sees the sickness unyielding, he does not stand aside or take it hard but then is all the more earnest. That then is what Christ orders us to do. You appeared too weak since you were alone, so become stronger with the help of others. Two are sufficient to reprove the wrongdoer. Do you see how he seeks the interest not of the aggrieved party alone but also that of the one who caused the grief? *The Gospel of Matthew, Homily 60.1.*

The Beauty of the Wholeness of the Body. PETER CHRYSOLOGUS:
There are those who presume that the congregation of the church can be disregarded. They assert that private prayers should be preferred to those of an honorable assembly. But if Jesus denies nothing to so small a group as two or three, will he refuse those who ask for it in the assemblies and congregation of the church? . . . Some, however, endeavor to excuse under an appearance of faith the idleness that prompts their contempt for assemblies. They omit participation in the fervor of the assembled congregation and pretend that they have devoted to prayer the time they have expended upon their household cares. While they give themselves up to their own desires, they scorn and despise the divine service. These are the people who destroy the body of Christ. They scatter its members. . . . Individual members do indeed have their own duty of personal prayer, but they will not be able to fulfill it if they come to the beauty of that perfect body wrapped up in themselves. *Sermon 132.4-5.*

CLOSING PRAYER

We ask you, O Lord, in your compassion to increase your faith in us, because you will not deny the aid of your loving-kindness to those on whom you bestow a steadfast belief in you; through Jesus Christ our Lord. [Amen.] *The Leonine Sacramentary*

God's Care

⌇ THEME

The Lord protects his people; just as he brought them safely out of
Egypt (Ex 14:19-31), so he will care for us. We praise God for his justice, healing, mercy and love (Ps 103:1-13), knowing that as Christians, we must consider the feelings of others (Rom 14:1-12). In the
same way God has forgiven us much, we are to forgive others with generosity (Mt 18:21-35).

⌇ OPENING PRAYER: *Proper 19*

We beg you, Master, be our help and strength. Save those among us
who are oppressed, have pity on the lowly, and lift up the fallen. Heal
the sick, bring back the straying, and feed the hungry. Release those
in prison, lift up those who falter, and strengthen the fainthearted. Let
all nations come to know you the one God, with your Son Jesus
Christ, and us your people and the sheep of your pasture. [Amen.]
Clement of Rome

⌇ OLD TESTAMENT READING: *Exodus 14:19-31*

REFLECTIONS FROM THE CHURCH FATHERS

The Body Stands Between Us and God. GREGORY OF NAZIAN-
ZUS: Therefore this darkness of the body has been placed between us
and God, like the cloud of old between the Egyptians and the Hebrews.

This is perhaps what is meant by "He made darkness his separate place," namely, our dullness, through which few can see even a little. *Theological Oration 2.12.*

The Law of God Delivers Us. ORIGEN: How hard a temptation it is to pass through the midst of the sea, to see the waves rise piled up, to hear the noise and rumbling of the raging waters! But if you follow Moses, that is, the law of God, the waters will become for you walls on the right and left, and you will find a path on dry ground in the midst of the sea. Moreover, it can happen that the heavenly journey that we say the soul takes may hold peril of waters. Great waves may be found there. *Homilies on Numbers 27.10.*

Water Saves and Destroys. AMBROSE: The waters of the sea were held back yet at the same time surround the Hebrews. They then poured back and brought death upon the Egyptians, so that they destroyed one people and saved the other. What too do we find in the Gospel itself? Did not our Lord show there that the sea grew calm at his word, that the storm clouds of heaven were scattered, that the blasts of the winds subsided and that the dumb elements obeyed him and the shores were quieted? *On His Brother Satyrus 2.74.*

⁑ PSALM OF RESPONSE: *Psalm 103:1-13*

⁑ NEW TESTAMENT READING: *Romans 14:1-12*

REFLECTIONS FROM THE CHURCH FATHERS

Cultural Sensitivity. GENNADIUS OF CONSTANTINOPLE: Who would be so inhumane as to lay aside any sympathy for the weak and trample on them, not even offering them the help they need in adversity? Paul makes this an absolute command and accompanies it with the teaching that the law and all the behavior it entailed has been abolished in Christ. Yet he was conscious that the ethnic heritage weighed more heavily on the Jew, who felt that he would be sinning against his brothers if he went against the law. *Pauline Commentary from the Greek Church.*

Not Passing Judgment. ORIGEN: Paul wants harmony to prevail in the church between those who are more mature and those who are less. *Commentary on the Epistle to the Romans.*

Personal Choice. AMBROSIASTER: What we eat or do not eat is a matter of personal choice and therefore it should not become a matter for argument. *Commentary on Paul's Epistles.*

GOSPEL READING: *Matthew 18:21-35*

REFLECTIONS FROM THE CHURCH FATHERS

No Time for Anger. HILARY OF POITIERS: When Peter asked him whether he should forgive his brother sinning against him up to seven times, the Lord replied, "Not up to seven times but up to seventy times seven times." In every way he teaches us to be like him in humility and goodness. In weakening and breaking the impulses of our rampant passions he strengthens us by the example of his leniency, by granting us in faith pardon of all our sins. For the vices of our nature did not merit pardon. Therefore all pardon comes from him. *On Matthew 18.10.*

The Seventy-Seven Generations from Adam to Christ. AUGUSTINE: What then does "seventy times seven" mean? Listen, my friends, to this great mystery, this wonderful gift. When the Lord was baptized, Luke the holy Evangelist there noted down his ancestry, in what order, series and stems that generation had reached in which Christ was born. . . . Note that in his account he enumerates seventy-seven generations! With whom did he begin his reckoning? Note carefully! He began to reckon from Christ up to Adam himself, who was the first sinner and who parented us into bondage to sin. Luke reckoned up to Adam, and so there are enumerated in toto seventy-seven generations—from Christ up to Adam and from Adam up to Christ. Note seventy-seven! So then if no generation was omitted, there is no exemption of any trespass that ought not to be forgiven. *Sermon 83.5.*

Forced Sale. CYRIL OF ALEXANDRIA: The sale of his wife and the rest of the family shows the complete and utter separation from the joys of God. For the sale shows quite clearly alienation from God. Those alienated from God are those who hear those bitter, fearful words, "Depart from me, you workers of iniquity, for I do not know you." *Fragment 217.*

So My Father Will Do to You. CHRYSOSTOM: For what then, can be a more grievous thing than to be vengeful, especially when it appears to overthrow so great a gift of God. The text does not simply say they "delivered him" but "in anger delivered him." For when he had earlier commanded him to be sold, his were not the words of wrath but, rightly understood, a moment of great mercy. He did not in fact show wrath at that point. But in this case it is a sentence of great anger, punishment and vengeance. So what does the parable mean? "So also my heavenly Father will do to you," he says, "if you do not forgive your brother from your heart." Note that he did not say "your Father" but "my Father." For it is not proper for God to be called the Father of one who is so wicked and malicious. *The Gospel of Matthew, Homily 61.4.*

✤ CLOSING PRAYER

Beloved, let us give thanks to God the Father, through his Son, in the Holy Spirit, because in his great love for us he took pity on us, "and when we were dead in our sins he brought us to life with Christ," so that in him we might be a new creation. Let us throw off our old nature and all its ways and, as we have come to birth in Christ, let us renounce the works of the flesh. [Amen.] *Leo the Great*

God's Generosity

THEME

We praise God and meditate on his glorious works (Ps 145:1-8). We may suffer for Christ's sake (Phil 1:21-30), but we know that God will be generous with us, beyond what we deserve (Mt 20:1-16). There is no need we have that God will not provide (Ex 16:2-15).

OPENING PRAYER: *Proper 20*

Eternal God, we bless you for all people holy and humble of heart who served you here of whom also you did make trial and found them worthy for yourself. Happy are the souls who, being loosed from the earthly prison, go freely into heaven, there to behold their dearest Lord face to face, and are no more disquieted by any fear of death but rejoice in glory everlasting. And we ask you so to guide and defend us that finally we may attain to that glory and to the gladsome praises of your godhead, Father, Son and Holy Spirit, forever and forevermore. Amen. *Augustine*

OLD TESTAMENT READING: *Exodus 16:2-15*

REFLECTIONS FROM THE CHURCH FATHERS

The True Renunciation of Egypt. JOHN CASSIAN: Although this manner of speaking first referred to that people, nonetheless we see it now daily fulfilled in our life and profession. For everyone who has first renounced this world and then returns to his former pursuits and his erstwhile desires proclaims that in deed and intention he is the same as they were, and he says, "It was well with me in Egypt." *Conference 3.7.6-7.*

The Meaning of Manna. CAESARIUS OF ARLES: Manna is interpreted as "What is this?" See whether the very power of the name does not provoke you to learn it, so that when you hear the law of God read in church you may always ask and say to the teachers: What is this? This it is that the manna indicates. Therefore if you want to eat the manna, that is, if you desire to receive the word of God, know that it is small and very fine like the seed of the coriander. *Sermon 102.3.*

The Bread Is God's Commandment. AMBROSE: "This is the bread that God gave" to you "to eat." Hear who this bread is: "The word," Scripture says, "which God has ordained." This then is the ordination of God; this food nourishes the soul of the wise. It illuminates and it sweetens, resplendent with the gleam of truth and soothing, as if with a honeycomb, by the sweetness of different virtues and the word of wisdom. For "good words are sweeter than a honeycomb," as it is written in Proverbs. *Letter 54 (64).2.*

⌁ **PSALM OF RESPONSE:** *Psalm 145:1-8*

⌁ **NEW TESTAMENT READING:** *Philippians 1:21-30*

REFLECTIONS FROM THE CHURCH FATHERS

Neither Death nor Torture Is Punishment If Christ Is Life. MARIUS VICTORINUS: It is not death itself that is gain, but to die in Christ. Life is Christ. The one who has hope in him is always alive, both now and forever. . . . Therefore they achieve nothing, whether they hand me over to death or to tortures in life. Neither alternative harms me. Life under torments is no punishment for me, since Christ is my life. And if they kill me, that too is no punishment for me, since Christ for me is life and to die is gain. *Epistle to the Philippians 1.21.*

That Your Boast May Abound. CHRYSOSTOM: What does he mean, that your boast may abound? All there was to glory in was their being established in the faith. This is what it means to boast in Christ, to live rightly. . . . He means "so that I may have more to boast of in you. . . . As you improve, I have more to boast of." *Homily on Philippians 5.1.22-26.*

Whether Absent or Present. CHRYSOSTOM: He does not imply by saying this that he is changing his mind or that he is not going to come. Rather he is saying whether he comes or not, regardless of what comes to pass, they may stand firm even in his absence. *Homily on Philippians 5.1.27.*

Be Ready to Suffer for His Sake. MARIUS VICTORINUS: It was therefore within his purpose that he gave to us the gift of trusting in him. This was an incomparable gift. It is only by faith in him that we are blessed with so great a reward. We are to believe in such a way as to be ready to suffer for him. *Epistle to the Philippians 1.29.*

The Special Gift to Those Who Love Christ. AMBROSIASTER: Although he extols the grace of Christ on many occasions, he offers a special kind of honor to the Philippians in this passage. He says: "God has allowed you to suffer for Christ." He does not propose this distinction to any but true lovers of Christ. His paradoxical reasoning is that this gift *is given to you for Christ!* This means that God the Father gives this special gift to lovers of his Son. Why? That their blessings might increase correspondingly through their participation in suffering on Christ's behalf. Paul speaks as one who himself has received this gift. *Epistle to the Philippians 1.30.*

GOSPEL READING: *Matthew 20:1-16*

REFLECTIONS FROM THE CHURCH FATHERS

Laborers for His Vineyard. ANONYMOUS: "To hire laborers for his vineyard." What is the vineyard of God here? Not men, as elsewhere; for men are called the cultivators of the vineyard. The vineyard is justice and in it different kinds of virtues are placed like vines. For example, gentleness, chastity, patience, high-mindedness, and countless other good qualities which are all in general called virtues. So let us note how earnestly we should cultivate the heavenly vineyard. *Incomplete Work on Matthew, Homily 34.*

Ready to Obey. CHRYSOSTOM: So what was the point of this parable and what does it want to accomplish? To make those who convert in their extreme old age more earnest and to make them better and not to let them think they have less. *The Gospel of Matthew, Homily 64.3.*

Is Your Eye Evil Because Mine Is Good? GREGORY THE GREAT: The householder said to them, "I wish to give to this last one as I give even to you." And since the obtaining of his kingdom comes from his good will, he properly adds, "Or I am not allowed to do what I wish? It is always foolish to question the goodness of God. There might have been reason for loud complaint if he did not give what he owed but not if he gives what he does not owe. And so he adds, "Or is your eye evil because I am good? . . . Indeed, we must all rejoice exceedingly to be even the last in the kingdom of God. *Forty Gospel Homilies 19.4.*

CLOSING PRAYER

May the yoke of the Law of God be on my shoulder,
The coming of the Holy Spirit on my head,
The sign of Christ on my forehead,
The hearing of the Holy Spirit in my ears,
The smelling of the Holy Spirit in my nose,

The vision of the people of heaven in my eyes,

The speech of the people of heaven in my mouth,

The work of the church of God in my hands,

The good of God and of neighbor in my feet.

May God dwell in my heart, and may I belong entirely to God the
Father.

Amen. *Breastplace Prayer of Fursa*

Humility and Service

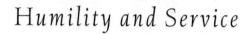

⊰ THEME

We cry out to God for help, trusting him and asking him to show us the right ways to live (Ps 25:1-9), and he meets our needs even when we are undeserving (Ex 17:1-7). In turn, we need to consider others better than ourselves and be willing to help them in their need (Phil 2:1-13). We repent of our sins and believe in God (Mt 21:23-32).

⊰ OPENING PRAYER: *Proper 21*

Lord, you know those who are sore stricken and heavy of heart. As their days, so let their strength be. Heal the sick, comfort the weary, succor the tempted, give peace to the dying and light at eventide. . . . Watch over us who are still in our dangerous voyage, and remember such as lie exposed to the rough storms of trouble and temptations. Frail is our vessel, and the ocean is wide; but as in your mercy you have set our course, so steer the vessel of our life toward the everlasting shore of peace, and bring us at length to the quiet haven of our heart's desire, where you, O our God, are blessed, and live and reign for ever and ever. [Amen.] *Augustine*

⊰ OLD TESTAMENT READING: *Ezekiel 18:1-4, 25-32*

REFLECTIONS FROM THE CHURCH FATHERS

The Justice of God. JEROME: How good and just is the God of the law and the prophets, who keeps quiet and remains silent before the sins of the fathers, and gives back to those who have not sinned! *Commentary on Ezekiel 6*.

It Is Our Fault If We Make Heavy Going of Taking the Yoke of Christ.
JOHN CASSIAN: When we make the Lord's yoke heavy, with blasphemous spirit we accuse as harsh and rough either the yoke itself or Christ who imposes it. *Conference 24.25.5*.

Repentance Leads to the Promised Land. JEROME: These words show us that the mind must not fail to believe in the promised blessings and give way to despair; and that the soul once marked out for perdition must not refuse to apply remedies on the ground that its wounds are past curing. *Letter 122.1*.

The God of the Living Is the God of the New Heart. JEROME: "Get yourselves a new heart and a new spirit" means leaving behind the old age of the letter, and living in the newness of the spirit. The new heart of Israel is to believe in him who before had denied them; the new heart is to forsake the idols of the Gentiles, to despise dead things, and to believe in him who is "God of the living." *Commentary on Ezekiel 6*.

Believers Must Live. PACHOMIUS: Why are you dying? Do not go into the trap. These are the reminders given to the believers, that by walking in them and striving in the commandments they will do the works worthy of eternal life. *Letters 3.9*.

Repentance Means Recognizing First of All That We Are Dead. JEROME: "I do not want you to die." He did not say "turn," unless those who were once with God and afterwards deserted his company and "live" through penitence, you who are dead through sin. Therefore Israel is believed to be dead because she does not turn back to her original state. *Commentary on Ezekiel 6*.

Forgiveness Means Healing. BASIL THE GREAT: Remember the compassion of God, how he heals with olive oil and wine. Do not despair of salvation. Recall the memory of what has been written, how he that falls rises again, and he that is turned away turns again, he that has been smitten is healed, he that is caught by wild beasts escapes, and he that confesses is not rejected. The Lord does not want the death of the sinner, but that he return and live. Do not be contemptuous like one who has fallen into the depths of sins. *Letter 44.*

Confession Means Asking for Forgiveness, a Prayer Always Heeded. CASSIODORUS: The prayer which frees us from faults wins the heart of the judge and wipes away sins; mercy cannot be withheld from the one who asks for it, as humility fires us to pray unceasingly for forgiveness. All this is achieved by the devoted Lord, for he does not wish to condemn those whom he forewarns. *Expositions of Psalm 140.1.*

PSALM OF RESPONSE: *Psalm 25:1-9*

NEW TESTAMENT READING: *Philippians 2:1-13*

REFLECTIONS FROM THE CHURCH FATHERS

Enslaved to Popularity. CHRYSOSTOM: Selfishness is the cause of all sorts of evils. From it comes strife and rivalry. From these come jealousy and contentiousness. Out of this that love grows cool when we are in love with human glory and become enslaved to the honors of popularity. One cannot be both a slave to popularity and a true servant of God. *Homily on Philippians 6.2.1-4.*

Equal to God. AUGUSTINE: God who is eternally wise has with him his eternal Wisdom [the Son]. He is not in any way unequal to the Father. He is not in any respect inferior. For the apostle too says "who, when he was in the form of God, thought it no robbery to be equal with God." *On Faith and the Creed 5.*

Whether Humility Is Lack of Power. CHRYSOSTOM: When someone who has the power to think great thoughts humbles himself, that one is humble. But when his humility comes from impotence, that is not what you would call humility. . . . It is a humility of a greater sort to refrain from *seizing* power, to be "obedient to death." *Homily on Philippians 7.2.5-8.*

The Emptying as a Lesson in Humility. AMBROSIASTER: Christ, therefore, knowing himself to be *in the form of God,* showed himself equal to God. But in order to teach the law of humility when the Jews were binding him, he not only refrained from resistance but *emptied himself,* that is, withheld his power from taking effect, so that in his humiliation he seemed to be weakened as his power lay idle. *Epistle to the Philippians 2.8.1.*

The Sovereignty Temporarily Under Submission. NOVATIAN: The sovereignty of the divine Word temporarily submitted to assume a man and for a season *humbled himself* and abased himself, not exercising his nature through his powers, while he bore the man that he had assumed. He *emptied himself* when he bowed to injuries and slanders, when he heard unspeakable insults and suffered indignities. *On the Trinity 22.8-9.*

His Humbling Becomes Our Example. CYRIL OF ALEXANDRIA: He *humbled himself,* according to the Scriptures, *taking on himself the form of a slave.* He became like us that we might become like him. The work of the Spirit seeks to transform us by grace into a perfect copy of his humbling. *Festal Letter 10.4.*

GOSPEL READING: *Matthew 21:23-32*

REFLECTIONS FROM THE CHURCH FATHERS

Liars Will Lie to Themselves. ANONYMOUS: "They answered Jesus, saying, 'We do not know.' And he said to them, 'Neither will I tell you by what authority I do these things.'" He did not say, "Neither do I know." It was as if he had said, "You know the truth because you are men, but you deny it because you are evil; I know it because I am God, but I will not tell you because you are unworthy." Liars will lie to themselves if they have no one to deceive. Similarly truth will keep itself pure if it finds no one to save. *Incomplete Work on Matthew, Homily 39.*

The Two Sons. ANONYMOUS: Who is this if not the God who created all people and loves them with a fatherly affection, the God who preferred to be loved as a father rather than feared as a lord, even though he was Lord by nature? On this account, at the beginning of the commandments of the law, he did not say," You shall fear the Lord with all your heart" but "you shall love the Lord with all your heart." To elicit love is not characteristic of a lord but of a father. *Incomplete Work on Matthew, Homily 40.*

Do Not Promise, Then Renege. ANONYMOUS: What does it mean to work in the vineyard? To work in the vineyard is to do justice. We noted above that the vineyard is the justice that God has planted generally in the nature of all people but more particularly in the Jewish Scriptures. Each vine in the vineyard represents a different type of justice, and each person, according to his individual virtues, produces either more or fewer vines. . . . It is better to do the righteousness of God without promising to do so than it is to promise and then to renege. *Incomplete Work on Matthew, Homily 40.*

CLOSING PRAYER

Lord Jesus Christ, who stretched out your hands on the cross and redeemed us by your blood, forgive me, a sinner, for none of my thoughts are hidden from you. Pardon I ask, pardon I hope for, pardon I trust to have. You who are pitiful and merciful, spare and forgive me. *The Ambrosian Liturgy*

Quietness and Rest

THEME

Moses was given the law, which calls us to honor the Lord as the one true God and to observe the sabbath (Ex 20:1-4, 7-9, 12-20). God is the creator and giver of the law; all we have to do is look to the heavens to see his handiwork and majesty (Ps 19). We press forward, desiring what is right, knowing that everything pales before what Christ offers (Phil 3:4b-14) and recognizing the sacrifice Christ made for our salvation and that our foundation in him is rock solid (Mt 21:33-46).

OPENING PRAYER: *Proper 22*

Through your works, you have manifested the eternal ordering of the world, Lord, creator of the universe. You remain the same throughout all generations; just in your judgments, admirable in power and magnificence, full of wisdom in creating and prudent in strengthening everything in existence. You manifest your goodness toward all visible things and your fidelity toward those who trust you, for you are merciful and compassionate. [Amen.] *Clement of Rome*

OLD TESTAMENT READING: *Exodus 20:1-4, 7-9, 12-20*

REFLECTIONS FROM THE CHURCH FATHERS

The Sabbath Means a Peaceful Mind. AUGUSTINE: The third commandment: "Remember the Sabbath day to sanctify it." This third commandment imposes a regular periodical holiday—quietness of heart, tranquility of mind, the product of a good conscience. Here is sanctification, because here is the Spirit of God. Well, here is what a true holiday, that is to say, quietness and rest, means. "Upon whom," he says, "shall my spirit rest? Upon one who is humble and quiet and trembles at my words." So unquiet people are those who recoil from the Holy Spirit, loving quarrels, spreading slanders, keener on argument than on truth, and so in their restlessness they do not allow the quietness of the spiritual Sabbath to enter into themselves. *Sermon 8.6.*

Acts and Thoughts. GREGORY THE GREAT: The law suppressed physical sins, but our Redeemer condemned even unlawful thoughts. And so "if they do not hear Moses and the prophets, neither will they believe one who rises from the dead." When will those who neglect to fulfill the less important commandments of the law be strong enough to obey our Savior's more demanding precepts? This much is clear: anyone whose sayings they decline to fulfill, they have refused to believe. *Homily 40.*

⁂ **PSALM OF RESPONSE:** *Psalm 19*

⁂ **NEW TESTAMENT READING:** *Philippians 3:4b-14*

REFLECTIONS FROM THE CHURCH FATHERS

Blameless Under the Law. AUGUSTINE: Before his conversion Paul fulfilled the law conspicuously, either through fear of the people or of God himself, even if he may have offended the law in his internal affections. But he was fulfilling the law through fear of punishment, not through love of righteousness. *On Two Letters of Pelagius 1.15.*

The Power of His Resurrection Known Through Faith. CHRYSOSTOM: Knowledge therefore comes through faith, and without faith there is no knowledge. How so? It is only through faith that we know the power of his resurrection. For what reasoning could demonstrate the resurrection to us? None, but it is through faith. And if the resurrection of Christ in the flesh is known through faith, how can the nativity of the Word be comprehended by reason? For the resurrection is far more plausible to reason than the virgin birth. *Homily on Philippians 12.3.10-11.*

Straining in Pursuit. CHRYSOSTOM: He says not "I run" but I press on. Consider how the pursuer strains in his pursuit. He sees nothing, he thrusts away all who impede him with great force, he cherishes his mind, his eye, his strength, his soul and his body, looking at nothing other than the crown. *Homily on Philippians 12.3.12.*

What Is Perfect Today May Be False Tomorrow. JEROME: Put the past out of mind. Set your mind to the future. What he has reckoned perfect today he ascertains to have been false tomorrow as he reaches for ever better and higher goals. By this gradual advance, never being static but always in progress, he is able to teach us that what we supposed in our human way to be perfect still remains in some ways imperfect. The only perfection is the true righteousness of God. *Dialogue Against the Pelagians 1.15.*

The Upward Call of God. MARIUS VICTORINUS: Here then are two precepts for the one who is going to live the rest of life walking in the Christian way. First, the one who is still living under divine governance, however well and rightly he has acted in the past, should not think about all the actions he has already done as though he deserved to obtain something by them. Rather he should cast them into oblivion, always seeking the new tasks that remain. Second, he should nonetheless keep living under the divine rule, continually pressing on toward these things and observing the rule of Christ, even to death. *Epistle to the Philippians 3.13-14.*

GOSPEL READING: *Matthew 21:33-46*

REFLECTIONS FROM THE CHURCH FATHERS

Hear Another Parable. CHRYSOSTOM: This parable suggests many things: God's providence had been at work toward them from the outset; their disposition was murderous from the beginning; nothing had been neglected of whatever pertained to an attentive care for them, even when prophets had been slain, God had not turned away from this people but had sent them his very Son; it is now clear that the God of both the New and the Old Testaments is one and the same; we know that the Son's death will effect great blessings; we here learn that they were to endure extreme punishment for the crucifixion; here we learn of the calling of the Gentiles and the turning aside of the unbelieving Jews. He presents this parable after the previous one that he may show the charge to be even greater in this case and highly unpardonable. In what way? Although the Jews had received so much care from God, they were now found to be worse than harlots and publicans, and that by a wide margin. *The Gospel of Matthew, Homily 68.1.*

He Set a Hedge Around the Vineyard. CHRYSOSTOM: Then he "went into a far country." He was patient with them. He did not always keep a close account of their sins. The meaning of "going into a far country" is God's great patience. *The Gospel of Matthew, Homily 68.1.*

The Householder and the Vineyard. EPIPHANIUS THE LATIN: The "only son" of the householder is the Lord, the Son of God, who came by the will of the Father to his vineyard, which is the Jewish people. "But when the tenants," who are the teachers of the law, "saw his son, they said to themselves, 'this is the heir; come let us kill him, and the inheritance will be ours,' and they threw him out of the vineyard and killed him." They also crucified our Lord outside the city, while they shouted, "Crucify him! Crucify him!" Yet they did not in fact come to possess the inheritance of the law; instead, they sentenced themselves to death, for the Lord asked, "What will the owner of the vineyard do to the tenants when he comes?" They responded, "He will destroy the evil tenants and give the vineyard to other tenants who will produce its fruit in a timely manner." They condemned themselves by their own words, as the Lord implies when he speaks about himself and their faithlessness: "The stone which the builders rejected has become the cornerstone; therefore, I say to you that the kingdom of God will be removed from you and given to a people producing its fruits." *Interpretation of the Gospels 31.*

CLOSING PRAYER

O You, who are the light of the minds that know You, the life of the souls that love You, and the Strength of the thoughts that seek You; help us to know You, that we may truly love You, so to love You that we may fully serve you, whose service is perfect freedom; through Jesus Christ our Lord. Amen. *The Gelasian Sacramentary*

Confession and Praise

◌ THEME

God allows us the chance to intercede for others through prayer (Ex 32:1-14). We come to him confessing our sins and praising him (Ps 106:1-6, 19-23), putting aside our anxieties and setting our minds on Christ (Phil 4:1-9) and recognizing the promise of eternal life with God (Mt 22:1-14).

◌ OPENING PRAYER: *Proper 23*

O God, the comforter of the humble and the strength of the faithful, be merciful to your suppliants; that human weakness, which by itself is prone to fall, may be evermore supported by you to stand upright; through Jesus Christ our Lord. [Amen.] *The Gelasian Sacramentary*

◌ OLD TESTAMENT READING: *Exodus 32:1-14*

REFLECTIONS FROM THE CHURCH FATHERS

The People Reject Moses. EPHREM THE SYRIAN: Bitter signs had accompanied [Israel] as far as the [Red] Sea so that they would fear [God]. And blessed wonders surrounded [Israel] in the desert waste so that they would be reconciled [to him]. But for want of faith [Israel] rejected [the signs] with the feeble excuse: "as for the man Moses who brought us out, we do not know what has become of him." They no longer considered the triumphs that had accompanied them. They only saw that Moses was not near. And so, with this as a convenient excuse, they could draw near to the paganism of Egypt. Therefore Moses was not seen by them for a while, so that the calf could be seen with them [and] so that they could worship openly what they had been worshiping in their hearts. When their paganism came out of hiding and into the open, Moses also came out of hiding and into the open to deliver openly the penalty to those whose paganism had become unrestrained beneath the holy cloud that overshadowed them. *Homily on Our Lord 17.3—18.1.*

Moses Prays As a Mother Does. AUGUSTINE: And in case you should suppose that he acted like this more from necessity than from charity, God actually offered him another people: "And I will make you," he said, "into a great nation," so leaving himself free to eliminate those others. But Moses wouldn't accept this: he sticks to the sinners; he prays for the sinners. And how does he pray? This is a wonderful proof of his love, brothers and sisters. How does he pray? Notice something I've often spoken of, how his love is almost that of a mother. When God threatened that sacrilegious people, Moses' maternal instincts were roused, and on their behalf he stood up to the anger of God. "Lord," he said, "if you will forgive them this sin, forgive; but if not, blot me out from the book you have written." What sure maternal and paternal instincts, how sure his reliance, as he said this, on the justice and mercy of God! He knew that because he is just he wouldn't destroy a just man, and because he is merciful he would pardon sinners. *Sermon 88.24.*

PSALM OF RESPONSE: *Psalm 106:1-6, 19-23*

NEW TESTAMENT READING: *Philippians 4:1-9*

REFLECTIONS FROM THE CHURCH FATHERS

Again I Say, Rejoice. **CHRYSOSTOM:** This rejoicing is not separable from grief, for indeed it is rather deeply connected with grief. The one who grieves for his own wrongdoing and confesses it is joyful. Alternatively it is possible to grieve for one's own sins but rejoice in Christ. . . . On this account he says *Rejoice in the Lord.* For this is nothing if you have received a life worthy of rejoicing. . . . He is right to repeat himself. For since the events are naturally grievous, it is through the petition that he shows that in all cases one should rejoice. *Homily on Philippians 15.4.5-7.*

God Provides All That Is Needful. **MARIUS VICTORINUS:** *Do not be anxious about anything.* This means: Do not be concerned for yourselves. Do not give unnecessary thought to or be anxious about the world or worldly things. For all that is needful for you in this life God provides. And it will be even better in that life which is eternal. *Epistle to the Philippians 4.6.*

The Comfort of Giving Thanks in Everything. **CHRYSOSTOM:** It is comforting to know that the Lord is at hand. . . . Here is a medicine to relieve grief and every bad circumstance and every pain. What is it? To pray and to give thanks in everything. He does not wish that a prayer be merely a petition but a thanksgiving for what we have received. . . . How can one make petitions for the future without a thankful acknowledgment of past things? . . . So one ought to give thanks for everything, even what seems grievous. That is the mark of one who is truly thankful. Grief comes out of the circumstances with their demands. Thanksgiving comes from a soul that has true insight and a strong affection for God. *Homily on Philippians 15.4.4-7.*

GOSPEL READING: *Matthew 22:1-14*

REFLECTIONS FROM THE CHURCH FATHERS

Invitation to the Feast. GREGORY THE GREAT: And so he sent his servants to invite his friends to the marriage feast. He sent once, and he sent again, because first he made the prophets and later the apostles preachers of the Lord's incarnation. He sent his servants twice with the invitation, because he said through the prophets that his only Son's incarnation would come about, and he proclaimed through the apostles that it had. *Forty Gospel Homilies 38.1, 3-4.*

No Wedding Garment. GREGORY THE GREAT: What do we think is meant by the wedding garment, dearly beloved? For if we say it is baptism or faith, is there anyone who has entered this marriage feast without them? A person is outside because he has not yet come to believe. What then must we understand by the wedding garment but love? That person enters the marriage feast, but without wearing a wedding garment, who is present in the holy church. He may have faith, but he does not have love. We are correct when we say that love is the wedding garment because this is what our Creator himself possessed when he came to the marriage feast to join the church to himself. Only God's love brought it about that his only begotten Son united the hearts of his chosen to himself. John says that "God so loved the world that he gave his only begotten Son for us." *Forty Gospel Homilies 38.9.*

Cast Him Out. AUGUSTINE: The garment that is required is in the heart, not on the body, for if it had been put on externally, it could not have been concealed even from the servants. But what is the wedding garment that must be put on? We learn it from these words, "May your priests be clothed with righteousness." It is of that garment of righteousness that the apostle speaks when he says, "Because when we are clothed, we are not found naked." In this way the unprepared man was discovered by the Lord of the feast, interrogated, bound and thrown out, one from among the many. *Sermon 90.4.*

CLOSING PRAYER

May God the Father bless us. May Christ the Son take care of us. The Holy Spirit enlighten us all the days of our life. The Lord be our defender and keeper of body and soul both now and for ever and to the ages of ages. Amen. *An Ancient Blessing*

Seeking God's Kingdom

THEME

God's power and glory are impossible for us to understand (Ex 33:12-
23), yet we recognize that God is great and to be praised (Ps 96:1-9,
10-13). We marvel at Jesus' wisdom (Mt 22:15-22) and eagerly anticipate his return (1 Thess 1:1-10).

OPENING PRAYER: *Proper 24*

O GOD Almighty, Father of our Lord Jesus Christ, grant us, we pray
thee, to be grounded and settled in the truth, by the coming down of
the Holy Spirit into our hearts. That which we know not, . . . reveal;
that which is wanting in us, . . . fill up; that which we know, . . . confirm, and keep us blameless in thy service; through the same Jesus
Christ our Lord. Amen. *Clement*

OLD TESTAMENT READING: *Exodus 33:12-23*

REFLECTIONS FROM THE CHURCH FATHERS

God Is Found in the Darkness. CLEMENT OF ALEXANDRIA: As a
result Moses, convinced that God will never be known to human wisdom, says, "Reveal yourself to me," and finds himself forced to enter
"into the darkness" where the voice of God was present; in other words,
into the unapproachable, imageless, intellectual concepts relating to ul-
timate reality. For God does not exist in darkness. He is not in space at

all. He is beyond space and time and anything belonging to created beings. Similarly he is not found in any section. He contains nothing. He is contained by nothing. He is not subject to limit or division. *Stromateis 2.2.6.*

God Is Incomprehensible by Eyes and by Mind. AUGUSTINE: Hence the answer made to Moses is true that no one can see the face of God and live, that is, no one living in this life can see him as he is. Many have seen, but they saw what his will chose, not what his nature formed, and this is what John said, if he is rightly understood: "Dearly beloved, we are the sons of God, and it has not yet appeared what we shall be. We know that when he shall appear, we shall be like to him, because we shall see him as he is"; not as men saw him when he willed under the appearance that he willed; not in his nature under which he lies hidden within himself even when he is seen, but as he is. This is what was asked of him by the one who spoke to him face to face, when he said to him, "Show me yourself," but no one can at any time experience the fullness of God through the eyes of the body any more than by the mind itself. *Letter 147.8-9.*

And the Rock Was Christ. ORIGEN: Like to these is the saying of God to Moses: "Lo, I have set you in a cleft of the rock, and you shall see my back parts." That rock which is Christ is therefore not completely closed but has clefts. But the cleft of the rock is he who reveals God to men and makes him known to them; for "no one knows the Father, save the Son." So no one sees the back parts of God—that is to say, the things that are come to pass in the latter time—unless he be placed in the cleft of the rock, that is to say, when he is taught them by Christ's own revealing. *Commentary on the Song of Songs 3.15.*

⛭ **PSALM OF RESPONSE:** *Psalm 96:1-9*

⛭ **NEW TESTAMENT READING:** *1 Thessalonians 1:1-10*

REFLECTIONS FROM THE CHURCH FATHERS

Receiving the Spirit. GREGORY OF NYSSA: Thus, the obedient and responsive soul gives itself over to the virtuous life. This life is freedom itself, on the one hand, from the chains of this life, separating itself from the slavery of base and empty pursuits. On the other hand, this soul devotes itself to faith and the life of God alone, because it sees clearly that where there is faith, reverence and a blameless life, there is present the power of Christ, there is flight from all evil and from death which robs us of life. For shameful things do not have in themselves sufficient power to compete with the power of the Lord. It is their nature to develop from disobedience to his commands. This was experienced in ancient times by the first man, but now it is experienced by all of us when we imitate Adam's disobedience through stubborn choice. *On the Christian Mode of Life.*

Grace Requires Cooperation. CHRYSOSTOM: Do you see what a great thing zeal is? It does not ask for more time or delay or procrastinate. It is sufficient simply to offer one's self, and all is fulfilled. *Homilies on 1 Thessalonians 1.*

The Foundation of Belief. BASIL THE GREAT: By what means do we become Christians? Through our faith would be the universal answer. And in what way are we saved? Plainly because we were regenerated through the grace given to us in our baptism. How else could we be? And after recognizing that this salvation is established through the Father and the Son and the Holy Spirit, shall we fling away "that form of doctrine" which we received? Would it not rather be grounds for great groaning if we are found now further off from our salvation "than when we first believed," and deny now what we then received? *On the Holy Spirit 10.26.*

GOSPEL READING: *Matthew 22:15-22*

REFLECTIONS FROM THE CHURCH FATHERS

The Pharisees Planned How to Entangle Him. ANONYMOUS: "They went out and planned how to catch him in his words." If anyone attempts to shut off a stream of running water by erecting some sort of blockade, the water will burst through and create a new path in another direction. Similarly the priests' frustrated evil intentions discovered other avenues for themselves. *Incomplete Work on Matthew, Homily 42.*

Teacher, We Know That You Are True. ANONYMOUS: They called him teacher, and truly he was. Yet they were only pretending that he was a teacher, one honored and praised. They pretended that he would simply open to them the ministry of his heart, as if they wanted to be his disciples. This is the first power of hypocrites, to simulate praise. They praise those whom they want to destroy. Their art is to incline human hearts toward simplicity of a kind confession through the delight of praise. They take small steps, a little at a time. *Incomplete Work on Matthew, Homily 42.*

The Image of God. ANONYMOUS:
So let us always reflect the image of God in these ways:
I do not swell up with the arrogance of pride;
nor do I droop with the blush of anger;
nor do I succumb to the passion of avarice;
nor do I surrender myself to the ravishes of gluttony;
nor do I infect myself with the duplicity of hypocrisy;
nor do I contaminate myself with the filth of rioting;
nor do I grow flippant with the pretension of conceit;
nor do I grow enamored of the burden of heavy drinking;
nor do I alienate by the dissension of mutual admiration;
nor do I infect others with the biting of detraction;
nor do I grow conceited with the vanity of gossip.
Rather, instead, I will reflect the image of God in that I feed on love;

grow certain on faith and hope;

strengthen myself on the virtue of patience;

grow tranquil by humility;

grow beautiful by chastity;

am sober by abstention;

am made happy by tranquility;

and am ready for death by practicing hospitality.

It is with such inscriptions that God imprints his coins with an impression made neither by hammer nor by chisel but has formed them with his primary divine intention. For Caesar required his image on every coin, but God has chosen man, whom he has created, to reflect his glory. *Incomplete Work on Matthew, Homily 42.*

CLOSING PRAYER

We ask not of you, O Father, silver and gold, honor and glory, nor the pleasures of the world, but grant us grace to seek your kingdom and your righteousness, and add to us things necessary for the body and for this life. Behold, O Lord, our desire; may it be pleasing in your sight. We present our petition to you through our Lord Jesus Christ, who is at your right hand, our mediator and advocate, through whom you sought us that we might seek you; your Word, through whom you made us and all things; your only begotten Son, through whom you called us to adoption, who intercedes with you for us, and in whom are hid all the treasures of wisdom and knowledge; to him, with yourself and the Holy Spirit, be all honor, praise and glory, now and forever. Amen. *Augustine*

Living Holy Lives

⸙ THEME

God is eternal, while our time on earth is fleeting (Ps 90:1-6, 13-17).
Because of this, we seek to share the gospel as Paul did (1 Thess 2:1-8),
loving the Lord and loving our neighbor as ourselves (Mt 22:34-46)
and living holy lives, as much as possible (Lev 19:1-2, 15-18).

⸙ OPENING PRAYER: *Proper 25*

Grant us, O Lord, not to mind earthly things but to love things heavenly; and even now, while we are placed among things that are passing
away, to cling to those that shall abide; through Jesus Christ our Lord.
[Amen.] *The Leonine Sacramentary*

⸙ OLD TESTAMENT READING: *Leviticus 19:1-2, 15-18*

REFLECTIONS FROM THE CHURCH FATHERS

The Two Great Commandments. AUGUSTINE: Long before Christ it
had been said, "You shall not covet"; long before it had been said, "You
shall love your neighbor as yourself," a phrase which, as the apostle
says, expresses the fulfillment of the whole law. And as no one loves
himself unless he loves God, the Lord says that the whole Law and the
Prophets depend on these two commandments. *Letter 177.*

Love in Practice. GREGORY THE GREAT: A person who does not divide with his needy neighbor what is necessary to him proves that he loves him less than himself. The command is to share two tunics with one's neighbor: he could not have spoken of a single tunic, since if one is shared no one is clothed. Half a tunic leaves the person who receives it naked, as well as the person who gives it. *Homily 6.*

PSALM OF RESPONSE: *Psalm 90:1-6, 13-17*

NEW TESTAMENT READING: *1 Thessalonians 2:1-8*

REFLECTIONS FROM THE CHURCH FATHERS

Frost and Fire. GREGORY THE GREAT: I beg you, in all this, recall to your mind what I believe you must never forget: "All who would live godly in Christ suffer persecution." And with regard to this I confidently say that you would live less godly if you suffered less persecution. For let us hear what else the same teacher of the Gentiles says to his disciples. "You yourselves know, brothers, how we came to you; we did not come in vain, for we had already suffered and been shamefully treated." My most sweet son, the holy preacher declared that his coming to the Thessalonians would have accomplished nothing if he had not been shamefully treated. . . . On the basis of Paul's example be even more disciplined in the midst of adverse circumstances. In this way adversity itself may increase significantly your desire for the love of God and your earnestness in good works. Similarly, the seeds planted for a future harvest germinate more fruitfully if they are covered over with frost. Likewise fire is increased by blowing on it that it may grow greater. *Letters 30.*

The Source of Success. CHRYSOSTOM: For Paul's work found its source in power, mighty power, power that surpassed mere human diligence. For Paul brought three qualifications to the preaching of the word: a fervent and adventurous zeal, a soul ready to undergo any possible hardship and the combination of knowledge and wisdom. Even with Paul's love of the difficult task, his blameless life would have accomplished little had he not also received the power of the Spirit. Examine the matter from Paul's own words: "That our ministry not be blamed." And again, "For our exhortation is not founded on error, nor uncleanness, nor guile nor hidden under a cloak of covetousness." Thus you have seen his blamelessness. And again, "For we aim at what is honorable, not only in the sight of the Lord, but also in the sight of men.". . . Without this, Paul's work would have been impossible. People were not converted because of Paul's miracles; no, it was not the miracles that produced faith, nor did Paul base his high calling upon the miraculous but upon other grounds: a man must be irreproachable in conduct, prudent and discreet in his dealings with others, regardless of the dangers involved, and apt to teach. These were the qualifications that enabled Paul to reach his goal. *Homilies on Ephesians 6.*

Motivation the Key. FULGENTIUS OF RUSPE: In all good works, be careful lest you be stirred by desire for human praise. You ought to be praised in your good works, but insofar as you do them, you ought not to expect human praises. The human tongue may praise you, but desire praise from God alone. And thus it may come about that while you do not seek human praise, God may be praised in your deeds. *Letters 2.35.*

Like a Nurse. AUGUSTINE: But there is no greater proof of charity in Christ's church than when the very honor which seems so important on a human level is despised. *Sermons 10.8.*

Fleshly Charity and Spiritual Charity. AUGUSTINE: Can we not see, even in dumb, unreasoning creatures, where there is no spiritual charity but only that which belongs to their nature as animals, with what eager insistence the mother's milk is demanded by her little ones? Yet, however rough be the nursing calf's mouth upon the udder, the mother likes it better than if there were no sucking, no demanding of the debt that charity admits. Indeed, we often see the bigger calf butting with its head at the cow's udders, and the mother's body forced upward by the pressure; yet she will never kick her calf away, but if the young one not be there to suck, she will low for him to come. Of spiritual charity, the apostle says: "I have become little among you, like a nurse cherishing her children." If such charity be in us, we cannot but love you when you press your demand upon us. We do not love backwardness in you. It makes us fearful that your strength is failing. *Homilies on 1 John 9.1.*

GOSPEL READING: *Matthew 22:34-46*

REFLECTIONS FROM THE CHURCH FATHERS

Heart, Mind and Soul. ORIGEN: Worthy is he, confirmed in all his gifts, who exults in the wisdom of God, having a heart full of the love of God, and a soul completely enlightened by the lamp of knowledge and a mind filled with the word of God. *Commentary on Matthew 4.*

With All Your Heart. CYRIL OF ALEXANDRIA: Therefore the first commandment teaches every kind of godliness. For to love God with the whole heart is the cause of every good. The second commandment includes the righteous acts we do toward other people. The first commandment prepares the way for the second and in turn is established by the second. For the person who is grounded in the love of God clearly also loves his neighbor in all things himself. The kind of person who fulfills these two commandments experiences all the commandments. *Fragment 251.*

What Do You Think of the Christ? CHRYSOSTOM: Remember how many miracles have preceded this dialogue—after how many signs, after how many questions, after how great a display of his union with the Father in deeds as well as in words—now Jesus asks his own question. After so many previous events, he is now quietly leading them to the point of confessing that he is God. He does this so that they may not be able to say that he is an adversary to the law and a foe to God, even though he has worked mighty miracles. . . . For since he was now about to go on to his passion, he sets forth the prophecy that plainly proclaims him to be Lord. It is not as if the call to confession has emerged without any precipitating occasion, or from no reasonable cause or as if he had this as his prior aim. For he had already brought the issue to their attention, and they had answered that he was a mere man, in opposition to the truth. Now he is overthrowing their mistaken opinion. This is why he introduces David into the discussion, that his true identity and divinity might be more clearly recognized. For they had supposed that he was a mere man, yet they also say that the Christ is "the Son of David." Hence he now brings in the prophetic testimony to his being Lord, and to the genuineness of his Sonship and his equality in honor with his Father. *The Gospel of Matthew, Homily 71.2.*

CLOSING PRAYER

To God's gracious mercy and protection we commit ourselves. The Lord bless us and keep us. The Lord make his face to shine on us and be gracious to us. The Lord lift up the light of his countenance on us and give us peace. *Aaronic Blessing*

Practicing Virtue

THEME

Look to God, and he will deliver you from trouble; praise him even in the most difficult circumstances (Ps 34:1-10, 22). We anticipate the return of Christ, when there will be no more sorrow or tears (Rev 7:9-17). Work to purify yourselves (1 Jn 3:1-3); practicing peace, mercy and humility (Mt 5:1-12).

OPENING PRAYER: *All Saints Day or First Sunday in November*

Almighty and everlasting God, who adorns the sacred body of your church by the confessions of holy martyrs; grant us, we pray you, that both by their doctrines and their pious example, we may follow after what is pleasing in your sight; through Jesus Christ our Lord. Amen. *The Leonine Sacramentary*

NEW TESTAMENT READING: *Revelation 7:9-17*

REFLECTIONS FROM THE CHURCH FATHERS

Rejoicing in Christ's Victory. OECUMENIUS: They are clothed in white robes as a sign of the purity of their life, and the palm branches are symbolic of victory and reveal that they rejoice in the victory of Christ against every spiritual and physical foe. *Commentary on the Apocalypse 7.9-17.*

***The Gift of the Spirit.* CAESARIUS OF ARLES:** By the white robes he means the gift of the Holy Spirit. *Exposition on the Apocalypse 7.9.*

***Baptism and the Eucharist Make White.* OECUMENIUS:** To be sure, one might think that robes dipped in blood would be red, not white. And so, how is it that they have become all white? Because, according to the opinion of the all-wise Paul, baptism is completed in the death of the Lord and wipes clean from every filth of sin, so that those baptized in him are made white and clean. *Commentary on the Apocalypse 7.9-17.*

***To Praise God.* BEDE:** To be continuously present at the praises of God is not a laborious servitude but a servitude that is pleasant and desirable. "Day and night," indeed, do not exclusively signify the vicissitude of time, but typologically [they signify] its perpetuity. *Homilies on the Gospels 1.10.*

***Perfect Knowledge and Incorruption.* ANDREW OF CAESAREA:** They will be led to the pure and clear fountains of divine thoughts, for the image of water already indicates the abundant stream of the divine Spirit. *Commentary on the Apocalypse 7.17.*

PSALM OF RESPONSE: *Psalm 34:1-10, 22*

NEW TESTAMENT READING: *1 John 3:1-3*

REFLECTIONS FROM THE CHURCH FATHERS

***As Children Love a Father.* BEDE:** The grace of our Creator is so great that he has allowed us both to know him and to love him, and moreover, to love him as children love a wonderful father. It would be no small thing if we were able to love God in the way that a servant loves his master or a worker his employer. But loving God as father is much greater still. *On 1 John.*

It Does Not Yet Appear What We Shall Be. BEDE: The believer in Christ has already died to his old life and has been born again by faith, but it is not yet clear what the full extent of that new life will be. However, we do at least know that we shall be immortal and unchanging, because we shall enjoy the contemplation of God's eternity. Because we shall be blessed we shall be like Christ, yet at the same time we shall be unlike him because he is our Creator and we are only creatures. *On 1 John.*

Purify Yourselves. THEOPHYLACT: Note that John uses the present tense when he talks about our need to purify ourselves. The practice of virtue is an ongoing thing and has its own inner dynamic. If we stop living this way or put it off until some future time, there is nothing virtuous about that at all. *Commentary on 1 John.*

GOSPEL READING: *Matthew 5:1-12*

REFLECTIONS FROM THE CHURCH FATHERS

Perfect Blessedness Is Humility of Spirit. HILARY OF POITIERS: "Blessed are the poor in spirit, for theirs is the kingdom of heaven." The Lord taught by way of example that the glory of human ambition must be left behind when he said, "The Lord your God shall you adore and him only shall you serve." And when he announced through the prophets that he would choose a people humble and in awe of his words, he introduced the perfect Beatitude as humility of spirit. Therefore he defines those who are inspired as people aware that they are in possession of the heavenly kingdom. . . . Nothing belongs to anyone as being properly one's own, but all have the same things by the gift of a single parent. They have been given the first things needed to come into life and have been supplied with the means to use them. *On Matthew 4.2.*

The Docile Heart. ANONYMOUS: Whoever hungers for righteousness wants to live actively according to God's righteousness; this is proper for the person with a good heart. One who thirsts for righteousness wants to acquire the knowledge of God that one can gain only by studying the Scriptures. This is fitting for the person with an attentive heart. *Incomplete Work on Matthew, Homily 9.*

Mercy Toward Enemies. ANONYMOUS: The kind of compassion referred to here is not simply giving alms to the poor or orphan or widow. This kind of compassion is often found even among those who hardly know God. But that person is truly compassionate who shows compassion even to his own enemy and treats the enemy well. For it is written, "Love your enemies, and treat well those who hate you." Remember that God too sends his rain and asks his sun to rise not only over the grateful but also over the ungrateful. So Jesus calls us to "be compassionate, just as your Father is compassionate." Such a person is truly blessed, for if in fact he hasn't sinned, which is difficult for us all, God's grace helps him along in increasing his sense of justice. So he prays, "Forgive me my debts, just as I too forgive my debtors." *Incomplete Work on Matthew, Homily 9.*

Seeing God in This Age and in the Age to Come. ANONYMOUS: There are two ways of seeing God: in this age and in the age to come. In this age, as has been written, "He who sees me sees my Father, too." For they have a pure heart who not only do no evil and intend no evil but who also always do and intend everything good. For it is possible now and then to do good but not to intend it. Those who do so may do good, but not on account of God. And God does not reward such good, for the good rewarded by God isn't the one that is merely done but the one that is well done. Moreover, a person who does good on account of God no doubt also intends the good. So whoever acts entirely justly and intends so with his mind sees God, for justice is the likeness of God. For God is just. So, to the extent that anybody has torn himself from evils and done good things, to that extent he also sees God, either dimly or clearly or slightly or to a greater degree, or partly or completely, or now and then or always, or in accordance with human possibility. *Incomplete Work on Matthew, Homily 9.*

Persecution for Righteousness' Sake. CHROMATIUS OF AQUILEIA: Not without reason did the Lord previously mention hungering and thirsting for justice. He instructs us so to thirst in our desire for justice that for its sake we should despise the world's persecutions, the punishments of the body and death itself. *Tractate on Matthew 17.8.1-2.*

Falsely on Christ's Account. CHRYSOSTOM: But to keep you from supposing that being slandered of itself makes people blessed, he has added two qualifications: first, that it happens for Christ's sake, and second, that what is said be false. Do not expect to be blessed if you are being reviled for something evil, and what is being said is true. *The Gospel of Matthew, Homily 15.4.*

CLOSING PRAYER

Mercifully regard, O Lord, the prayers of your family; and while we submit ourselves to you with our whole heart, prosper, support and encompass us, that, relying on you as our guide, we may be entangled in no evils and replenished with all good; through Jesus Christ our Lord. Amen. *The Leonine Sacramentary*

Worthy Lives

⁜ THEME

Even when circumstances are overpoweringly difficult, God "turns deserts into pools of water, a parched land into springs of water" (Ps 107:1-7, 33-37). We desire to live worthy lives (1 Thess 2:9-13), not for the praise of other people but in order to please God (Mt 23:1-12) and to walk in the light rather than the darkness (Mic 3:5-12).

⁜ OPENING PRAYER: *Proper 26*

Merciful God, good Lord, I wish that you would unite me to that fountain, that there I may drink of the living spring of the water of life with those others who thirst after you. There in that heavenly region may I ever dwell, delighted with abundant sweetness, and say, "How sweet is the fountain of living water which never fails, the water welling up to eternal life." O God, you are yourself that fountain ever and again to be desired ever and ever and again to be consumed. Lord Christ, always give us this water to be for us the "source of the living water which wells up to eternal life." *Columbanus*

⁜ OLD TESTAMENT READING: *Micah 3:5-12*

REFLECTIONS FROM THE CHURCH FATHERS

The Prophets Knew the Spirit of the Lord. CYRIL OF JERUSALEM: If, further, one works through the twelve minor prophets, many testimonies to the Holy Spirit are to be found. Thus Micah speaks as God's mouthpiece and says, "Truly I am full of power by the Spirit of the Lord." Joel cries, "And it shall come to pass afterwards," says God, "that I will pour out my Spirit upon all flesh" and what follows. Haggai said, 'For I am with you,' says the Lord of hosts . . . 'my Spirit remained among you.'" And in like manner Zechariah says, "Receive my words and my statutes which I commanded my servants the prophets." *Catechetical Lecture 15.29.*

The Destruction of Jerusalem Foretold. GREGORY OF NAZIANZUS: Meanwhile, these heads of the house of Jacob abhorred justice. The priests were teaching for hire. The prophets were prophesying for money! What does Micah say will be the result of this? "Zion shall be plowed as a field, and Jerusalem shall be as a storehouse of fruit, and the mountain of the house shall be as the grove of the forest." *In Defense of His Flight to Pontus, Oration 2.58.*

PSALM OF RESPONSE: *Psalm 107:1-7, 33-37*

NEW TESTAMENT READING: *1 Thessalonians 2:9-13*

REFLECTIONS FROM THE CHURCH FATHERS

The Balance of Work and Prayer. CAESARIUS OF ARLES: Perhaps someone says: Who can always be thinking of God and eternal bliss, since all men must be concerned for food, clothing and the management of their household? God does not bid us be free from all anxiety over the present life, for he instructs us through his apostle: "If any man will not work, neither let him eat." The same apostle repeats the idea with reference to himself when he says: "We worked night and day so that we might not burden any of you." Since God especially advises reasonable thought of food and clothing, so long as avarice and ambition which usually serve dissipation are not linked with it, any action or thought is might rightly considered holy. The only provision is that those preoccupations should not be so excessive that they do not allow us to have time for God, according to the words: "The burdens of the world have made them miserable." *Sermons 45.1.*

The Balance of Work and Prayer. CHRYSOSTOM: "The sleep of a working man is sweet, whether he eats little or much." Why does he add, "Whether he eat little or much"? Both these things usually bring sleeplessness, namely, poverty and abundance; . . . but the effect of hard work is such that neither poverty nor excess disrupt this servant's sleep. Though throughout the whole day they are running about everywhere, ministering to their masters, being knocked about and hard pressed, having little time to catch their breath, they receive a sufficient recompense for their toils and labors in the pleasure of sleeping. And thus it has happened through the goodness of God toward humanity, that these pleasures are not to be purchased with gold and silver but with labor, with hard toil, with necessity and every kind of discipline. *Homilies Concerning the Statues 2.8.*

GOSPEL READING: *Matthew 23:1-12*

REFLECTIONS FROM THE CHURCH FATHERS

They Allow Themselves Privilege. CHRYSOSTOM: He mentions here a twofold wickedness. First they require great and extreme strictness of life, without any indulgence, from those over whom they rule. Yet they are much less stringent with themselves. This is opposite from what the truly good pastor ought to hold. He ought to be a rigorous and severe judge in things that concern himself. But in the matters of those whom he rules, he ought to be gentle and ready to make allowances. What these men do is just the opposite. For such are all they who practice self-restraint in mere words while being unforgiving and grievous to bear when they have had no experience of the difficulty in actions. This is no small fault. In no small way does Jesus increase the former charge. *The Gospel of Matthew, Homily 72.2.*

Deacons and Bishops Who Love the Place of Honor. ORIGEN: What are we to say about those who "love the places of honor at banquets and the front seats in synagogues and the highest respect in public places and to be called rabbi by everyone"? We must first admit that this kind of delight is found not only among the scribes and Pharisees but also in the church of Christ, and not only at dinner, while taking places at the table, but also the front seats in church. *Commentary on Matthew 12.*

The Best Seats. CHRYSOSTOM: Everything he accused them of was small and trifling. Yet he was dealing with the cause of all the evils: ambition, the violent seizing of the teacher's chair, and so on. These he brings forward and corrects with diligence, confronting this strongly and earnestly charging them. His own disciples needed to be warned about these matters. *The Gospel of Matthew, Homily 72.3.*

The Humble Exalted. CHRYSOSTOM: For nothing is as crucial as the practice of modesty. This is why he is continually reminding them of this virtue, both when he brought the children into the midst and now. Even when he was preaching on the mount, beginning the Beatitudes, this is where he began. And in this passage he plucks up pride by the roots, saying, "Whoever humbles himself will be exalted." See how he draws off the hearer right over to the contrary thing. For not only does he forbid him to set his heart upon the first place but also requires him to follow after the last. For so shall you obtain your desire, he says. So one who pursues his own desire for the first must follow after in the last place: "Whoever humbles himself will be exalted." *The Gospel of Matthew, Homily 72.3.*

One Who Exalts Will Be Humbled. ORIGEN: They had not thought of critically examining their false humility. They would have done better to have remembered the word of wisdom that says, "The greater you are, the more you must humble yourself, and you will find grace before God." It was the Lord who provided the pattern for this process. No matter how great he was, he humbled himself. *Commentary on Matthew 12.*

⊰ CLOSING PRAYER

O Lord our God, teach us, we ask you, to ask you aright for the right blessings. Steer the vessel of our life toward yourself, you tranquil haven of all storm-tossed souls. Show us the course wherein we should go. Renew a willing spirit within us. Let your Spirit curb our wayward senses and guide and enable us unto that which is our true good, to keep your laws, and in all our works evermore to rejoice in your glorious and gladdening presence. For yours is the glory and praise from all your saints, for ever and ever. Amen. *Basil the Great*

Obedience

THEME

God does not want lip service; he wants obedience from us (Amos 5:18-24). God is our help and deliverer (Ps 70); because we love him, we seek a pure heart and pure motives (Mt 25:1-13), knowing that in Jesus, we have the assurance of salvation and eternal life (1 Thess 4:13-18).

OPENING PRAYER: *Proper 27*

We ask you, Lord Jesus, that to whom you vouchsafe sweet draughts of the words of your knowledge, you will also, of your goodness, grant that we may in due time come to you, the fountain of all wisdom, and ever stand before your face; for your sake. [Amen.] *Bede*

OLD TESTAMENT READING: *Amos 5:18-24*

REFLECTIONS FROM THE CHURCH FATHERS

They Loved Darkness Rather Than Light. THEODORET OF CYR: Since there were some buoyed up by audacity and temerity who resisted the prophetic oracles, raging against them, calling the divine pronouncements false and demanding the fulfillment of the prophecies, the Lord declares these people lamentable for longing to see darkness instead of light. Those who long to see the fulfillment of prophecy, he is saying, are no different than a person fleeing an attacking lion and after that running into a bear, or fearfully going into a house and, with one's soul in the grip of panic, putting a hand on the wall and being bitten by a venomous snake. In other words, as that person on that day sees darkness and not a gleam of light, so these people will be given over to deep darkness on the day of punishment. *Commentary on Amos 5.18-20.*

Sacrifices Are Not Needed. CHRYSOSTOM: This brings us to a conclusion on another matter of great importance. The observances regarding sacrifices, sabbaths, new moons, and all such things prescribed by the Jewish way of life of that day—they are not essential. Even when they were observed they could make no great contribution to virtue; nor when neglected could they make the excellent person worthless or degrade in any way the sanctity of his soul. People of old, while still on earth, manifested by their piety a way of life that rivals the way angels live. Yet they followed none of these observances, they slew no beasts in sacrifice, they kept no fast, they made no display of fasting. They were so pleasing to God that they surpassed this fallen human nature of ours and, by the lives they lived, drew the whole world to a knowledge of God. *Discourses Against Judaizing Christians 4.6.*

Justice Better Than Sacrifice. APOSTOLIC CONSTITUTIONS: According to Jeremiah, "For in the day that I brought them out of the land of Egypt, I did not speak to your fathers or command them concerning burnt offerings and sacrifices." And we hear similarly through Isaiah, "'To what purpose do you bring me a multitude of sacrifices?' says the Lord. 'I am full of the burnt offerings of rams, and I will not accept the fat of lambs and the blood of bulls and of goats. Nor do you come and appear before me; for who has required these things at your hands? Do not go on to tread my courts any more. If you bring me fine flour, it is vain; incense is an abomination unto me; your new moons, and your sabbaths, and your great day, I cannot bear them. Your fasts, and your

rests, and your feasts, my soul hates them; I am overfull of them.'" . . .
For, behold, the Lord does not so much delight in sacrifice as in obeying him." *Constitutions of the Holy Apostles 6.5.12.*

PSALM OF RESPONSE: *Psalm 70*

NEW TESTAMENT READING: *1 Thessalonians 4:13-18*

REFLECTIONS FROM THE CHURCH FATHERS

Final Reunion. AUGUSTINE: And you should not grieve as the heathen do who have no hope, because we have hope, based on the most assured promise, that as we have not lost our dear ones who have departed from this life but have merely sent them ahead of us, so we also shall depart and shall come to that life where, more than ever, their dearness to us will be proportional to the closeness we shared on earth and where we shall love them without fear of parting. *Letters 92.1.1.*

God's Good Purpose. BASIL THE GREAT: All things are directed by the goodness of the Master. Nothing which happens to us should be received as distressful, although at present it affects our weakness. In fact, even if we are ignorant of the reasons for which each event is applied as a blessing to us from the Master, nevertheless, we ought to be convinced of this—that what happens is assuredly advantageous either for us as a reward for our patience or for the soul that was taken up, lest tarrying too long in this life it should be filled with the evil which exists in this world. For if the hope of Christians were limited to this life, for what reason would the premature separation from the body be considered difficult? If however, the beginning of true life for those living in God is the release of the soul from these corporeal chains, why do you grieve, even as those who have no hope? Therefore, be encouraged. Do not succumb to your afflictions, but show that you are superior and have risen above them. *Letters 101.*

The Reversal of Human Wisdom. PRUDENTIUS:
When at the awful trumpet's sound
The earth will be consumed by fire,
And with a mighty rush the world
Unhinged, will crash in dreadful ruin. *Hymns 11, 105.8.*

Final Bliss. GREGORY OF NAZIANZUS: Why, then, be faint-hearted in my hopes? Why behave like a mere creature of the day? I await the voice of the archangel, the last trumpet, the transformation of the heavens, the transfiguration of the earth, the liberation of the elements, the renovation of the universe. *On His Brother St. Caesarius 21.*

 GOSPEL READING: *Matthew 25:1-13*

REFLECTIONS FROM THE CHURCH FATHERS

Division Between Good and Bad. HILARY OF POITIERS: The whole story is about the great day of the Lord, when those things concealed from the human mind will be revealed through our understanding of divine judgment. Then the faith true to the Lord's coming will win the just reward for unwavering hope. *On Matthew 27.3.*

What the Oil Signifies. AUGUSTINE: I will tell you why charity seems to be signified by the oil. The apostle says, "I will show you a still more excellent way." "If I speak with the tongue of mortals and of angels but do not have love, I am a noisy gong or a clanging cymbal." This is charity. It is "that way above the rest," which is with good reason signified by the oil. For oil swims above all liquids. Pour in oil, pour in water upon it; the oil will swim above. If you keep the usual order, it will be uppermost; if you change the order, it will be uppermost. "Charity never fails." *Sermon 93.4.*

The Virgins and Their Lamps. AUGUSTINE: But if it is good to abstain from the unlawful excitements of the senses, and on that account every Christian soul has received the name of virgin, why then are five admitted and five rejected? They are both virgins, and yet half are rejected. It is not enough that they are virgins but that they also have lamps. They are virgins by reason of abstinence from unlawful indulgence of the senses. But they have lamps by reason of good works. Of these good works the Lord says," Let your works shine before men, that they may see your good works and glorify your Father in heaven." Again he said to his disciples, "Let your loins be girded and your lamps burning." In the "girded loins" is virginity. In the "burning lamps" is good works. *Sermon 93.2.*

CLOSING PRAYER

O Lord, our Savior, who has warned us that you will require much of those to whom much is given; grant that we whose lot is cast in so goodly a heritage may strive together more abundantly by prayer, by almsgiving, by fasting, and by every other appointed means, to extend to others what we so richly enjoy; and as we have entered into the labors of other men, so to labor that in their turn other men may enter into ours, to the fulfillment of your holy will, and our own everlasting salvation; through Jesus Christ our Lord. Amen. *Augustine*

Using Our Talents

◈ THEME

We plead with God for mercy on our situations, submitting to him and looking to him for help (Ps 123). We use our gifts and talents wisely (Mt 25:14-30) until his anticipated return (1 Thess 5:1-11) and judgment (Zeph 1:7, 12-18).

◈ OPENING PRAYER: *Proper 28*

O Christ, who knows our sorrows: comfort our brethren who are lonely and heavy with griefs. Give courage to those who are assailed by vehement temptations; give strength to them who have no might, and when they are tried, grant them the victory. Remember the sick and afflicted, especially such as are dear to us whom we name in our hearts . . . and if so it seems good to you, give health again, in body and soul, for your tender mercies' sake. [Amen.] *Augustine*

◈ OLD TESTAMENT READING: *Zephaniah 1:7, 12-18*

REFLECTIONS FROM THE CHURCH FATHERS

Money and Things to Be Shunned. CYPRIAN: The lust of possessions and money are not to be sought for. In Solomon, in Ecclesiastes: "He that loves silver shall not be satisfied with silver." Also in Proverbs: "He who holds back the corn is cursed among the people; but blessing is on the head of him that communicates it." Also in Isaiah: "Woe to them who join house to house, and lay field to field, that they may take away something from their neighbor. Will you dwell alone upon the earth?" Also, in Zephaniah: "They shall build houses, and shall not dwell in them; and they shall appoint vineyards, and shall not drink the wine of them, because the Day of the Lord is near." Also in the Gospel according to Luke: "For what does it profit a man to make a gain of the whole world, but that he should lose himself?" *To Quirinus, Testimonies Against the Jews 12.3.61.*

Always Room to Repent. CASSIODORUS: That is why the penitent now introduced before us earnestly supplicates in the ordered divisions of his prayer that he may not be convicted for his deeds on that day of judgment. What is more beneficial and farsighted for the person who could have no hope in his own deserts because of the sins which he has committed than to decide to pray to God's fatherly love while in this world, where there is opportunity for repentance? *Exposition of the Psalms 6.1.*

False Hearts Revealed on the Day of Judgment. GREGORY THE GREAT: For what is expressed by fenced cities but minds suspected and surrounded ever with a fallacious defense; minds which, as often as their fault is attacked, suffer not the darts of truth to reach them? And what is signified by lofty corners (a wall being always double in corners) but insincere hearts; which, while they shun the simplicity of truth, are in a manner doubled back on themselves in the crookedness of duplicity, and, what is worse, from their fault of insincerity lift themselves in their thoughts with the pride of prudence? *Pastoral Care 11.*

PSALM OF RESPONSE: *Psalm 123*

NEW TESTAMENT READING: *1 Thessalonians 5:1-11*

REFLECTIONS FROM THE CHURCH FATHERS

The Divine Intention. CHRYSOSTOM: Do not place your confidence in your youth, nor think that you have a very fixed term of life, "For the day of the Lord comes as a thief in the night." On this account he has made our end invisible, so that we might demonstrate clearly our diligence and forethought. Do you not see men taken away prematurely day after day? On this account a certain one admonishes, "don't delay in turning to the Lord, and don't put things off from day to day," lest at any time, while you delay, you are destroyed. Let the old man keep this admonition, let the young man heed this advice. Indeed, are you in insecurity and are you rich, and do you abound in health, and does no affliction happen to you? Still hear what Paul says: "when they say peace and safety then sudden destruction comes upon them." Affairs change often. We are not masters of our end. Let us be masters of virtue. Our Master Christ is loving. *The Second Homily Concerning the Power of Demons 2.*

Affliction and Watchfulness. CHRYSOSTOM: Nothing puts carelessness and negligence to flight the way grief and affliction do. They bring together our thoughts from every side and make our mind turn back to ponder itself. The man who prays in this way, in his affliction, after many a prayer, can bring joy into his own soul. *On the Incomprehensible Nature of God 5.6.*

Dawn's Approach. PRUDENTIUS:
The winged messenger of day
Sings loud, foretelling dawn's approach,
And Christ in stirring accents calls
Our slumbering souls to life with him.
"Away," he cries, "with dull repose,
The sleep of death and sinful sloth,
With hearts now sober, just and pure,

Keep watch, for I am very near." *Hymns 1.1-8.*

Seeing the Church Grow. CHRYSOSTOM: God, you know, does not wish Christians to be concerned only for themselves but also to edify others, not simply through their teaching but also through their behavior and the way they live. After all, nothing is such an attraction to the way of truth as an upright life—in other words, people pay less attention to what we say than to what we do. *Homilies on Genesis 8.4-5.*

GOSPEL READING: *Matthew 25:14-30*

REFLECTIONS FROM THE CHURCH FATHERS

A Man Going on a Journey. GREGORY THE GREAT: Who is the man who sets out for foreign parts but our Redeemer, who departed to heaven in a body he had taken on? Earth is the proper place for his body. It is transported to foreign parts, so to speak, when he establishes it in heaven. *Forty Gospel Homilies 9.1.*

I Hid Your Talent. GREGORY THE GREAT: For many people in the church resemble that servant. They are afraid to attempt a better way of life but not of resting in idleness. When they advert to the fact that they are sinners, the prospect of grasping the ways of holiness alarm them, but they feel no fear at remaining in their wickedness. *Forty Gospel Homilies 9.3.*

From One Who Has Not. CHRYSOSTOM: Let no one say, "I have but one talent and can do nothing with it." You are not poorer than the widow. You are not more uninstructed than Peter and John, who were both "unlearned and ignorant men." Nevertheless, since they demonstrated zeal and did all things for the common good, they were received into heaven. For nothing is so pleasing to God as to live for the common advantage. *The Gospel of Matthew, Homily 78.3.*

The Worthless Servant Cast into Darkness. CHRYSOSTOM: "The unprofitable servant is to be cast into outer darkness, where there shall be weeping and gnashing of teeth." Do you see how sins of omission also are met with extreme rejection? It is not only the covetous, the active doer of evil things and the adulterer, but also the one who fails to do good. Let us listen carefully then to these words. As we have opportunity, let us work to cooperate with our salvation. Let us get oil for our lamps. Let us labor to add to our talent. For if we are backward and spend our time in sloth here, no one will pity us any more hereafter, though we should wait ten thousand times. . . . Remember the virgins who again entreated and came to him and knocked, all in vain and without effect. *The Gospel of Matthew, Homily 78.3.*

CLOSING PRAYER

Forgive our transgressions, our errors, our lapses and our weaknesses. Do not keep count of the sins of your servants but purify us through the gift of your truth and direct our steps. Help us to walk in holiness of heart and to do what is good and pleasing to your eyes. [Amen.] *Clement of Rome*

Praising the Good Shepherd

⊰ THEME

God is the good shepherd (Ezek 34:11-16, 20-24) who made the wonders of creation; we praise him, who made all things (Ps 95:1-7a). We pray that our hearts may be opened (Eph 1:15-23) and that we may be confident that we have done our best to serve others for his sake on the day of Christ's return (Mt 25:31-46).

⊰ OPENING PRAYER: *Proper 29, Reign of Christ*

Stir up, O Lord, your power, and come; mercifully fulfill that which you have promised to your church unto the end of the world! [Amen.]
The Gelasian Sacramentary

⊰ OLD TESTAMENT READING: *Ezekiel 34:11-16, 20-24*

REFLECTIONS FROM THE CHURCH FATHERS

Shepherds Do Not Desert the Flock in Any Weather. AUGUSTINE:
Rain and fog, the errors of this world; a great darkness arising from the lusts of men, a thick fog covering the earth. And it is difficult for the sheep not to go astray in this fog. But the shepherd doesn't desert them. He seeks them, his piercing gaze penetrates the fog, the thick darkness of the clouds does not prevent him. *Sermon 46.23.*

The Scriptures Are the Pastures. AUGUSTINE: He established the mountains of Israel, the authors of the divine Scriptures. Feed there, in order to feed without a qualm. Whatever you hear from that source, let that taste good to you; anything from outside, spit it out. In order not to go astray in the fog, listen to the voice of the shepherd. Gather yourselves to the mountains of holy Scripture. There you will find your heart's desire, there is nothing poisonous there, nothing unsuitable; they are the richest pastures. *Sermon 46.24.*

God Does Not Desert Us. GREGORY THE GREAT: If we are negligent, does almighty God desert his sheep? No; he himself will pasture them, as he promised through the prophet. *Homily 19.*

We Can All Shepherd Each Other. GREGORY THE GREAT: We must all of us strive zealously to make known to the church both the dreadfulness of the coming judgment and the kingdom of heaven's delight. Those who are not in a position to address a large assembly should instruct individuals, offering instruction in personal talks; they should try to serve those around them through simple encouragement. You who are pastors, consider that you are pasturing God's flock. We often see a block of salt put out for animals to lick for their well-being. Priests among their people should be like blocks of salt. They should counsel everyone in their flocks in such a way that all those with whom they come in contact may be seasoned with eternal life as if they had been sprinkled with salt. We who preach are not the salt of the earth unless we season the hearts of those who listen to us. We are really preaching to others if we ourselves do what we say, if we are pierced with God's love, if, since we cannot avoid sin, our tears wash away the stains on our life that come with each new day. We truly feel remorse when we take to heart the lives of our forebears in the faith so that we are diminished in our own eyes. Then do we truly feel remorse, when we attentively examine God's teachings, and adopt for our own use what those we revere themselves used for theirs. And while we are moved to remorse on our own account, let us also take responsibility for the lives of those entrusted to our care. Our own bitter compunction should not divert us from concern for our neighbor. What good to love and strive to do good for our neighbor and abandon ourselves? We must realize that our passion for justice in the face of another's evil must never cause us to lose the virtue of gentleness. Priests must not be quick-tempered or rash; they must instead be temperate and thoughtful. We must support those we challenge and challenge those we support. If we neglect this, our work will lack either courage or gentleness. What shall we call the human soul but the food of the Lord? It is created to become nothing less than Christ's body, and to bring about growth in the eternal church. We priests are to season this food. Cease to pray, cease to teach, and the salt loses its taste. *Be Friends of God 35.*

Shepherds Bring Back the Lost, Bind Up the Broken and Heal the Sick. BASIL THE GREAT: If you are a shepherd, take care that none of your pastoral duties is neglected. And what are these duties? To bring back that which is lost, to bind up that which was broken, to heal that which is diseased. *Homily on the Words "Give Heed to Thyself."*

PSALM OF RESPONSE: *Psalm 95:1-7a*

NEW TESTAMENT READING: *Ephesians 1:15-23*

REFLECTIONS FROM THE CHURCH FATHERS

Paul Remembers the Ephesians in His Prayers. MARIUS VICTORINUS: Every prayer that we offer up to God is made either in thanks for what we have received or in petition to receive something else. We are encouraged to pray both for ourselves and for those we love. So Paul says, "I make mention of you in my prayer." "Therefore my chief prayer is first on my account, then on yours." *Epistle to the Ephesians 1.1.16.*

For What Does Paul Pray? AMBROSIASTER: The hope of their faith lies in a heavenly reward. When they truly know what the fruit of believing is, they will become more eager in acts of worship. *Epistle to the Ephesians 1.18.1.*

The Eyes of the Heart. JEROME: His phrase *eyes of the heart* clearly refers to those things we cannot understand without sense and intelligence. . . . Faith sees beyond what the physical eyes see. Physical eyes are in the heads of not only the wise but the unwise. *Epistle to the Ephesians 1.1.15.*

GOSPEL READING: *Matthew 25:31-46*

REFLECTIONS FROM THE CHURCH FATHERS

Inherit the Kingdom. CHRYSOSTOM: He did not say "take" but "inherit" as one's own, as your Father's, as due to you from the first. "For before you were," he says, "these things had been prepared and made ready for you, because I knew you would be such as you are." *The Gospel of Matthew, Homily 79.2.*

The Lord Hungers in His Saints. EPIPHANIUS THE LATIN: "I was hungry, and you gave me something to drink." [Jesus mentioned] many other things, which we have recited. Having been given the faith, the righteous say, "Lord, when did we see you hungry and fed you, thirsty, and gave you something to drink, naked and clothed you?" Other things also follow. What then, my most beloved? Does our Lord hunger and thirst? Is he who himself made everything in heaven and on earth, who feeds angels in heaven and every nation and race on earth, who needs nothing of an earthly character, as he is unfailing in his own nature, is this one naked? It is incredible to believe such a thing. Yet what must be confessed is easy to believe. For the Lord hungers not in his own nature but in his saints; the Lord thirsts not in his own nature but in his poor. The Lord who clothes everyone is not naked in his own nature but in his servants. The Lord who is able to heal all sicknesses and has already destroyed death itself is not diseased in his own nature but in his servants. Our Lord, the one who can liberate every person, is not in prison in his own nature but in his saints. Therefore, you see, my most beloved, that the saints are not alone. They suffer all these things because of the Lord. In the same way, because of the saints the Lord suffers all these things with them. *Interpretation of the Gospels 38.*

Eternal Punishment, Eternal Life. EPIPHANIUS THE LATIN: You see, my beloved, there is no excuse for it. They knew what they had to do in this world. But greed and ill-will prevented them, so they laid up for themselves not treasures for the future but the world of the dead. Neither were they condemned because of the active wrong they did, nor did the Lord say to them, Depart from me, you wicked, because you committed murder or adultery or theft. But instead: because I was hungry and thirsty in my servants, and you did not minister to me. If those who did no wrong are thus condemned, what must be said of those who do the works of the devil? *Interpretation of the Gospels 38.*

CLOSING PRAYER

O God, who art the unsearchable abyss of peace, the ineffable sea of love, the fountain of blessings, and bestower of affection, who sendest peace to those who receive it; open up to us this day the sea of thy love, and water us with plenteous streams from the riches of thy grace. Make us children of quietness, and heirs of peace. Enkindle in us the fire of thy love; strengthen our weakness by thy power; bind us closely to thee and each other in one firm and indissoluble bond. *Syrian Clementine Liturgy.*

Ancient Christian Commentary
CITATIONS

The following volumes from the Ancient Christian Commentary on Scripture, Thomas C. Oden, General Editor, from InterVarsity Press, Downers Grove, Illinois, were cited in this book.

Acts, edited by Francis Martin, ©2006.

Colossians, 1-2 Thessalonians, 1-2 Timothy, Titus, Philemon, edited by Peter Gorday, ©2000.

1-2 Corinthians, edited by Gerald Bray, ©1999.

Exodus, Leviticus, Numbers, Deuteronomy, edited by Joseph T. Lienhard, ©2001.

Ezekiel, Daniel, edited by Kenneth Stevenson and Michael Glerup, forthcoming.

Galatians, Ephesians, Philippians, edited by Mark J. Edwards, ©1999.

Genesis 1-11, edited by Andrew Louth, ©2001.

Genesis 12-50, edited by Mark Sherida, ©2002.

Isaiah 1-39, edited by Steven A. McKinion, ©2004.

Isaiah 40-66, edited by Mark W. Elliott, forthcoming.

James, 1-2 Peter, 1-3 John, Jude, edited by Gerald Bray, ©2000.

John 1-10, edited by Joel C. Elowsky, ©2006.

John 11-21, edited by Joel C. Elowsky, ©2007.

Joshua, Judges, Ruth, 1-2 Samuel, edited by John R. Franke, ©2005.

Luke, edited by Arthur A. Just Jr., ©2003.

Matthew 1-13, edited by Manlio Simonetti, ©2001.

Matthew 14-28, edited by Manlio Simonetti, ©2002.

Revelation, edited by William C. Weinrich, ©2005.

Romans, edited by Gerald Bray, ©1998.

The Twelve Prophets, edited by Alberto Ferreiro, ©2003.

PRAYER CITATIONS

WEEK 1

Opening: Thomas Spidlik, *Drinking from the Hidden Fountain: A Patristic Breviary, Ancient Wisdom for Today's World* (Kalamazoo, Mich.: Cistercian Publications, 1994), pp. 389-90.

Closing: J. Robert Wright, *Readings for the Daily Office from the Early Church* (New York: The Church Hymnal Corporation, 1991), p. 393.

WEEK 2

Opening: Selina Fitzherbert Fox, *A Chain of Prayer Across the Ages: Forty Centuries of Prayer, 2000 B.C.-A.D. 1916* (New York: E. P. Dutton, 1943), p. 218.

Closing: James Ferguson and Charles L. Wallis, eds., *Prayers for Public Worship: A Service Book of Morning and Evening Prayers Following the Course of the Christian Year* (New York: Harper & Brothers, 1958), p. 19.

WEEK 3

Opening: J. Robert Wright, *Readings for the Daily Office from the Early Church,* pp. 21-22.

Closing: James Ferguson and Charles L. Wallis, eds., *Prayers for Public Worship: A Service Book of Morning and Evening Prayers Following the Course of the Christian Year,* p. 7.

WEEK 4

Opening: Roger Geffen, *The Handbook of Public Prayer* (New York: Macmillan, 1963), p. 163.

Closing: J. Robert Wright, *Readings for the Daily Office from the Early Church,* pp. 31-32.

WEEK 5 *(CHRISTMAS)*

Opening: James Ferguson and Charles L. Wallis, *Prayers for Public Worship: A Service Book of Morning and Evening Prayers Following the Course of the Christian Year,* p. 34.

Closing: J. Robert Wright, *Readings for the Daily Office from the Early Church,* p. 33.

WEEK 6

Opening: Selina Fitzherbert Fox, *A Chain of Prayer Across the Ages: Forty Centuries of Prayer from 2000 B.C.-A.D. 1916,* p. 221.

Closing: James Ferguson and Charles L. Wallis, *Prayers for Public Worship: A Service Book of Morning and Evening Prayers Following the Course of the Christian Year,* p. 49.

WEEK 7

Opening: Roger Geffen, *The Handbook of Public Prayer,* p. 111.

Closing: William Bright, *Ancient Collects and Other Prayers: Selected for Devotional Use from Various Rituals,* 8th ed. (Oxford and London: James Parker, 1908), pp. 29-30.

WEEK 8

Opening: James Ferguson and Charles L. Wallis, *Prayers for Public Worship: A Service Book of Morning and Evening Prayers Following the Course of the Christian Year,* p. 71.

Closing: Selina Fitzherbert Fox, *A Chain of Prayer Across the Ages: Forty Centuries of Prayer from 2000 B.C.-A.D. 1916,* p. 70.

WEEK 9
Opening: William Bright, *Ancient Collects and Other Prayers: Selected for Devotional Use from Various Rituals,* p. 28.

Closing: Selina Fitzherbert Fox, *A Chain of Prayer Across the Ages: Forty Centuries of Prayer from 2000 B.C.-A.D. 1916,* p. 68.

WEEK 10
Opening: J. Robert Wright, *Readings for the Daily Office from the Early Church,* p. 118.

Closing: Selina Fitzherbert Fox, *A Chain of Prayer Across the Ages: Forty Centuries of Prayer from 2000 B.C.-A.D. 1916,* p. 68.

WEEK 11
Opening: William Bright, *Ancient Collects and Other Prayers: Selected for Devotional Use from Various Rituals,* p. 121.

Closing: Roger Geffen, *The Handbook of Public Prayer,* pp. 117-18.

WEEK 12
Opening: Selina Fitzherbert Fox, *A Chain of Prayer Across the Ages: Forty Centuries of Prayer from 2000 B.C.-A.D. 1916,* p. 86.

Closing: Selina Fitzherbert Fox, *A Chain of Prayer Across the Ages: Forty Centuries of Prayer from 2000 B.C.-A.D. 1916,* p. 86.

WEEK 13 *(LENT)*
Opening: William Bright, *Ancient Collects and Other Prayers: Selected for Devotional Use from Various Rituals,* p. 32.

Closing: Roger Geffen, *The Handbook of Public Prayer,* p. 154.

WEEK 14
Opening: Roger Geffen, *The Handbook of Public Prayer,* p. 74.

Closing: Selina Fitzherbert Fox, *A Chain of Prayer Across the Ages: Forty Centuries of Prayer from 2000 B.C.-A.D. 1916,* p. 111.

WEEK 15

Opening: William Bright, *Ancient Collects and Other Prayers: Selected for Devotional Use from Various Rituals,* p. 39.

Closing: John Wallace Suter Jr., ed., *The Book of English Collects* (New York: Harper, 1940), p. 76.

WEEK 16

Opening: James Ferguson and Charles L. Wallis, eds., *Prayers for Public Worship: A Service Book of Morning and Evening Prayers Following the Course of the Christian Year,* p. 123.

Closing: Phyllis Tickle, *The Divine Hours: Prayers for Summertime* (New York: Doubleday, 2000), p. 312.

WEEK 17

Opening: James Ferguson and Charles L. Wallis, eds., *Prayers for Public Worship: A Service Book of Morning and Evening Prayers Following the Course of the Christian Year,* p. 89.

Closing: John Wallace Suter Jr., ed., *The Book of English Collects,* p. 77.

WEEK 18

Opening: Selina Fitzherbert Fox, *A Chain of Prayer Across the Ages: Forty Centuries of Prayer from 2000 B.C.-A.D. 1916,* p. 226.

Closing: William Bright, *Ancient Collects and Other Prayers: Selected for Devotional Use from Various Rituals,* p. 51.

WEEK 19 *(EASTER)*

Opening: William Bright, *Ancient Collects and Other Prayers: Selected for Devotional Use from Various Rituals,* p. 54.

Closing: Selina Fitzherbert Fox, *A Chain of Prayer Across the Ages: Forty Centuries of Prayer from 2000 B.C.-A.D. 1916,* p. 234.

WEEK 20

Opening: William Bright, *Ancient Collects and Other Prayers: Selected for Devotional Use from Various Rituals,* p. 58.

Closing: Roger Geffen, *The Handbook of Public Prayer,* p. 105.

WEEK 21

Opening: James Ferguson and Charles L. Wallis, eds., *Prayers for Public Worship: A Service Book of Morning and Evening Prayers Following the Course of the Christian Year,* p. 155.

Closing: William Bright, *Ancient Collects and Other Prayers: Selected for Devotional Use from Various Rituals,* p. 159.

WEEK 22

Opening: Selina Fitzherbert Fox, *A Chain of Prayer Across the Ages: Forty Centuries of Prayer from 2000 B.C.-A.D. 1916.* p. 86.

Closing: James Ferguson and Charles L. Wallis, eds., *Prayers for Public Worship: A Service Book of Morning and Evening Prayers Following the Course of the Christian Year,* pp. 179-80.

WEEK 23

Opening: Selina Fitzherbert Fox, *A Chain of Prayer Across the Ages: Forty Centuries of Prayer from 2000 B.C.-A.D. 1916,* p. 172.

Closing: Joel C. Elowsky, ed., *John 11-21,* Ancient Christian Commentary on Scripture (Downers Grove, Ill.: InterVarsity Press, 2007), p. 126.

WEEK 24

Opening: Roger Geffen, *The Handbook of Public Prayer,* p. 196.

Closing: Selina Fitzherbert Fox, *A Chain of Prayer Across the Ages: Forty Centuries of Prayer from 2000 B.C.-A.D. 1916,* p. 196

WEEK 25

Opening: Selina Fitzherbert Fox, *A Chain of Prayer Across the Ages: Forty Centuries of Prayer from 2000 B.C.-A.D. 1916,* p. 236.

Closing: William Bright, *Ancient Collects and Other Prayers: Selected for Devotional Use from Various Rituals,* p. 60.

WEEK 26 *(PENTECOST)*

Opening: Selina Fitzherbert Fox, *A Chain of Prayer Across the Ages: Forty Centuries of Prayer from 2000 B.C.-A.D. 1916,* p. 237.

Closing: Ancient Collects and Other Prayers: Selected for Devotional Use from Various Rituals, p. 61.

WEEK 27

Opening: Selina Fitzherbert Fox, *A Chain of Prayer Across the Ages: Forty Centuries of Prayer from 2000 B.C.-A.D. 1916,* p. 239.

Closing: James Ferguson and Charles L. Wallis, eds., *Prayers for Public Worship: A Service Book of Morning and Evening Prayers Following the Course of the Christian Year,* p. 203.

WEEK 28

Opening: William Bright, *Ancient Collects and Other Prayers: Selected for Devotional Use from Various Rituals,* p. 81.

Closing: Roger Geffen, *The Handbook of Public Prayer,* p. 115.

WEEK 29

Opening: James Ferguson and Charles L. Wallis, eds., *Prayers for Public Worship: A Service Book of Morning and Evening Prayers Following the Course of the Christian Year,* p. 335.

Closing: Selina Fitzherbert Fox, *A Chain of Prayer Across the Ages: Forty Centuries of Prayer from 2000 B.C.-A.D. 1916,* p. 2.

WEEK 30

Opening: William Bright, *Ancient Collects and Other Prayers: Selected for Devotional Use from Various Rituals,* p. 77.

Closing: Selina Fitzherbert Fox, *A Chain of Prayer Across the Ages: Forty Centuries of Prayer from 2000 B.C.-A.D. 1916,* p. 138.

WEEK 31

Opening: William Bright, *Ancient Collects and Other Prayers: Selected for Devotional Use from Various Rituals,* pp. 80-81.

Closing: J. Robert Wright, *Readings for the Daily Office from the Early Church,* pp. 299-300.

WEEK 32

Opening: Roger Geffen, *The Handbook of Public Prayer,* p. 193.

Closing: James Ferguson and Charles L. Wallis, eds., *Prayers for Public Worship: A Service Book of Morning and Evening Prayers Following the Course of the Christian Year,* p. 222.

WEEK 33

Opening: J. Robert Wright, *Readings for the Daily Office from the Early Church,* p. 310.

Closing: James Ferguson and Charles L. Wallis, eds., *Prayers for Public Worship: A Service Book of Morning and Evening Prayers Following the Course of the Christian Year,* pp. 321-22.

WEEK 34

Opening: William Bright, *Ancient Collects and Other Prayers,* pp. 127-28.

Closing: James Ferguson and Charles L. Wallis, eds., *Prayers for Public Worship: A Service Book of Morning and Evening Prayers Following the Course of the Christian Year,* p. 290.

WEEK 35

Opening: J. Robert Wright, *Readings for the Daily Office from the Early Church,* pp. 327-28.

Closing: Phyllis Tickle, *The Divine Hours: Prayers for Autumn and Wintertime* (New York: Doubleday, 2000), p. 208.

WEEK 36

Opening: William Bright, *Ancient Collects and Other Prayers: Selected for Devotional Use from Various Rituals,* p. 2.

Closing: James Ferguson and Charles L. Wallis, eds., *Prayers for Public Worship: A Service Book of Morning and Evening Prayers Following the Course of the Christian Year,* pp. 298-99.

WEEK 37

Opening: Selina Fitzherbert Fox, *A Chain of Prayer Across the Ages: Forty Centuries of Prayer from 2000 B.C.-A.D. 1916,* p. 72.

Closing: James Ferguson and Charles L. Wallis, eds., *Prayers for Public Worship: A Service Book of Morning and Evening Prayers Following the Course of the Christian Year,* pp. 74-75.

WEEK 38

Opening: Selina Fitzherbert Fox, *A Chain of Prayer Across the Ages: Forty Centuries of Prayer from 2000 B.C.-A.D. 1916,* p. 195.

Closing: Phyllis Tickle, *The Divine Hours: Prayers for Autumn and Wintertime,* p. 89.

WEEK 39

Opening: Selina Fitzherbert Fox, *A Chain of Prayer Across the Ages: Forty Centuries of Prayer from 2000 B.C.-A.D. 1916,* p. 176.

Closing: Phyllis Tickle, *The Divine Hours: Prayers for Autumn and Wintertime,* p. 312.

WEEK 40

Opening: William Bright, *Ancient Collects and Other Prayers: Selected for Devotional Use from Various Rituals,* p. 149.

Closing: William Bright, *Ancient Collects and Other Prayers: Selected for Devotional Use from Various Rituals,* p. 74.

WEEK 41

Opening: J. Robert Wright, *Readings for the Daily Office from the Early Church,* p. 21.

Closing: J. Robert Wright, *Readings for the Daily Office from the Early Church,* p. 31.

WEEK 42

Opening: James Ferguson and Charles L. Wallis, eds., *Prayers for Public Worship: A Service Book of Morning and Evening Prayers Following the Course of the Christian Year,* p. 237.

Closing: Richard J. Foster, *Prayers from the Heart* (San Francisco: HarperSanFrancisco, 1994), p. 63.

WEEK 43

Opening: James Ferguson and Charles L. Wallis, eds., *Prayers for Public Worship: A Service Book of Morning and Evening Prayers Following the Course of the Christian Year,* pp. 252-53.

Closing: William Bright, *Ancient Collects and Other Prayers: Selected for Devotional Use from Various Rituals,* p. 44.

WEEK 44

Opening: J. Robert Wright, *Readings for the Daily Office from the Early Church,* pp. 21-22.

Closing: Selina Fitzherbert Fox, *A Chain of Prayer Across the Ages: Forty Centuries of Prayer from 2000 B.C.-A.D. 1916,* p. 164.

WEEK 45

Opening: James Ferguson and Charles L. Wallis, eds., *Prayers for Public Worship: A Service Book of Morning and Evening Prayers Following the Course of the Christian Year,* p. 72.

Closing: Selina Fitzherbert Fox, *A Chain of Prayer Across the Ages: Forty Centuries of Prayer from 2000 B.C.-A.D. 1916,* p. 293.

WEEK 46

Opening: James Ferguson and Charles L. Wallis, eds., *Prayers for Public Worship: A Service Book of Morning and Evening Prayers Following the Course of the Christian Year,* p. 203. (Source does not identify whether the author of the prayer is Clement of Rome or Clement of Alexandria.)

Closing: Selina Fitzherbert Fox, *A Chain of Prayer Across the Ages: Forty Centuries of Prayer from 2000 B.C.-A.D. 1916,* p. 163.

WEEK 47

Opening: William Bright, *Ancient Collects and Other Prayers: Selected for Devotional Use from Various Rituals,* p. 79.

Closing: Selina Fitzherbert Fox, *A Chain of Prayer Across the Ages: Forty Centuries of Prayer from 2000 B.C.-A.D. 1916,* p. 292.

WEEK 48 *(ALL SAINTS DAY)*

Opening: Selina Fitzherbert Fox, *A Chain of Prayer Across the Ages: Forty Centuries of Prayer from 2000 B.C.-A.D. 1916,* p. 241.

Closing: James Ferguson and Charles L. Wallis, eds., *Prayers for Public Worship: A Service Book of Morning and Evening Prayers Following the Course of the Christian Year,* p. 353.

WEEK 49

Opening: J. Robert Wright, *Readings for the Daily Office from the Early Church,* pp. 393-94.

Closing: Selina Fitzherbert Fox, *A Chain of Prayer Across the Ages: Forty*

Centuries of Prayer from 2000 B.C.-A.D. 1916, p. 86.

WEEK 50

Opening: James Ferguson and Charles L. Wallis, eds., *Prayers for Public Worship: A Service Book of Morning and Evening Prayers Following the Course of the Christian Year,* p. 126.

Closing: Selina Fitzherbert Fox, *A Chain of Prayer Across the Ages: Forty Centuries of Prayer from 2000 B.C.-A.D 1916,* p. 27.

WEEK 51

Opening: James Ferguson and Charles L. Wallis, eds., *Prayers for Public Worship: A Service Book of Morning and Evening Prayers Following the Course of the Christian Year,* pp. 295-96.

Closing: J. Robert Wright, *Readings for the Daily Office from the Early Church,* pp. 21-22.

WEEK 52

Opening: William Bright, *Ancient Collects and Other Prayers: Selected for Devotional Use from Various Rituals,* p. 16.

Closing: Roger Geffen, *The Handbook of Public Prayer,* p. 128.

BIOGRAPHICAL
SKETCHES

Ambrose of Milan (c. 333 or 339-397; fl. 374-397). Bishop of Milan and teacher of Augustine who defended the divinity of the Holy Spirit and the perpetual virginity of Mary. He was known as a pastor of souls as well as a scholar, a good listener and counselor. Among his chief works are *On the Gospel of Luke, On the Holy Spirit* and *Mysteries.*

Ambrosian. One of three surviving distinct liturgical rites regularly used in the Latin Church, and attributed to St. Ambrose for the first time in the eighth century.

Ambrosiaster (fl. c. 366-384). Name given by Erasmus to the author of a work once thought to have been composed by Ambrose.

Andreas (c. seventh century). Monk who collected commentary from earlier writers to form a catena on various biblical books.

Apostolic Constitutions (c. 381-394). Also known as *Constitutions of the Holy Apostles* and thought to be redacted by Julian of Neapolis. The work is divided into eight books and is primarily a collection of and expansion on previous works such as the *Didache* (c. 140) and the *Apostolic Traditions.* Book 8 ends with 85 canons from various sources and is elsewhere known as the *Apostolic Canons.*

Athanasius (c. 295-373). A native of Alexandria and secretary/deacon to his bishop at the Council of Nicaea (325), Athanasius was elevated to the Episcopal See of Alexandria. He was exiled more than four times.

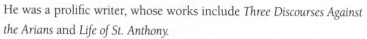

He was a prolific writer, whose works include *Three Discourses Against the Arians* and *Life of St. Anthony.*

Augustine of Hippo (354-430). Bishop of Hippo and a voluminous writer on philosophical, exegetical, theological and ecclesiological topics. He formulated the Western doctrines of predestination and original sin in his writings against the Pelagians. He was very involved in the theological controversies of the time period.

Basil the Great (b. c. 330; fl. 357-379). One of the Cappadocian fathers, bishop of Caesarea and champion of the teaching on the Trinity propounded at Nicaea in 325. He was a great administrator and founded a monastic rule. His devotion to the cause of the poor earned him the title of "Great."

Bede the Venerable (c. 672/673-735). Born in Northumbria, at the age of seven he was put under the care of Benedictine monks and received a broad classical education in the monastic tradition. Considered one of the most learned men of his age, he is the author of *An Ecclesiastical History of the English People.*

Brigid (460-528). Born to a slave woman, she founded numerous monasteries and is considered one of the three patron saints of Ireland.

Caesarius of Arles (c. 470-543). Bishop of Arles renowned for his attention to his pastoral duties. Among his surviving works, the most important is a collection of some 238 sermons that display an ability to preach Christian doctrine to a variety of audiences.

Canons of Hippolytus. Originally written in Greek, this book, attributed to Hippolytus, is divided into 38 canons. It contains instructions on ordination, regulations regarding widows and virgins, conditions for the reception of converts, counsel on the preparations for baptism, rules for fasting and celebration of the Eucharist, and various prayers and other rituals.

Cassiodorus (c. 485-580). Founder of the monastery of Vivarium, Calabria, where monks transcribed classic sacred and profane texts, Greek and Latin, preserving them for the Western tradition.

Chromatius of Aquileia (fl. 400). Bishop of Aquileia, friend of Rufinus and Jerome, and author of tracts and sermons.

Chrysostom (John Chrysostom) (344/354-407; fl. 386-407). Bishop of Constantinople who was noted for his orthodoxy, his eloquence (hence his nickname Chrysostom = "Golden-tongued") and his attacks on Christian laxity in high places.

Clement of Alexandria (c. 150-215). Born to pagan parents, Clement is sometimes called "the first Christian scholar." He was a highly educated Christian convert from paganism, head of the catechetical school in Alexandria and pioneer of Christian scholarship. His major works, *Protrepticus, Paedagogus* and the *Stromata,* bring Christian doctrine face to face with the ideas and achievements of his time.

Clement of Rome (fl. c. 92-101). Pope whose *Epistle to the Corinthians* is one of the most important documents of subapostolic times.

Columba (521-597). Irish abbot of Iona and founder of monasteries at Derry and Durrow. He was called the apostle of Caledonia because of his evangelization of the Picts and Scots.

Columbanus (Columban) (543-615). A teacher, missionary and founder of monasteries who fought against corruption in the church. His Irish Latin poetry, rules and letters were formational for the culture of the time period.

Coptic Liturgy of St. Basil. Several liturgies or "Anaphoras" have been attributed to St. Basil, bishop of Cæsarea in Cappadocia (370 to 379). This is one of three major liturgies of the Coptic Church and the most frequently used (St. Gregory and St. Cyril are the others).

Cyprian (fl. 248-258). Martyred bishop of Carthage who maintained that those baptized by schismatics and heretics had no share in the blessings of the church. He was generous with his wealth, and dedicated to chastity.

Cyril of Alexandria (375-444; fl. 412-444). Patriarch of Alexandria whose extensive exegesis, characterized especially by a strong espousal of the unity of Christ, led to the condemnation of Nestorius in 431.

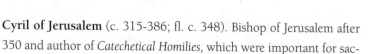

Cyril of Jerusalem (c. 315-386; fl. c. 348). Bishop of Jerusalem after 350 and author of *Catechetical Homilies,* which were important for sacramental theology and baptism.

Didymus the Blind (c. 313-398). Blind from the age of four or five, this Alexandrian exegete was much influenced by Origen and admired by Jerome, who considered him his master.

Diodore (d. c. 394). Bishop of Tarsus and Antiochene theologian. He authored a great scope of exegetical, doctrinal and apologetic works, which come to us mostly in fragments because of his condemnation as the predecessor of Nestorianism. Diodore was a teacher of John Chrysostom and Theodore of Mopsuestia.

Ephrem the Syrian (b. c. 306; fl. 363-373). A Syrian writer of commentaries and devotional hymns that are sometimes regarded as the greatest specimens of Christian poetry prior to Dante.

Epiphanius the Latin. Author of the late fifth-century or early sixth-century Latin text *Interpretation of the Gospels,* with constant references to early patristic commentators. He was possibly a bishop of Benevento or Seville.

Eusebius of Caesaria (c. 260/263-340). Bishop of Caesarea, partisan of the Emperor Constantine and first historian of the Christian church. He argued that the truth of the gospel had been foreshadowed in pagan writings but had to defend his own doctrine against suspicion of Arian sympathies.

Fulgentius of Ruspe (c. 467-532). Bishop of Ruspe and author of many orthodox sermons and tracts under the influence of Augustine.

Fursa (c. 650). An Irish missionary who saw visions that gained him great literary fame during the Middle Ages.

Gallican Litanies, Sacramentary, Old Gallican Missal. From the fifth century to the ninth century, these were chants of the ancient liturgies as practiced in French Gaul.

Gelasian Sacramentary. The most complete and oldest extant manuscript of the Roman Sacramentary. Its ancestry is believed to date back to between 628 and 715. Trium Magorum ("Three Magi") refers to the prayers associated with the Feast of the Epiphany.

Gennadius of Constantinople (d. 471). Patriarch of Constantinople, author of numerous commentaries and an opponent of the Christology of Cyril of Alexandria.

Gothic Missal. An ancient service book deriving from southern Gaul.

Gregorian Sacramentary. A service book with a complex history, whose date and authenticity are still debated. It has been suggested it dates back to 593. It received its definitive form under Gregory II.

Gregory the Great (c. 540-604). Pope from 590, the fourth and last of the Latin "Doctors of the Church." He was a prolific author and a powerful unifying force within the Latin Church, initiating the liturgical reform that brought about the Gregorian Sacramentary and Gregorian chant.

Gregory of Nazianzus (b. 329/330; fl. 372-389). Cappadocian father, bishop of Constantinople, friend of Basil the Great and Gregory of Nyssa, and author of theological orations, sermons and poetry.

Gregory of Nyssa (c. 335-394). Bishop of Nyssa and brother of Basil the Great. A Cappadocian father and author of catechetical orations, he was a philosophical theologian of great originality.

Hilary of Arles (c. 401-449). Archbishop of Arles and leader of the Semi-Pelagian party. Hilary incurred the wrath of Pope Leo I when he removed a bishop from his see and appointed a new bishop. Leo demoted Arles from a metropolitan see to a bishopric to assert papal power over the church in Gaul.

Hilary of Poitiers (c. 315-367). Bishop of Poitiers and called the "Athanasius of the West" because of his defense (against the Arians) of the common nature of Father and Son.

Ignatius (c. 35-107/112). Bishop of Antioch who wrote several letters to local churches while being taken from Antioch to Rome to be martyred. In the letters, which warn against heresy, he stresses orthodox Christology, the centrality of the Eucharist and unique role of the bishop in preserving the unity of the church.

Incomplete Work on Matthew. A widely disseminated commentary on the Gospel of Matthew, once thought to be the work of John Chrysostom, containing 54 homilies. It lacks comment, however, on Matthew 8:11—10:15 and 13:14—18:35; hence, the attribution "incomplete."

Irenaeus (c. 135-c. 202). Bishop of Lyons who published the most famous and influential refutation of Gnostic thought.

Isaac of Nineveh (d. c. 700). Also known as Isaac the Syrian or Isaac Syrus, this monastic writer served for a short while as bishop of Nineveh before retiring to live a secluded monastic life. His writings on ascetic subjects survive in the form of numerous homilies.

Isho'dad of Merv (fl. c. 850). Nestorian bishop of Hedatta. He wrote commentaries on parts of the Old Testament and all of the New Testament, frequently quoting Syriac fathers.

Jacobite Liturgy of Dionysius. A West Syrian liturgy of the Syrian Orthodox Church, incorporating elements attributed to Dionysius of Athens.

Jerome (c. 347-420). Gifted exegete and exponent of a classical Latin style, now best known as the translator of the Latin Vulgate. He defended the perpetual virginity of Mary, attacked Origen and Pelagius, and supported extreme ascetic practices.

John Cassian (360-432). Author of the *Institutes* and the *Conferences,* works purporting to relay the teachings of the Egyptian monastic fathers on the nature of the spiritual life which were highly influential in the development of Western monasticism.

John of Carpathos. A seventh-century Greek monk.

John of Damascus (c. 650-750). Arab monastic and theologian whose writings enjoyed great influence in both the Eastern and Western Churches. His most influential writing was the *Orthodox Faith.*

John the Monk. Traditional name found in *The Festal Menaion,* believed to refer to John of Damascus. *See* John of Damascus.

Justin Martyr (c. 100/110-165; fl. c. 148-161). Palestinian philosopher who was converted to Christianity, "the only sure and worthy philosophy." He traveled to Rome where he wrote several apologies against both pagans and Jews, combining Greek philosophy and Christian theology; he was eventually martyred.

Lactantius (c. 260-c. 330). Christian apologist removed from his post as teacher of rhetoric at Nicomedia upon his conversion to Christianity. He was tutor to the son of Constantine and author of *The Divine Institutes*.

Leo the Great (regn. 440-461). Bishop of Rome whose *Tome to Flavian* helped to strike a balance between Nestorian and Cyrilline positions at the Council of Chalcedon in 451.

Leonine (Sacramentary). Mass prayer formularies with a Roman origin, which have been variously attributed, including to Leo I. It was likely written in the seventh century.

Liturgy of Dioscorus. Variation of the West Syrian rite, incorporating prayers attributed to Dioscorus of Alexandria.

Liturgy of St. James. Considered by some to be the oldest surviving liturgy for general church use. Some date it around A.D. 60.

Liturgy of St. Mark. The traditional main liturgy of the Orthodox Church of Alexandria.

Luculentius (fifth century). Unknown author of a group of short commentaries on the New Testament, especially Pauline passages. His exegesis is mainly literal and relies mostly on earlier authors such as Jerome and Augustine. The content of his writing may place it in the fifth century.

Marius Victorinus (b. c. 280/285; fl. c. 355-363). Grammarian of African origin who taught rhetoric at Rome and translated works of Platonists. After his conversion (c. 355), he wrote against the Arians and commentaries on Paul's letters.

Methodius (d. 311). Bishop of Olympus who celebrated virginity in a Symposium partly modeled on Plato's dialogue of that name.

Nerses of Clajes (d. 323). An Armenian patriarch who initiated reform of the church.

Novatian (fl. 235-258). Roman theologian, otherwise orthodox, who formed a schismatic church after failing to become pope. His treatise on the Trinity states the classic Western doctrine.

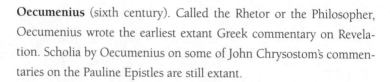

Oecumenius (sixth century). Called the Rhetor or the Philosopher, Oecumenius wrote the earliest extant Greek commentary on Revelation. Scholia by Oecumenius on some of John Chrysostom's commentaries on the Pauline Epistles are still extant.

Origen (b. 185; fl. c. 200-254). Influential exegete and systematic theologian. He was condemned (perhaps unfairly) for maintaining the preexistence of souls while purportedly denying the resurrection of the body. His extensive works of exegesis focus on the spiritual meaning of the text.

Pachomius. (c. 292-347). Founder of cenobitic monasticism. A gifted group leader and author of a set of rules, he was defended after his death by Athanasius of Alexandria.

Patrick (Breastplate of). This beautiful prayer is attributed to St. Patrick (c. 389-461), but is probably dated after his death.

Pelagius (c. 354-c. 420). Contemporary of Augustine whose followers were condemned in 418 and 431 for maintaining that even before Christ there were people who lived wholly without sin and that salvation depended on free will.

Peter Chrysologus (c. 380-450). Latin archbishop of Ravenna whose teachings included arguments for adherence in matters of faith to the Roman see, and the relationship between grace and Christian living.

Phos Hilaron. This is attributed by some to the matyr and bishop Athenogenes (d. c. 305), who is said by tradition to have sung this hymn ("O Cheerful Light") as he was burned for his faith.

Prudentius (c. 348-c. 410). Latin poet and hymn-writer who devoted his later life to Christian writing. He wrote didactic theological poetry.

Pseudo-Constantius. Designation of the unknown author of a fifth-century commentary on Romans. Constantius may have been its author, but this is uncertain.

Pseudo-Dionysius the Areopagite (fl. c. 500). Author who assumed the name of Dionysius the Areopagite mentioned in Acts 17:34, and who composed the works known as the Corpus Areopagiticum (or Dionysiacum). These writings were the foundation of the apophatic school of mysticism in their denial that anything can be truly predicated of God.

Romanus the Melodist (fl. c. 536-556). A Jewish convert to Christianity, who may have written as many as eighty metrical sermons, which were sung rather than preached.

Severian of Gabala (fl. c. 400). A contemporary of John Chrysostom, he was a highly regarded preacher in Constantinople, particularly at the imperial court, and ultimately sided with Chrysostom's accusers. He wrote homilies on Genesis.

Slavonic Liturgy of John Chrysostom. A Slavonic version of John Chrysostom's shortened version of St. Basil's Liturgy.

Symeon the New Theologian (c. 949-1022). Compassionate spiritual leader known for his strict rule. He believed that the divine light could be perceived and received through the practice of mental prayer.

Synesius of Cyrene (c. 370 or 375-c.414). A bishop of Ptolemais and a fourth-century philosopher who left behind numerous letters, several hymns, and other writings and homilies.

Syrian Clementine Liturgy. This Syrian liturgical rite is similar to the ancient rite of the fourth-century Antiochene Church.

Theodore of Heraclea (d. c. 355). An anti-Nicene bishop of Thrace. He was part of a team seeking reconciliation between Eastern and Western Christianity. In 343 he was excommunicated at the council of Sardica. His writings focus on literal interpretations of Scripture.

Theodore of Mopsuestia (c. 350-428). Bishop of Mopsuestia, founder of the Antiochene, or literalistic, school of exegesis. A great man in his day, he was later condemned as a precursor of Nestorius.

Theodoret of Cyr (c. 393-466). Bishop of Cyr (Cyrrhus), he was an opponent of Cyril who commented extensively on Old Testament texts as a lucid exponent of Antiochene exegesis.

Theophylact (c. 1050-c. 1108). Byzantine archbishop of Ohrid (or Achrida) in what is now Bulgaria. Drawing on earlier works, he wrote commentaries on several Old Testament books and all of the New Testament except for Revelation.

Index of Names and Sources

Ambrose of Milan, 16, 17, 35, 44, 51, 52, 57, 68, 82, 84, 89, 96, 120, 124, 141, 146, 173, 180, 186, 210, 214, 283

Ambrosian, 62, 222, 283

Ambrosiaster, 18, 39, 49, 53, 54, 59, 64, 78, 83, 87, 132, 136, 137, 142, 152, 157, 162, 178, 182, 196, 201, 211, 215, 221, 265, 283

Andreas, 122, 127, 283

Apostolic Constitutions, 254, 283

Athanasius, 34, 283

Augustine of Hippo, 17, 21, 23, 27, 28, 29, 31, 46, 47, 50, 58, 61, 65, 71, 73, 74, 76, 80, 83, 84, 94, 103, 113, 116, 119, 123, 126, 127, 128, 129, 133, 135, 141, 144, 152, 157, 164, 167, 173, 178, 179, 187, 191, 192, 194, 196, 200, 204, 206, 211, 213, 218, 220, 223, 224, 227, 229, 231, 234, 237, 238, 240, 255, 256, 257, 258, 263, 283, 284, 286, 289, 290

Basil the Great, 44, 67, 79, 83, 91, 122, 152, 156, 219, 235, 252, 255, 265, 284, 287

Bede the Venerable, 16, 23, 24, 27, 67, 69, 101, 106, 107, 111, 112, 115, 117, 122, 126, 130, 132, 134, 168, 171, 244, 245, 253, 284

Brigid, 193, 284

Caesarius of Arles, 33, 77, 81, 82, 146, 156, 161, 165, 171, 181, 190, 205, 206, 214, 244, 249, 256, 284

Canons of Hippolytus, 109, 284

Cassiodorus, 32, 220, 259, 284

Chromatius of Aquileia, 19, 23, 30, 55, 60, 99, 170, 173, 191, 247, 285

Chrysostom (John Chrysostom), 14, 17, 18, 19, 29, 30, 33, 34, 35, 40, 44, 48, 49, 50, 53, 54, 57, 59, 63, 64, 65, 74, 75, 78, 82, 83, 87, 88, 90, 92, 93, 98, 99, 104, 105, 111, 112, 116, 117, 121, 122, 126, 128, 131, 133, 137, 141, 142, 143, 147, 148, 149, 151, 153, 154, 157, 163, 165, 166, 168, 176, 179, 180, 181, 183, 185, 186, 187, 188, 189, 190, 195, 196, 197, 201, 202, 205, 206, 212, 215, 216, 220, 224, 225, 226, 230, 235, 239, 241, 247, 250, 251, 254, 260, 261, 266, 285, 286, 288, 290, 291

Clement of Alexandria, 43, 118, 122, 125, 128, 233, 280, 285

Clement of Rome, 22, 115, 196, 209, 223, 233, 262, 280, 285

Columba, 188, 285

Columbanus (Columban), 15, 248, 285

Coptic Liturgy of St. Basil, 185, 285

Cyprian, 170, 258, 285

Cyril of Alexandria, 20, 22, 23, 29, 40, 49, 54, 79, 84, 88, 94, 98, 107, 108, 134, 138, 163, 168, 190, 202, 212, 221, 241, 248, 285, 287

Cyril of Jerusalem, 47, 136, 137, 138, 286

Didymus the Blind, 112, 128, 286

Diodore, 74, 162, 177, 187, 196, 286

Ephrem the Syrian, 33, 113, 131, 141, 194, 228, 286

Epiphanius the Latin, 97, 98, 226, 266, 267, 286

Eusebius of Caesaria, 43, 199, 286

Fulgentius of Ruspe, 240, 286

Fursa, 217, 286

Gallican Litanies, Sacramentary, Old Gallican Missal, 100, 105, 150, 176, 286

Gelasian Sacramentary, 26, 37, 42, 61, 72, 81, 101, 114, 130, 174, 228, 263, 286

Gennadius of Constantinople, 92, 162, 167, 210, 287

Gothic Missal, 46, 287

Gregorian Sacramentary, 41, 76, 85, 95, 139, 287

Gregory of Nazianzus, 118, 209, 249, 256, 287

Gregory of Nyssa, 22, 34, 73, 102, 235, 287

Gregory the Great, 25, 39, 55, 75, 104, 148, 149, 179, 216, 224, 231, 238, 239, 259, 261, 264, 287

Hilary of Arles, 107, 117, 121, 127, 287

Hilary of Poitiers, 14, 45, 64, 99, 123, 137, 140, 154, 158, 178, 183, 187, 200, 211, 245, 256, 287

Ignatius, 187, 287

Incomplete Work on Matthew, 15, 21, 30, 31, 41, 46, 54, 60, 61, 153, 216, 222, 236, 237, 246, 247, 288

Irenaeus, 42, 110, 138, 288

Isaac of Nineveh, 79, 102, 288

Isho'dad of Merv, 24, 288

Jacobite Liturgy of Dionysius, 145, 288

Jerome, 24, 39, 62, 63, 65, 70, 71, 91, 132, 141, 158, 168, 172, 173, 183, 218, 219, 225, 266, 285, 286, 288, 289

John Cassian, 213, 219, 288

John of Carpathos, 109, 288

John of Damascus, 9, 28, 29, 72, 191, 288

John the Monk, 36, 288

Justin Martyr, 17, 92, 288

Lactantius, 43, 86, 289

Leo the Great, 34, 36, 53, 70, 134, 212, 289

Leonine Sacramentary, 32, 96, 110, 134, 155, 169, 199, 208, 238, 243, 247, 289

Liturgy of Dioscorus, 204, 289

Liturgy of St. James, 125, 289

Liturgy of St. Mark, 66, 289

Luculentius, 196, 289

Marius Victorinus, 39, 132, 133, 214, 215, 225, 230, 265, 289

Methodius, 38, 289

Nerses of Clajes, 80, 135, 289

Novatian, 97, 98, 177, 221, 290

Oecumenius, 68, 69, 112, 152, 243, 244, 290

Origen, 14, 29, 37, 48, 49, 53, 58, 64, 69, 77, 78, 122, 140, 147, 150, 155, 156, 158, 160, 166, 172, 177, 182, 200, 201, 205, 210, 211, 234, 241, 251, 286, 288, 290

Patrick (Breastplate of), 86, 90, 179, 203, 290

Pelagius, 224, 288, 290

Peter Chrysologus, 68, 93, 103, 108, 207, 290

Phos Hilaron, 198, 290

Prudentius, 127, 195, 256, 260, 290

Pseudo-Constantius, 290

Pseudo-Dionysius the Areopagite, 11, 290

Romanus the Melodist, 94, 291

Severian of Gabala, 103, 291

Slavonic Liturgy of John Chrysostom, 149, 291

Symeon the New Theologian, 69, 291

Synesius of Cyrene, 184, 291

Syrian Clementine Liturgy, 160, 267, 291

Theodore of Heraclea, 75, 197, 286, 291

Theodore of Mopsuestia, 26, 58, 59, 88, 163, 177, 192, 197, 206, 286, 291

Theodoret of Cyr, 43, 48, 62, 74, 78, 97, 102, 106, 133, 157, 172, 178, 201, 253, 291

Theophylact, 27, 68, 245, 291

formatio
TRADITION. EXPERIENCE.
TRANSFORMATION.

Formatio books from InterVarsity Press follow the rich tradition of the church in the journey of spiritual formation. These books are not merely about being informed, but about being transformed by Christ and conformed to his image. Formatio stands in InterVarsity Press's evangelical publishing tradition by integrating God's Word with spiritual practice and by prompting readers to move from inward change to outward witness. InterVarsity Press uses the chambered nautilus for Formatio, a symbol of spiritual formation because of its continual spiral journey outward as it moves from its center. We believe that each of us is made with a deep desire to be in God's presence. Formatio books help us to fulfill our deepest desires and to become our true selves in light of God's grace.